Coaching
TENNIS
Technical and
Tactical Skills

American Sport
Education Program
with Kirk Anderson

HUMAN KINETICS

Library of Congress Cataloging-in-Publication Data

Coaching tennis technical and tactical skills / American Sport Education Program.
     p. cm.
 Includes index.
 ISBN-13: 978-0-7360-5380-8 (soft cover)
 ISBN-10: 0-7360-5380-8 (soft cover)
 1. Tennis--Coaching. I. American Sport Education Program.
 GV1002.9.C63C63 2009
 796.342--dc22

2009002238

ISBN-10: 0-7360-5380-8 (print)   ISBN-10: 0-7360-8607-2 (Adobe PDF)
ISBN-13: 978-0-7360-5380-8 (print)   ISBN-13: 978-0-7360-8607-3 (Adobe PDF)

The Web addresses cited in this text were current as of April 2009 unless otherwise noted.

Acquisitions Editor: Pat Sammann; **Project Writers:** United States Tennis Association with Kirk Anderson; **Developmental Editor:** Laura Floch; **Assistant Editors:** Elizabeth Watson and Laura Podeschi; **Copyeditor:** Patsy Fortney; **Proofreader:** Sarah Wiseman; **Indexers:** Robert and Cynthia Swanson; **Permission Manager:** Martha Gullo; **Graphic Designer:** Nancy Rasmus; **Graphic Artist:** Tara Welsch; **Cover Designer:** Keith Blomberg; **Photographer (cover):** Dan Wendt; **Photographer (interior):** Jay Adkins; **Visual Production Assistant:** Joyce Brumfield; **Photo Production Manager:** Jason Allen; **Art Manager:** Kelly Hendren; **Associate Art Manager:** Alan L. Wilborn; **Printer:** McNaughton & Gunn

Copies of this book are available at special discounts for bulk purchase for sales promotions, premiums, fund-raising, or educational use. Special editions or book excerpts can also be created to specifications. For details, contact the Special Sales Manager at Human Kinetics.

Printed in the United States of America   10   9   8   7   6   5   4   3   2   1

The paper in this book is certified under a sustainable forestry program.

Human Kinetics
Web site: www.HumanKinetics.com

United States: Human Kinetics
P.O. Box 5076
Champaign, IL 61825-5076
800-747-4457
e-mail: humank@hkusa.com

Canada: Human Kinetics
475 Devonshire Road Unit 100
Windsor, ON N8Y 2L5
800-465-7301 (in Canada only)
e-mail: info@hkcanada.com

Europe: Human Kinetics
107 Bradford Road
Stanningley
Leeds LS28 6AT, United Kingdom
+44 (0) 113 255 5665
e-mail: hk@hkeurope.com

Australia: Human Kinetics
57A Price Avenue
Lower Mitcham, South Australia 5062
08 8372 0999
e-mail: info@hkaustralia.com

New Zealand: Human Kinetics
Division of Sports Distributors NZ Ltd.
P.O. Box 300 226 Albany
North Shore City
Auckland
0064 9 448 1207
e-mail: info@humankinetics.co.nz

contents

If you are a seasoned tennis coach, surely you have experienced the frustration of watching your players perform well in practice, only to find them underperforming in matches. In your own playing days, you likely saw the same events unfold. In practice, your teammates, or perhaps even you, could hit the first serve with good pace and spin forcing your opponent wide on the court. You could then move forward to the net and hit the first volley crisply to the opening on the opposite side of the court, but you could not transfer that kind of performance to the match. Although this book will not provide you with a magical quick fix to your players' problems, it will help you prepare your players for match day. Whether you are a veteran coach or are new to coaching, *Coaching Tennis Technical and Tactical Skills* will help you take your players' games to the next level by providing you with the tools you need to teach them the game of tennis.

Every tennis coach knows the importance of technical skills. The ability to hit groundstrokes accurately and with a variety of spins, as well as powerful, directed serves, and win points at the net with decisive volleys and overheads can significantly affect the outcome of a match. This book discusses the basic and intermediate technical skills necessary for your players' success, including offensive, defensive, and neutral skills. You will learn how to detect and correct errors in your players' performances of those skills and then help them transfer the knowledge and ability they gain in practice to matches.

Besides covering technical skills, this book also focuses on tactical skills, including offensive skills such as hitting groundstrokes from the backcourt, approaching the net to hit volleys and overheads, and playing the serve-and-volley style. Your players will learn to identify the style that works best for them and is the most effective against the preferred style of the opponent. The book discusses the tactical triangle, an approach that teaches players to read a situation, acquire the knowledge they need to make a tactical decision, and apply decision-making skills to the problem. To advance this method, the book covers important cues that help athletes respond appropriately when they see a play developing, including important rules, match strategies, and the strengths and weaknesses of opponents.

In addition to presenting rigorous technical and tactical training to prepare your athletes for match situations, this book also provides guidance in how to improve their match performance by incorporating matchlike situations into daily training. We describe many traditional drills that can be effective but also show you how to shape, focus, and enhance drills and minigames to help players transfer their technical skills to tactical situations that occur during matches. For example, you can change a tedious crosscourt groundstroke drill into an exciting, competitive contest by keeping score of the number of balls that land behind the service line and how many times the opponent has to play the shot from outside the doubles alley.

This book also covers planning at several levels—the season plan, practice plans, and match plans. We offer a set of eight-session practice plans based on the games approach, which cover the length of the practice session, objective of the practice, equipment needed, warm-up, practice of previously taught skills, teaching and practicing new skills, cool-down, and evaluation.

Of course, playing in matches is what your practices eventually lead to. This book shows you how to prepare long before the first match, addressing such issues as communicating with players and parents, scouting your opponents, and motivating your players. You will learn how to control your players' performances on match day by establishing routines, as well as how to help them play at optimal pace, maintain focus between points, and hit every shot with purpose. You will also learn how to manage around such elements as wind, sun, and court surface.

PART I

Teaching and Evaluating

Being a good coach requires more than simply knowing the sport of tennis. You have to go beyond the sport and find a way to teach your athletes how to be better players. To improve your players' performance, you must know how to teach and evaluate them.

In chapter 1 we go over the fundamentals of teaching sport skills. We first provide a general overview of tennis and talk about the importance of being an effective teacher. Next, we define some important skills, helping you gain a better understanding of technical and tactical skills before discussing the traditional and games approaches to coaching.

We build on the knowledge of how to teach sport skills by addressing the evaluation of technical and tactical skills in chapter 2. We discuss the importance of evaluating athletes and review the core skills you should assess and how you can best do so. This chapter stresses the importance of preseason, in-season, and postseason evaluations and provides you with tools you can use to evaluate your players.

By learning how to teach and evaluate your players, you will be better prepared to help them improve their performance.

chapter 1

Teaching Sport Skills

Tennis is a very simple sport. The object is to hit the ball over the net and inside the boundary lines one more time than the opponent does. As simple as that sounds, the task of hitting a ball over a net and into the court has multiple variables that each player must master to be a successful competitor.

The most obvious skills are the strokes used to hit the ball over the net: forehand and backhand groundstrokes, first and second serves, serve returns, volleys, and overheads. Other shots are lobs, approach shots, and drop shots.

In addition, a good tennis player must understand the five controls for each of the preceding strokes: direction, distance, height, spin, and speed. With all of these variables to master, every player must also adjust to an opponent's shots so as to keep the ball away from the opponent.

To get to every ball, players must learn how to move before playing a shot and how to recover after a shot. In addition, they must adjust to their own strengths, the weaknesses of the opponent, their position on the court, and the playing conditions.

Players must also be aware of the mental side of the game. Keeping track of the score; calling balls in and out; controlling their thoughts and emotions; and dealing with errors, conditions, and idiosyncrasies of their opponents are all parts of the game.

Players on a doubles team must do all of the preceding while also working with a partner on the same side of the court. Doubles players need to have all of the skills of singles players while also understanding doubles formations. The team must do everything possible to return balls to openings on the opponents' side of the court and fill the gaps before the opponents can hit their shot to these openings.

Although tennis is a simple game, there is always something new that players can learn, either tactics or techniques, that will make them better players or teams. The learning and playing take place in almost every country, where players are playing on the same-size court and with identical rules. These rules apply to men and women, children and seniors. Tennis is truly a game for every person, in any country, and it's a game that can be played for a lifetime.

Effective Teaching

Effective tennis coaches must be well schooled in teaching both singles and doubles skills, shot selection, and movement and recovery. Coaches who are tennis players have to learn about all styles of play because players come in all sizes and temperaments. Because they must be able to teach more than one stroke or style of play, coaches must learn much more than the style and strokes they use when they play.

If you, like many coaches, play the game, you must master the transition from playing the game to teaching the game, a more difficult step than most people realize. To perform successfully, athletes need to gain a sense of how each skill feels—how they have to move and think. As a teacher, you have to search for ways to help your players gain that sense, that feeling, of how to perform skills, and you must understand that different athletes often perceive the same skill in different ways.

Additionally, to be an effective teacher, you must accept responsibility for the performance of your athletes. If you hide behind the tired excuse that your athletes just can't play, you will never be motivated to find the teaching strategy that will produce improvement. But if you adopt the credo that the team reflects everything the coach has taught the players, or everything the coach has allowed them to do, then you will understand that every player can improve. Even if an athlete's skill level is average, you can motivate her to hustle and give great effort, you can drill her until she executes perfectly, and you can inspire her to help the whole be greater than the sum of the parts. If you continually search for new ways to teach the same skill, you will eventually find a phrase, drill, or concept that triggers the athlete's reactions in such a way that she finally starts showing improvement in areas where she previously struggled.

You have the responsibility of finding a way to teach, or motivate, your players to improve their skills. This concept alone—your acceptance of responsibility for your players' performances—will produce creative, exciting, and extremely effective teaching, the kind of teaching that results in improved skills and performances by both the individual players and the team as a whole.

Technical and Tactical Skills

As a coach, you are responsible for patiently and systematically explaining and drilling your athletes on the basic skills and shot patterns that make up the game. These skills, called technical skills, are the fundamentals that provide each player with the tools to execute the physical requirements of the game. Each day at practice, you also must create scenarios on the court in which players have to use their technical skills in matchlike situations, forcing them to make decisions that simulate the choices they will have to make in a match. These skills, called tactical skills, are the bridge between practice performance and match performance. Although the proper execution of technical skills is necessary for success, the tactical skills (i.e., the ability to make the appropriate decisions) are the key to having everything come together when it counts—in the match.

Obviously, other types of skills, such as pure physical capacity, mental skills, communication ability, and character traits, all contribute to athletic performance (Rainer Martens, *Successful Coaching, Third Edition*, Champaign, IL: Human Kinetics, 2004, p. 170). Although all these skills are important, effective teaching of the technical and tactical skills provides the foundation for successful tennis coaching.

The variety of skills used in tennis is massive and impossible to chronicle in one text. Consequently, this book focuses on the basic to intermediate technical and tactical skills in tennis. These skills were compiled with the help of the United States Tennis Association. The goal is to provide a resource that will help you improve your understanding and instructional methods as you strive to teach your players the great game of tennis.

Technical Skills

Technical skills are "the specific procedures to move one's body to perform the task that needs to be accomplished" (Martens, *Successful Coaching*, p. 169). The proper execution of the technical skills of tennis is, obviously, crucial to successful performance. Most coaches, even those with little experience, know what the basic technical skills of tennis are: serves, serve returns, groundstrokes, volleys, approach shots, lobs, and overheads. But your ability to teach athletes how to perform those skills usually develops only over a long period, as you gain coaching experience.

The goal of this book is to speed up the timetable of teaching skills by improving your ability to do the following:

- Clearly communicate the basic elements of each skill to the athlete.
- Construct drills and teaching scenarios to rehearse those skills.
- Detect and correct errors in the athletes' performance of skills.
- Help athletes transfer knowledge and ability from practice to matches.

Effective coaches have the capacity to transfer their knowledge and understanding of skills into improved performance of those skills by their athletes. This book outlines a plan that will help you do just that by teaching you how to become a master of the basic to intermediate technical skills of tennis and provide your athletes with the resources necessary for success.

Tactical Skills

Mastery of the technical skills of tennis is important, but athletes must also learn the tactics of the game. Tactical skills are defined as "the decisions and actions of players in the contest to gain an advantage over the opposing team or players"

(Martens, *Successful Coaching*, p. 170). Many tennis resources overlook the tactical aspects of the game. Coaches even omit tactical considerations from practice because they are focused so intently on teaching technical skills. Another reason for this omission is that tactics are difficult to teach. One way that you can approach tactical skills is by focusing on the following three critical aspects, the "tactical triangle" (Martens, *Successful Coaching*, p. 215):

○ Reading the play or situation
○ Acquiring the knowledge needed to make an appropriate tactical decision
○ Applying decision-making skills to the problem

This book as a whole provides you with the knowledge you need to teach players how to use the tactical triangle. Part III covers cues that help athletes respond appropriately when they see a play developing, including rules of the game, game strategies, and opponents' strengths and weaknesses that affect match situations, as well as ways to teach athletes how to acquire and use this knowledge. Part III will also help you teach athletes how to make appropriate choices in given situations and show you how to empower players to recognize emerging situations on their own and make sound judgments.

Perhaps the greatest frustration for a coach is to witness athletes making errors in matches on skills they have repeatedly drilled in practice. For example, in practice a player demonstrates perfect footwork while moving forward to play an approach shot and continues to the net where he hits a controlled and well-placed volley. During a match, however, he rushes his steps and overhits the approach shot and volleys wildly without getting set at the net. Transferring skills from practice to the match can be difficult, but you can reduce errors by placing the athletes in matchlike situations in practice to work on tactical skill decisions. Only after rehearsing the tactical decision repeatedly in practice will the athletes be prepared to execute those decisions (while maintaining their execution of the related technical skills) in the match.

Traditional Versus Games Approach to Coaching

As mentioned, transferring skills from practice to matches can be difficult. A sound background of technical and tactical training prepares athletes for match situations. Incorporating matchlike situations into daily training, however, increases the likelihood that players will transfer skills from practices to matches. To understand how to accomplish this, you must be aware of two approaches to coaching—the traditional approach and the games approach.

Part IV of this book provides examples of both the traditional approach and the games approach to coaching. Although each style has its particular advantages, the concept favored in this book is the games approach. The games approach provides athletes with a competitive situation governed by clear objectives and focused on specific individuals and concepts. The games approach creates a productive and meaningful learning environment in which athletes are motivated by both the structure of the drills and the improvements they make. Finally, the games approach prepares athletes for competition because they have experienced situations that closely resemble the tactical situations they will see in the match.

Traditional Approach

Although the games approach to coaching has much merit, the traditional approach to coaching also has value. The traditional approach often begins with a warm-up period, followed by individual drills, group drills, and then a substantial team period, or scrimmage, at the end of the practice. The traditional approach can be helpful in teaching the technical skills of tennis. But unless you shape, focus, and enhance the team period, the athletes may be unable to transfer the skills they learn in the drills to the scrimmage situation in practice or, worse, into effective performance, especially of tactical skills, in matches.

Games Approach

The games approach emphasizes the use of games and minigames to provide athletes with situations that are as close to a real match as possible (Alan G. Launder, *Play Practice,* Champaign, IL: Human Kinetics, 2001). But this method requires more than just putting the players on the court, throwing out a ball, and letting them play. You should use the following three components any time you use the games approach:

1. Shaping
2. Focusing
3. Enhancing

Shaping play allows you to modify the game in a way that is conducive to learning the skills your athletes are working on. You can shape play by modifying the rules, the environment (playing area), the objectives of the game, and the number of players (Launder, p. 56). In scrimmage situations the stronger players often dominate, and the weaker players merely get through the scrimmage without playing a strong, active role. If you shape play by reducing the playing area, every athlete will have the opportunity to learn and practice the skills required for tennis.

You also need to be sure to *focus* the athletes on the specific objectives of the game. Players are more apt to learn, or at least be open to learning, if they know why they are playing the game and how the tactics they are rehearsing fit into the bigger picture. Provide the athletes with clear objectives and a straightforward explanation of how those objectives will help them become better tennis players.

Finally, you must play an active role throughout the game, *enhancing* the play by stopping the game at the teachable moment and instructing the athletes about how they could improve their decision-making or technical skills.

A game called Half-Court Singles is an example of the games approach to teaching tactical skills. This game involves two singles players playing points using only half the singles court. The regular singles court is divided down the middle so the center service line is extended to the baseline, making the court 78 feet long but only 13.5 feet wide. This narrow court forces the players to use short and deep shots to move their opponents and create openings. The objective of the game is to move the opponent very deep in the court so the player can hit a short ball by using a drop shot or drop volley in front of her, or to draw her opponent to the net so she can hit a lob over her head into the backcourt. Because the court is narrow, hitting the ball with angles will be ineffective, so players will need to think about and work short and deep ball sequences.

To play this game, have players play to 10 points. Each player serves 2 points before changing serves. To emphasize the deep and short openings, players are awarded 2 points for hitting a successful drop shot or drop volley (a shot that bounces on the court twice before the opponent can play the shot). Also, award 2 points for a successful lob that the player at the net cannot touch.

This game forces all players to think about keeping the ball in play and not giving the opponent free points with unforced errors. It also makes players think about how to win points by hitting a series of shots rather than a one-shot winner. In this situation players are forced to use a combination of short and deep shots to win points. This is a great learning situation for all players because it makes them think about hitting every shot with a purpose.

The game seems simple, but some fascinating scenarios invariably unfold, creating vivid opportunities for teaching. For example, if a player has an opening shot in the court but hits a poor drop shot, it gives the opponent time to move forward, play the shot, and take an offensive position at the net. Players will learn that they must create an opening by forcing the opponent behind the baseline, but they must be inside the baseline themselves to execute a successful drop shot. This scenario illustrates some intriguing dimensions of the games approach to coaching. Later sections of the text will offer more examples of this approach for you to use in creating great learning experiences for your athletes.

Coaching tennis is a complex yet rewarding job. Tennis coaches are responsible not only for the development of good players but also for the development of young people who know right from wrong and how to make good behavioral decisions. The emphasis of this book is on the concepts and strategies of teaching the basic to intermediate technical and tactical skills of tennis, using both the traditional and games approaches. The foundation of effective teaching that this book provides will help you master the art of helping your athletes refine and improve the array of skills and techniques that make up the diverse, complex, and fascinating game of tennis.

chapter 2

Evaluating Technical and Tactical Skills

Tennis is both an individual sport and a team sport. In building your team, you should use specific evaluation tools to assess the development of the individual parts that make up the whole of the team. You must remember that basic physical skills contribute to the performance of the technical and tactical skills. In addition, an array of nonphysical skills, such as mental capacity, communication skills, and character skills, overlay athletic performance and affect its development (Rainer Martens, *Successful Coaching, Third Edition*). In this chapter we examine evaluation guidelines, exploring the specific skills you should evaluate and the tools to use to accomplish those evaluations. Evaluations as described in this chapter will help you critique your players objectively, something that you should continually strive to do.

Guidelines for Evaluation

Regardless of the skill you are measuring and the evaluation tool you are using, you should observe the basic guidelines that govern the testing and evaluation process. First, the athletes need to know and understand the purpose of the test and its relationship to the sport. If you are evaluating a technical skill, the correlation should be easy. But when you are evaluating physical skills, or mental, communication, or character skills, you must explain the correlation between the skill and the aspect of the game that will benefit.

Second, you must motivate your athletes to improve. Understanding the correlation to the game will help, but sometimes the matches seem a long way away during practices and training. In the physical skills area, elevating the status of the testing process can help inspire the athletes. If you can create a match-day atmosphere with many players present and watching as you conduct the testing, the athletes will compete with more energy and enthusiasm than they would if you ran the tests in a more clinical fashion. Goal boards and record boards posting all-time best performances can also motivate the athletes. The best of these boards have several categories, including the longest rally from baseline to baseline, the longest rally from the baseline to the net, the longest rally at the net from volley to volley, and target hits with the serve. You could also include tournament results as a team or even individual results or rankings for those playing in sanctioned tournaments.

The best motivation, though, comes from a personal best effort in physical skills testing, or an improved score in technical, tactical, communication, or mental skills. When athletes compare their performances today to those of yesterday, they can always succeed and make progress, regardless of the achievements of their teammates. When they see themselves making progress, they will be motivated to continue to practice and train. This concept, while focusing on the individual, is not antithetical to the team concept. You simply need to remind the team that if every player gets better every day, the team will get better every day!

Third, all testing must be unbiased, formal, and consistent. Athletes will easily recognize flaws in the testing process and subsequently lose confidence in the results. You must be systematic and accurate, treating every athlete the same way, in order for the test to have any integrity. No athlete should be credited with a test result on a physical skill if she does not execute the test regimen perfectly. You must mandate good form and attention to the details of the test. The same is true of evaluation tools that do not measure quantitatively. A coach who wants to evaluate technical skills must use the same tool for all athletes and score them fairly and consistently for them to trust the conclusions reached.

Fourth, you must convey your feedback to the athletes professionally and, if possible, personally. No athlete wants to fail, and all are self-conscious to a certain extent when they don't perform to their expectations or the expectations of their coach. At the same time, all athletes have areas in which they need to improve, and you must communicate those needs to them, especially if they do not see or understand that they need to improve! Personal, private meetings with athletes are crucial to the exchange of this information. Factual results, comparative ranking charts, historical records of previous test results, and even videos of athletes' performances can discretely communicate both areas in which they are doing well and areas in which they need to make progress.

If you have a large number of athletes, you can accomplish these individual meetings in occasional and subtle ways—by asking the athlete to stay for a few minutes in the office after a team meeting, by finding the athlete after practice or a workout in the locker room, by going out to practice early and creating an opportunity to talk to the athlete individually, or by calling the athlete in to the office at random times just to talk. These in-person, one-on-one meetings are by far the best method of communicating to your athletes the areas in which they need to improve.

Finally, you must apply the principles that you are asking of your players to the process of evaluating them. You must be an expert in your field in terms of your knowledge of the technical and tactical skills for your sport, so that you can accurately and consistently evaluate the skill that you see your players perform. You must understand the value and importance of the physical skills (perhaps even in your personal lifestyle and health habits) to convey the importance of these skills to the game. You must have outstanding communication skills to be effective in your teaching, and you must exhibit those skills in your dealings with other staff members, especially when you are visible to the players, so that you can establish credibility with the players regarding communication.

Evaluating Skills

Clearly, players must know the technical skills demanded by their sport, and they must know how to apply those skills in tactical situations when they compete. You must remember, however, that basic physical skills contribute to the performance of the technical and tactical skills and must be consciously incorporated into the athlete's training plan. In addition, various nonphysical skills such as mental capacity, communication skills, and character skills also overlay athletic performance and affect its development.

As you evaluate your athletes, one concept is crucial: Athletes should focus on trying to improve their own previous performance, as opposed to comparing their performances to those of their teammates. Certainly, comparative data help athletes see where they rank on the team and perhaps among other players, and these data may motivate them or help them set goals. However, because all rankings place some athletes on the team below others, these athletes can easily become discouraged, especially if they consistently rank at the bottom of the team. Conversely, if the focus of the evaluation is personal improvement, every player on the team has the possibility of being successful every time tests are conducted. Whether you are looking at physical skills or nonphysical skills, encourage your athletes to achieve their own personal bests.

Evaluating Physical Skills

The essential physical skills for tennis are strength, speed, agility, power, and flexibility. The training and evaluation of those five physical skills are especially important in the off-season and preseason periods, when athletes are concentrating on overall improvement. In-season evaluation, however, also ensures that any off-season gains, especially in strength, do not deteriorate because the players and coaches are devoting much of their time and attention to match-plan preparation and practice.

Testing should occur at least three times a year—once immediately before the tennis season begins to gauge athletes' readiness for the season, once after the season to measure the retention of physical skills during competition, and once in the spring to evaluate athletes' progress and development in the off-season program. In addition, you will be constantly evaluating your athletes throughout the season to make slight adjustments, about which you will learn more in chapter 8.

Of course, training programs can positively affect several skills. For example, improvements in leg strength and flexibility will almost certainly improve speed.

Furthermore, no specific workout program will ensure gains for every athlete in each of the five skill areas. Consequently, testing and measuring gains in these areas is critical in showing you and your athletes where they are making gains and where to place the emphasis of subsequent training programs.

Strength

Strength testing can be done safely and efficiently using multiple-rep projections of athletes' maximum performance. The risk of injury for the athletes is minimal because they are working with weights that are less than their maximum load. After properly warming up, athletes should select a weight that they believe they can rep at least three but no more than seven times. Using a chart of projected totals, the number of reps that they accomplish will yield their max. This type of test is slightly less accurate than a one-rep max, in which athletes continue to work with heavier weights until they find the highest load that they can rep one time. But the one-rep test takes much longer to administer and is less safe because the athletes are working with peak loads. Furthermore, the accuracy of the test would be critical only if the athletes were competing with each other. Because the focus of the off-season training program is personal development and improvement, the multiple-rep projection is adequate for allowing athletes to compare their performances with their previous performances.

Speed

Speed testing for tennis has always focused on the 10-yard dash. Rarely does a tennis athlete run longer than 10 yards to hit a shot, so longer distances are not indicative of the type of speed needed to play the game. Running from sideline to sideline and from the net to the baseline both require sprints that are in the 10-yard range, so the athlete's time over that distance is crucial. Nevertheless, the majority of runs that a tennis player makes in a match are short bursts, so a test of the player's initial 10-yard speed from a standing start also correlates well with the type of speed needed to play the game. The 10-yard test can be administered

CORE STRENGTH

Like the proverbial chain that is only as strong as its weakest link, the athlete's core ultimately determines whether she can put it all together and translate her strength, speed, or agility into successful tennis performance. The core refers to the midsection of the body—the abdominal muscles, the lower-back muscles, and the muscles of the hip girdle—that connect lower-body strength and functions with upper-body strength and functions. Core strength, then, is essential for tennis, but at the same time it is extremely difficult to isolate and evaluate.

Without a strong core, the tennis athlete will experience great difficulty in keeping low as he plays the game. The core also must be strong for the tennis athlete to be able to play with great explosiveness—combining strength, power, and speed into movement around the court and powerful groundstrokes and serves. Every physical training program for tennis, therefore, must include exercises that strengthen and develop the core. A core training program must go beyond sit-ups and crunches, which, although important, are not comprehensive enough to develop true core strength. Tennis athletes must incorporate active exercises such as lunges, step-ups, and squat jumps to focus on developing the core.

Isolating core strength is difficult because it is involved in the performance of every physical skill. But any exercise that recruits one or more large muscle areas and two or more primary joints (such as the bench press) can be used to test core strength (See NSCA's *Essentials of Personal Training*, 2003). The ultimate evaluation of core strength, however, is the athlete's performance of tennis skills on the practice court and on match day.

with an electronic timer to record times. You want the test situation to resemble the game situation as closely as possible.

Agility

Tennis also requires athletes to change direction quickly in short spaces and use quality footwork to get into the proper position for groundstrokes moving side to side and forward and back. Quick lateral movement is essential for successful volleys, and a quick drop step and crossover step are necessary when moving back for an overhead. For this reason, agility and footwork are physical skills that must be trained and measured. The most common agility test for tennis is the spider run, in which five balls are placed on a racket on the baseline at the center mark. The player starts at that point and runs with the first ball to the sideline/baseline intersection and returns for the second ball. The player places the second ball on the intersection of the service line and singles sideline; the third ball, on the intersection of the service line and center service line; the fourth ball, on the intersection of the opposite service line and singles sideline; and the fifth ball, on the intersection of the singles sideline and baseline. This test measures the athlete's ability to plant and change directions and requires her to keep her core low and maintain the athletic body position frequently mentioned throughout the skills section of this book.

Power

Power is the fourth primary skill required for tennis. The emphasis here is on the lower-body explosiveness that helps the tennis athlete to set, load, and drive with the legs on groundstrokes; load and drive with the legs on the serve; and jump in the air for the overhead. The two simplest and best tests for power are the standing long jump and the vertical jump. Administer both tests with the athlete in a stationary position so that the test measures pure explosiveness unassisted by a running start. Allow the athlete to take several trials at each event, using his best effort as his recorded score.

Flexibility

Flexibility is the most neglected physical skill but one of the most important. Enhanced flexibility will help athletes improve just about every other physical skill. Off-season programs should stress stretching, and you should encourage, or require, athletes to stretch for at least 15 minutes each day. In addition, the training program should include exercises that require athletes to bend and move, such as lunges and step-ups, so they are stretching and training the hip girdle and lower-back area as they work on strength and power. Flexibility is difficult to measure, but the classic sit-and-reach test provides a reasonable indication of athletes' ranges and gives them a standard from which to improve.

Evaluating Nonphysical Skills

Athletic performance is not purely physical; a number of other factors influence it. You must recognize and emphasize mental skills, communication skills, and character skills to enable your athletes to reach peak athletic performance.

Despite the importance of the physical, mental, communication, and character skills, however, the emphasis in this book is on the coaching of essential technical and tactical skills. For an in-depth discussion of teaching and developing both physical and nonphysical skills, refer to chapters 9 through 12 in Rainer Martens' *Successful Coaching, Third Edition.*

Mental Skills

Tennis is a complex game that requires players to maintain focus on their match plan; keep positive when opponents have the momentum; play at the right pace and not rush; and deal with the strengths, weaknesses, and idiosyncrasies of opponents.

Most important to tennis players' success, however, is the mental ability to sort out and isolate the cues that allow them to execute the proper shot at the right time. They must work hard on every point and must continually monitor what is successful and not successful. Can they play by using their strengths, or should they attack an opponent's weakness? Players must gauge the pace of play and adjust based on their own momentum swings, emotional status, and fitness level, and those of their opponents. Players need to focus on what works best based on the physical conditions of the court and ball and environmental conditions of sun, wind, and temperature. The performance of these skills takes study, discipline, focus, and a belief that the system of cues will produce the desired results. The term *mental toughness* might be the best and simplest way to describe the concentration and determination required to perform these skills in the course of a tennis match.

Communication Skills

Tennis also requires communication skills at several levels—among the players on the court and between the coaches and the players in classrooms and during practices and matches. As a coach, you must convey adjustments to the match plan and strategy at changeovers and between sets. Because communication skills are essential to tennis, you should spend considerable time coordinating your system of communication.

Character Skills

Finally, character skills help shape the performance of the team. Tennis is a game that requires (and reveals) character because in most cases players officiate their matches by calling their own lines and keeping track of the score.

Evaluation Tools

Tennis coaches are making more use of videos of practices and matches to evaluate athletes' performance of basic technical and tactical skills. Video is useful because so many players are participating at one time and it is difficult, if not impossible, to watch each of them on every court. The video becomes an excellent teaching tool in individual, group, or team meetings because the players can see themselves perform and listen to your comments evaluating that performance.

You can evaluate videos of your players in several ways. The most common way is to simply watch the video without taking notes or systematically evaluating every player. The purpose is to gather impressions to share with your players when you watch the video together later. Many coaches use this method because of time and staff limitations.

Other coaches systematically grade athletes from the video, evaluating their performances on every play in terms of whether they executed the correct assignment, technique, and tactical decision. This grading process can be simple; for example, you can simply mark a plus or a minus on each play and score the total number of pluses and minuses for the match. Alternatively, you can score athletes on each aspect of play, giving them grades for their assignments, their technique, and their tactical decision making.

Regardless of the level of sophistication or detail of the grading instrument, most coaches use a grading system of some kind for evaluating match videos. Most grading systems are based on a play-by-play (or rep-by-rep in practices) analysis of performance; some are coupled with an analysis of productivity totals such as the ones listed previously. Rarely does a coach systematically evaluate the technical and tactical skills required for tennis on a skill-by-skill basis.

Furthermore, when coaches evaluate a skill, they generally evaluate only the result (did the player return the ball or not?), not the key elements that determine the player's ability to hit the ball (eye contact, hand position, and so on).

Figure 2.1 *a* and *b* (page 16), are examples of an evaluation tool that allows you to isolate technical and tactical skills. By breaking down the whole skill into its component parts, this tool enables a more objective assessment of an athlete's skill performance than statistics can produce. By using these figures and the technical and tactical skills in parts II and III as a guide, you can create an evaluation tool for each of the technical and tactical skills that you want to evaluate during your season. In figure 2.1*a*, using the technical skill of the forehand ground stroke as an example, we have broken down the skill by pulling out each of the key points from the skills found in chapters 3 and 4 so that you can rate your players' execution of the skill in specific targeted areas.

As you may already know, evaluating tactical skills is more difficult than evaluating technical skills because many outside influences factor into how and when the skill comes into play. However, as a coach, you can evaluate your players' execution of tactical skills using a format that is similar to the one you use for technical skills. You will need to do the legwork in breaking down the skill into targeted areas. In figure 2.1*b*, we have used a generic format to show you how to break down a tactical skill into its component parts so you can do the same with the skills outlined in chapters 6 and 7.

The evaluation tool shown in figure 2.1 and the process of scoring that it advocates may help you avoid the common pitfall of becoming preoccupied with the result of the skill and coaching and evaluating only the outcome. This tool will help you pinpoint where errors are occurring and enable you to focus on correcting those errors with your athletes.

This tool is admittedly somewhat subjective because the ratings are simply an opinion based on observation. You can add some statistical weight to the process by scoring players each time they perform the skill. For example, a player might play hundreds of shots during the course of a match but hit only six lobs. Of these six lobs, only two are offensive lobs. Most coaches would grade the player on whether she executed the lob, but this tool allows you to evaluate the elements that make up a successful lob. You can pinpoint where the player is making mistakes by breaking down the skill and analyzing the component parts.

When you go beyond the result and focus on the cues and knowledge needed to execute a specific skill, you alert the player to the key elements of the skill that need improvement. Using this type of evaluation, you may sometimes be critical of an athlete's technique even when the result is positive.

For example, if your player is working on a topspin lob using a sharp-angled upward swing pattern with an open racket face, you need to reinforce the importance of a sharp-angled swing with a fast racket head and open racket face, whether or not the ball lands in the court. If the swing is fast and sharply angled and the racket face is open, you must be positive about the player's use of that technique and avoid comments about the ball landing beyond the baseline. Likewise, if the

Figure 2.1a Forehand groundstroke technical skill evaluation

Key focal points	Weak 1	2	3	4	Strong 5	Notes
Ready position	1	2	3	4	5	
Movement to the ball	1	2	3	4	5	
Preparation for the hit	1	2	3	4	5	
Loading on the back foot	1	2	3	4	5	
Contact point	1	2	3	4	5	
Balance	1	2	3	4	5	
Follow-through	1	2	3	4	5	
Recovery	1	2	3	4	5	

From *Coaching Tennis Technical and Tactical Skills* by ASEP, 2009, Champaign, IL: Human Kinetics.

Figure 2.1b Offensive lob tactical skill evaluation

Player's ability	Weak 1	2	3	4	Strong 5	Notes
Avoids distractions as discussed in Watch Out!	1	2	3	4	5	
Reads the situation	1	2	3	4	5	
Understands physical playing conditions and reacts appropriately	1	2	3	4	5	
Recognizes the skill level of opponents and reacts appropriately	1	2	3	4	5	
Recognizes own skill level and reacts appropriately	1	2	3	4	5	
Makes appropriate decisions based on the match situation	1	2	3	4	5	

From *Coaching Tennis Technical and Tactical Skills* by ASEP, 2009, Champaign, IL: Human Kinetics.

player hits a lob that lands in the court but it does not have topspin, you need to tell him that he is using an unacceptable technique. You cannot give the player mixed messages; you must focus on the process of hitting a lob with topspin, not the result, if you truly want to improve his use of this technique.

The evaluation tool shown in figure 2.1 *a* and *b* is a simple way to use the details of each technical and tactical skill, providing an outline for both the player and you to review and a mechanism for understanding the areas in which the player needs to improve. The tool also can be used as a summary exercise. After a match, after a week of practice, or after a preseason or spring practice segment, athletes can score themselves on all the essential technical and tactical skills, including all the cues and focal points, and on as many of the corollary skills as desired. You can also score the athletes and then compare the two score sheets. The ensuing discussion will give both you and your players a direction for future practices and drills, and help you decide where you need to focus to improve individual athletes' performances. You can repeat this process later, so the athletes can look for improvement in the areas in which they have been concentrating their workouts. As the process unfolds, the athletes' score sheets and yours should begin to match more closely.

Because your players will mirror your mental outlook, you must display the mental skills you ask of them—such as emotional control, self-confidence, and a motivation to achieve. Likewise, players will model your character, in terms of your trustworthiness, fairness, and ability to earn respect. You are a role model, whether you want to be or not, and your athletes will develop the proper mental and character skills only if you display those skills.

The process of teaching, evaluating, and motivating athletes to improve defines the job of the coach, which is to take athletes somewhere they could not get to by themselves. Without you, the athletes would not have a clear idea of the steps they need to take to become better players. You provide the expertise, guidance, and incentive that allow them to make progress.

One final point caps this discussion of evaluating athletes. Athletes in every sport want to know how much you care before they care how much you know. Keep in mind that at times you must suspend the process of teaching and evaluating to deal with the athlete as a person. Spend time with your athletes discussing topics other than their sport and their performance. Show them that you are interested in and concerned about them as people, that you are willing to listen to their issues, and that you are willing to help them if doing so is legal and they wish to be helped. Events in athletes' personal lives can overshadow their athletic quests, and you must be sensitive to that reality.

Athletes will play their best and their hardest for the coach who cares. Their skills will improve, and their performances will improve, because they want to reward the coach's caring attitude with inspired performance. They will finish their athletic careers for that coach having learned a lifelong lesson that care and concern are as important as any skill in the game of tennis.

Teaching Technical Skills

Now that you know how to teach and evaluate sport skills, you are ready to dive into the specific skills necessary for success in tennis. Part II focuses on the basic and intermediate skills necessary for your players' success, including offensive technical skills related to serving, groundstrokes, volleys, and overheads; and defensive technical skills related to lobs, returning the serve, and groundstrokes hit from deep or wide positions of the court. This part also focuses on other shots such as drop shots, second serves, approach shots, and midcourt volleys.

Chapters 3 and 4 present the material in a way that is clear and easy to understand. More important, you can immediately incorporate the information into your practices. Whether you are a seasoned veteran or a new coach, you will find the presentation of skills in this part helpful as you work with your athletes.

For each skill we first present a list of what we call the key points, which are the most important aspects of the skill. This list is a road map to the proper execution of the skill. Following is a detailed explanation of these key points, including instructional photos and diagrams to guide you along the way.

At the end of each skill description is a table of common errors that includes instructions for how to correct those errors in your athletes. We also include a useful At a Glance section to guide you to other tools in the book that will help you teach your athletes this particular skill—whether it is another technical skill that they need to be able to perform to be successful or a tactical skill that uses this technical skill.

chapter 3

Foundational Skills

This chapter covers the foundational skills players must know to be successful. In this chapter you will find the following skills:

Square Groundstroke Stance

Groundstrokes, about which you will learn more in chapter 4, can be hit using one of three stances. In the square stance, the entire body (feet, hips, and shoulders) face the sideline. This basic stance is the most traditional and is similar to a golfer addressing a ball on the tee or a baseball player waiting for a pitch in the batter's box.

The advantage of the square stance is that the hitter can have a long contact zone because the path of the racket and racket face are in line with the target for the longest period of time, compared with the open and closed stances (see pages 25 and 28). The square stance allows a weight shift forward as well as a proper hip and shoulder turn from facing the sideline to facing the net during the stroke.

INITIAL BODY AND FOOT POSITION

To assume the square groundstroke stance from the ready position, as shown in figure 3.1a, the player turns the hips, trunk, and feet 90 degrees, so that the body goes from facing the net to facing the sideline, as shown in figure 3.1b. The back foot is parallel to the baseline as the player sets up to hit with a square stance. The front foot is also parallel to the baseline.

a   b

Figure 3.1 **Body positioning for the square groundstroke stance.**

WEIGHT TRANSFER

As the player turns to the sideline, the weight shifts and loads on the back foot during the backswing, as shown in figure 3.1b. Just before the racket moves forward, the front foot steps forward and turns 45 degrees. The weight shifts to the forward foot from the back foot during the swing.

TRUNK ROTATION

As the weight shifts to the forward foot, the hips and shoulders rotate so the player is facing the net directly. The sequence begins with the weight loaded on the back foot and the transfer of weight to the front foot. This is followed by the hip, trunk, and shoulder turn (see figure 3.2), ending with the weight on the front foot and the back foot rotated so the toe is down and the sole of the foot is facing the back fence (see figure 3.3).

At a Glance

The following parts of the text offer additional information on the square groundstroke stance:

Forehand Groundstroke	66
One-Handed Backhand Groundstroke	73
Two-Handed Backhand Groundstroke	80
Passing Shot	131

Figure 3.2 Trunk rotation during the swing.

Figure 3.3 Final body position for the groundstroke when using the square stance.

(continued)

Common Errors

Following are several common errors that you might run into when teaching your athletes how to hit using the square groundstroke stance:

Error	Error correction
The player prepares perfectly but fails to rotate the body for the forward swing.	Once the player sets up and is prepared in the correct square stance position, he must transfer the weight from the back foot to the front foot and rotate the body from the hips so the trunk and shoulders face directly forward during the follow-through. Have him assume a finish position so his belt buckle faces the net on the follow-through. This will ensure that the hips rotate forward from the starting position facing the sideline.
The player prepares perfectly and rotates for the stroke, but does not transfer the weight from the back foot to the front foot.	When the player does not shift from the back foot to the front foot, she loses power in the stroke. Many times this happens because the player swings late and contacts the ball even with the back hip rather than the front hip. Make sure the player is preparing early enough so she can transfer the weight to the forward foot, rotate the hips, and make contact even with the front hip.
The player does not get a complete hip rotation so the hips don't finish facing the net on the follow-through.	Watch to see if the front foot opens from being at 90-degree angle to the net to being at a 45-degree angle. If the foot does not turn so it points more toward the net, the body will not be able to open properly during the hit.

Open Groundstroke Stance

Because of the speed of the game, the open stance has become the preferred stance of most experienced players when hitting groundstrokes. This stance allows the player to hit with a full body rotation and also recover back into position after the hit.

The open stance has become so common that it is used when playing very wide balls where the player will move wide, plant, drive, and recover from the back foot. It is also used when hitting the inside-out forehand, a preferred stroke by most top players when the ball is hit at the body or slightly to the backhand side. The player side steps from the ready position and the stance remains open for the forehand groundstroke.

KEY POINTS

The most important components of the open groundstroke stance are as follows:

- Initial body and foot position
- Weight transfer
- Trunk rotation

INITIAL BODY AND FOOT POSITION

To assume the open groundstroke stance, from the ready position, as shown in figure 3.4a, the player turns the hips, trunk, and feet 90 degrees, so that the body goes from facing the net to facing the sideline, as shown in figure 3.4b. The back foot should point at the sideline and be parallel with the baseline. The front foot is pointed toward the net.

a   b

Figure 3.4 **Body positioning for the open groundstroke stance.**

(continued)

At a Glance

The following parts of the text offer additional information on the open groundstroke stance:

Forehand Groundstroke	66
One-Handed Backhand Groundstroke	73
Two-Handed Backhand Groundstroke	80
Forehand as a Weapon	122

WEIGHT TRANSFER

Once the player has turned to the sideline, the weight is transferred to the back, or outside, foot during the backswing. Just before moving the racket forward, the player pushes off the back foot to initiate the body rotation toward the net.

TRUNK ROTATION

As the player prepares the racket in the backswing position, the body rotates forward, beginning from the outside foot to the hips and shoulders (see figure 3.5). The rotation shifts the weight from the back (outside) foot to a neutral position, with the weight evenly distributed on both feet during the follow-through, so that the body faces the net (see figure 3.6).

Figure 3.5 **Trunk rotation during the swing.**

Figure 3.6 **Final body position for the groundstroke when using the open groundstroke stance.**

Common Errors

Following are several common errors you may encounter when teaching your athletes the open groundstroke stance:

Error	Error correction
The player moves into position and the feet are in an open stance position, but the body does not turn and coil from the hips so it faces the sideline, leading to a less powerful hit.	The easiest correction is to have the player maintain contact with the nondominant hand from the ready position to the backswing position. As the racket goes back, this will turn the shoulders, trunk, and hips so they all face the sideline with the proper turn and coil before the hit.
Because the player is trying to hit with an open stance, she stays facing the net and shuffles for a wide ball.	Although a few shuffle steps work well for a ball that is only a step or two away, the wide ball requires that the player turn and run into position. As she turns and runs, the hips, trunk, and shoulders will face the sideline and the racket will be behind the body in the early stage of the backswing. The player simply needs to make the final stride with the outside foot so she can load and push off to generate the body turn and weight transfer during the forward swing.
The racket hits across the ball rather than directly into and through the ball.	It is easy to hit across the ball with an open stance. Even though the body is facing the net at contact, the arm, hand, and racket must all drive through the ball for optimal control. Rather than a glancing blow, the player should win the collision with the oncoming ball, and the hand and racket should extend out toward the target.

KEY POINTS

The most important components of a closed groundstroke stance are as follows:

o Initial body and foot position
o Weight transfer
o Trunk rotation

The closed stance is the least effective groundstroke stance because it restricts forward weight transfer, severely limits body rotation, and generally forces the hitter to take extra steps to recover after contact. The lack of rotation makes it difficult to generate a powerful stroke.

However, at times your players will have no other option than to use the closed stance. One example would be on a very wide ball that your player has to run down; if the last stride is with the front foot, the player will have to hit with a closed stance. Another example would be on a hard-hit ball, such as a serve return or volley, in which the player has time for only one step. In this situation the player simply pivots and steps across with the front foot and hits with a closed stance.

The closed stance is more common with the one-handed backhand groundstroke, because the hips and shoulders don't rotate as much and the weight can shift forward.

INITIAL BODY AND FOOT POSITION

In the closed groundstroke stance both feet are parallel to the baseline, but the front foot is closer to the sideline (see figure 3.7). The hips, trunk, and shoulders all turn 90 degrees from the ready position, in which the hips and shoulders are facing the net directly, to a position in which the hips, trunk, and shoulders are facing the sideline.

Figure 3.7 Body positioning for the closed groundstroke stance.

WEIGHT TRANSFER

Before contact, the weight shifts from the back foot to the forward foot. The direction of the transfer is inefficient because it is going toward the sideline rather than toward the net.

TRUNK ROTATION

Because the forward foot is across the body, there is very little rotation of the hips and minimal rotation of the trunk and shoulders. The body simply cannot rotate and open toward the net because the front leg crosses the body making it impossible for the hips to turn forward. The arm swings forward and makes contact with the ball. The arm then follows through, and the weight shifts to the front foot (see figure 3.8a). After contact, the back foot steps across so the body can maintain balance (see figure 3.8b). This extra balance step is necessary for recovering into position.

At a Glance

The following parts of the text offer additional information on the closed groundstroke stance:

Forehand Groundstroke	66
One-Handed Backhand Groundstroke	73
Two-Handed Backhand Groundstroke	80
Volley	105
Lob	126

a   b

Figure 3.8 **Contact with the ball (a) and recovery (b) when using a closed groundstroke stance.**

(continued)

Common Errors

Following are common errors you may run into when teaching the closed groundstroke stance:

Error	Error correction
The player hits many shots with a closed stance rather than using the more efficient and powerful square or open stance.	Make sure the player moves to the ball quickly so he can set up, either with a square or an open stance. He should try as much as possible to avoid hitting with a closed stance, because it has very limited power and the recovery requires an extra step to get back in position.
When a player hits with a closed stance, the body cannot rotate forward, often leading to a very short and weak swing.	Even though the hips are not turning and the body is not rotating, make sure the player swings the racket using a full follow-through from the shoulder. The player can still be somewhat effective if the swing with the closed stance is long and complete.

Players use the open volley stance when they can hit the ball within arm's reach or at the body. They also use this stance when they have little or no time to move their feet before playing the ball.

INITIAL BODY AND FOOT POSITION

The usual sequence for a volley is to prepare the racket, turn the body, and move across and forward with the feet. Ideally, players play volleys with the body moving forward and with the side of the body facing the net.

However, at times the ball is moving so quickly that the hitter has time only to prepare the racket. At these times the hitter must prepare the racket and hit the volley without turning and stepping. Because the ball is either hit directly at the body or coming quickly, the player has no time to move the feet. The feet are in the same position at contact as they were during the ready position.

KEY POINTS

The most important components of the open volley stance are as follows:

○ Initial body and foot position
○ Weight transfer
○ Trunk rotation

WEIGHT TRANSFER

The weight transfer is directly forward if there is time to take a step (see figure 3.9). If there is no time to step before the volley, the weight should be forward so the player doesn't contact the ball with the weight on the heels (see figure 3.10). Note that when the ball is coming quickly and is only a short distance away, the player can step quickly to the right or left with the outside foot. The stance remains open, but the player has additional reach for the shot.

Figure 3.9 Weight transfer for the open volley stance when there is time to take a step.

Figure 3.10 Weight transfer for the open volley stance when there is no time to take a step.

(continued)

At a Glance

The following parts of the text offer additional information on the open volley stance:

Volley	105
Volley and Overhead	175

TRUNK ROTATION

Because the feet are not turning right or left to play this shot because of time or distance, there is no body rotation. The hips and shoulders remain in the same position as in the ready position (facing the net).

Common Errors

Following are common errors you may run into when teaching your athletes the open volley stance:

Error	Error correction
The player hits the volley flat footed or with the weight back on the heels.	Make sure the player is in a good athletic ready position when she is at the net. The feet should be shoulder-width apart, the knees should be flexed, and the weight should be forward in anticipation of the opponent's shot. If the ball is hit at the body or very hard, the player should hit the shot early with the weight forward rather than late and moving back on the heels.
The player tries to turn sideways to play a volley that is hit directly at the body, turning and stepping back to get the body out of the way to play the shot.	Because the player should not be moving back as he plays the volley, he should hit the ball on the backhand side of the racket and simply block the ball into the open court. If the ball is hit so hard that the player has no time to move, he should use that speed to generate power for the volley. He should grip the racket firmly and play a solid backhand volley in front of the body without any body turn or stepping with either foot.

A player at the net has less time to react and move to the ball. If the player has to move one step to hit a ball at the net, he must use a crossover step. The crossover step should be across and forward so the player in the volley position moves closer to the net so he can hit a more aggressive shot. As the player turns to face the ball, he steps across with the forward foot to be in a position to hit the return volley. With a turn and crossover step on the forehand and backhand sides, the player at the net should be able to reach from almost singles sideline to singles sideline with only one step, giving the opponent little room to hit a passing shot.

KEY POINTS

The most important components of the crossover volley stance are as follows:

○ Initial body and foot position
○ Weight transfer
○ Trunk rotation

Figure 3.11   Initial body positioning for the crossover volley stance.

INITIAL BODY AND FOOT POSITION

From the ready position, as shown in figure 3.11, the outside foot then turns and points at the sideline so that the body turns sideways to the net. When the back foot turns and points at the sideline, the body begins to turn, first with the hips and then the shoulders, so they rotate 90 degrees from the ready position. The outside foot becomes the back foot and the opposite foot steps across and forward for maximum reach so the player can hit the volley with just one step.

WEIGHT TRANSFER

For the ideal volley, the hitter will be sideways to the net with the back foot parallel to the net and the front foot at a 45 degree angle to the net. As the player steps across and forward, the weight shifts from the back foot to the forward foot. Note that timing for this depends on the speed of the oncoming ball; the step and weight transfer could happen before, during, or even after contact.

At a Glance

The following parts of the text offer additional information on the crossover volley stance:

Continental Grip	41
Applying Backspin	51
Controlling Shot Angle	57
Volley	105

(continued)

TRUNK ROTATION

Once the player turns and steps forward and across, the racket is in position for the volley (see figure 3.12). Because the player hits the volley with a very short stroke, there is no need for the body to rotate. In fact, the body is not able to rotate when the player has a long crossover stride to reach the ball because the step across will not permit the body to rotate forward.

Figure 3.12   Racket in position for the volley when using the crossover step.

Common Errors

Following are several common errors that you might run into when teaching your athletes how to hit using the crossover volley stance:

Error	Error correction
The player steps across but not forward to play the volley.	When the player turns and steps across but not forward, she loses the power generated by the forward weight transfer for the volley. Make sure, whenever possible, that the player steps across but also forward. Not only will she have more power on the shot, but she will also make contact earlier. This earlier contact will allow the player to create a better angle on the volley. It will also prevent her from having to volley the ball up defensively rather than down and offensively.
The player moves only sideways for the volley without a crossover step.	Moving only sideways severely limits the player's reach and restricts the power possible with the weight shift. Prevent the side step by getting the player to first move the hands and racket so the racket is lined up for the volley. The body will have to turn so it faces the contact point. When the body turns, the weight transfers to the back foot and only one foot is free to move. The front foot will step across and forward to make the volley.
The player steps forward, but with the wrong foot.	When the player steps forward with the wrong foot (outside foot), he is not facing the ball at the contact point (note that the same correction can be used as with the previous error, as well). Have the player prepare the hands and racket first rather than moving the feet first. This will turn the body and load the weight on the outside foot so he can step forward and across with the front foot.

The Eastern forehand grip is the standard forehand grip for players with linear strokes or strokes with flat to moderate spin. The Eastern forehand is a traditional grip used when the weight is transferred from the back foot to the front foot and for flat to moderate topspin shots played at waist level. At the net, players can use the Eastern forehand grip for high forehand volleys. However, they must change to a Continental grip for low forehand volleys, and it is very weak on the backhand side. The Eastern forehand grip is not as strong as the semi-Western grip (see page 37) for the modern game, because it does not generate as much topspin and it is difficult to drive the ball when the contact point is above the waist.

For the Eastern forehand grip, the hand is positioned so the V formed by the thumb and first finger is directly on top of the handle (see figure 3.13). The palm is on the flat side of the handle in the same plane as the racket face.

HIGH FOREHAND VOLLEYS

The Eastern forehand grip is effective for volleys that are hit shoulder height or above with little or no spin. When players use this grip, the racket face is closed on low balls (see figure 3.14a) and open on balls hit at head level and above (see figure 3.14b), so they must use the wrist to get the racket face perpendicular on both types of balls.

KEY POINTS

The eastern forehand grip is used in the following situations:

- High forehand volleys
- Beginner serves

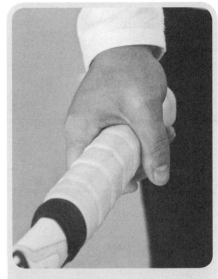

Figure 3.13 Eastern forehand grip.

a   b

Figure 3.14 Hitting a high forehand volley using the Eastern forehand grip: (a) low balls and (b) balls at head level and higher.

(continued)

At a Glance

The following parts of the text offer additional information on the Eastern forehand grip:

Forehand Groundstroke	66
Drop Shot	118
Lob	126
Groundstroke From Deep in the Court	134

BEGINNER SERVES

Players at the beginning skill level can also use the Eastern forehand grip. Learning spin is easier with an Eastern forehand grip than with another grip, such as a Continental grip, which creates a lot of spin. The Eastern forehand grip imparts minimal topspin on the serve, generally not enough to pull a hard-hit serve into the court, and creates sidespin. Because beginning players generally do not hit hard enough to need topspin to pull the ball down in the court, the Eastern forehand grip is a good grip to use to get a feel for imparting moderate spin while hitting the serve.

Common Errors

Following are several common errors that you might run into when teaching your athletes how to hit using the Eastern forehand grip:

Error	Error correction
The player tries to use the Eastern forehand grip to generate power and spin on the forehand side.	The Eastern forehand grip simply does not generate power and spin when hitting a forehand groundstroke. This grip is functional for flat to moderate topspin and can also be used for backspin and sidespin. Players wanting to hit powerful topspin forehands should move to a semi-Western (see page 37) or Western grip (see page 39).
The player serves without much spin using the Eastern forehand grip.	The Eastern forehand grip allows only minimal spin and wrist flexibility when used for the serve. The spin is limited to sidespin because it is difficult to hit up on the ball for topspin using this grip. A Continental grip (see page 41) would be a much better choice for the service grip.
The player volleys weakly using the Eastern forehand grip.	The Eastern forehand grip can be used when hitting volleys that are medium to high at the contact point. For low volleys the wrist must lay back, so this grip is not as strong when playing any ball below the height of the net. On the backhand side, this grip requires a large adjustment at the wrist; all backhand volleys played with an Eastern forehand grip tend to be very weak because of the unstable position at the wrist.

The semi-Western grip provides a good balance of power and spin. In this grip, the hand is in a strong and solid position in back of the handle for strength and control. The semi-Western grip is the most common grip used for playing aggressive forehand groundstrokes. With the move to more powerful, oversized rackets and the need for additional topspin and speed, most top players in the world use the semi-Western grip.

Although this grip is well suited for topspin forehand drives, it's a liability for serving. It has almost no value as a service grip because it cannot hit serves with spin. All the server can do is pop the ball up softly so it drops in the service court. It also is a very ineffective grip for volleys, because it closes the racket face on the forehand side and opens the racket face on the backhand side.

For the semi-Western grip, the palm is between the side and bottom of the handle (see figure 3.15). The racket face with this grip is slightly closed at waist level and below, and perpendicular to the court on balls struck above the waist.

KEY POINTS

The semi-Western grip is used in the following situations:

- Forehands
- High-bouncing forehands
- Forehand groundstrokes with power

FOREHANDS

The semi-Western grip works best for hitting forehands with moderate to heavy topspin. The player can hit the ball slightly later with this grip than with an Eastern forehand grip, and the hit is much stronger when the contact point is above waist level. This grip allows players to hit shots flat with no spin to heavy topspin shots.

HIGH-BOUNCING FOREHANDS

Because the modern game is primarily played with moderate to heavy topspin on all groundstrokes, balls bounce higher after hitting the

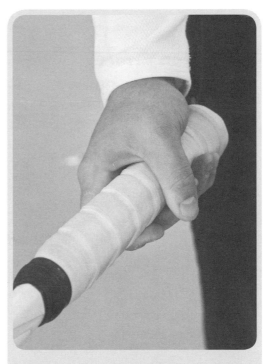

Figure 3.15 Semi-Western grip.

court. The semi-Western grip is a very strong grip for forehands that are hit in a higher contact area, between the waist and shoulder. It's easy to swing the racket from low to high with the arm, forearm, and wrist, keeping the racket face perpendicular to the court.

(continued)

At a Glance

The following parts of the text offer additional information on the semi-Western grip:

Forehand Groundstroke	66
Forehand as a Weapon	122
Passing Shot	131

FOREHAND GROUNDSTROKES WITH POWER

For a player to hit with power and keep the ball in the court, the hand must be in a strong position behind the handle and the shot must be hit with moderate to heavy topspin. The semi-Western forehand grip is well suited for the power game because it puts the hand in a strong position behind the handle allowing the player to generate the topspin necessary to pull the ball down in the court.

Common Errors

Following are several common errors that you might run into when teaching your athletes how to hit using the semi-Western grip:

Error	Error correction
The player uses the semi-Western grip when he is in trouble and must play very low or very wide balls.	The semi-Western grip is an ideal grip for playing power shots. It is a great topspin grip and is perfect for balls hit high in the contact zone. However, topspin is difficult to generate on very wide or very low balls, and the racket face should actually be open when hitting these difficult shots. It would be much better to play these defensive shots with either an Eastern (see page 35) or Continental grip (see page 41).
The player uses a semi-Western grip at the net.	Many players like to lock in on the semi-Western grip and use it for groundstrokes at the baseline, aggressive groundstrokes from inside the baseline, and even forcing approach shots. The problem occurs when they get to the net and have to volley. Any medium to low ball on the forehand side will be very difficult to play with this grip because the racket face will be naturally closed for balls at those heights. The result will probably be a volley into the net or a volley that pops up weakly over the net. Backhand volleys are even worse, and all shots will be hit up and without any force. Players must learn to change that comfortable semi-Western grip to a Continental grip (see page 41) when going to the net to volley.
The player uses a flat swing pattern on medium to low balls that results in forehand drives into the net.	The semi-Western grip is a strong grip when the ball is played above waist level, but when the ball is lower, the racket face is closed. If the player uses a flat swing pattern, she will hit balls into the net. The player must hit balls with good racket head speed and a sharp low-to-high swing pattern.

The Western grip is the ultimate power and spin grip for forehands and is best suited for balls hit high in the contact zone. This grip gives players maximum topspin, even on high balls. However, it does not have the flexibility of the semi-Western grip, because the racket face is closed on all balls but those hit well above waist level. For this reason, this grip can cause problems with medium to low balls. It also tends to give players excessive topspin, which will keep the ball in the court but may not allow the player to flatten out a shot and hit with more power and depth.

The Western grip has become more popular as the speed of the game increases. More players are hitting with topspin to keep powerful groundstrokes in play. These hard-hit shots with a lot of topspin bounce higher after contacting the court. The Western grip is the strongest grip for playing balls higher in the contact area.

The Western grip is limited to forehand groundstrokes; it is very ineffective for volleys. When this grip is used for the serve, it is sometimes called the "frying pan grip." The server can hit only a flat serve using this grip.

For the Western grip, the palm is under the handle, and the racket face is slightly closed with the wrist and hand in a neutral position when contact is at waist level (see figure 3.16).

KEY POINTS

The Western grip is used in the following situations:

- Forehand groundstrokes
- Forehand groundstrokes with heavy topspin

FOREHAND GROUNDSTROKES

The Western grip is the best grip for forehand groundstrokes hit with a high contact point, at shoulder level or higher. It gives the most amount of topspin because the racket face is closed and the hitter must swing with a more acute low-to-high swing path. This extra topspin is best suited for players who prefer to hit groundstrokes with power or for looping strokes from the baseline.

The Western grip is a strong grip for playing high-bouncing forehand groundstrokes with topspin, but it is not well suited for balls at waist level or below. Because the racket face is slightly closed when the hand is in a neutral position, the wrist must open the racket face on low balls.

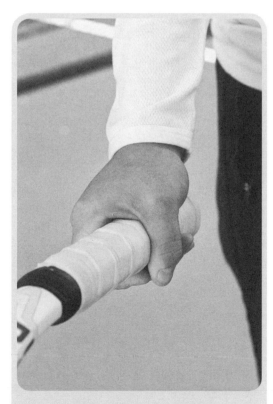

Figure 3.16 Western grip.

(continued)

At a Glance

The following parts of the text offer additional information on the Western grip:

Forehand Groundstroke	66
Forehand as a Weapon	122
Passing Shot	131

FOREHAND GROUNDSTROKES WITH HEAVY TOPSPIN

Using the Western grip generates a great deal of topspin on the forehand groundstroke. The player can hit the ball with a large margin of error over the top of the net and still dip down in the court. Hitting with heavy topspin is advantageous for most shots, but not when players need less spin to drive through the court rather than have the ball hit and bounce up.

Common Errors

Following are several common errors that you might run into when teaching your athletes how to hit using the Western grip:

Error	Error correction
The player hits very wide and very low balls into the net when using a Western grip.	The Western grip is a power and spin grip and is ideal on high balls, but it is difficult to get the racket open and under the ball for very wide and very low balls. The player needs to change to the Eastern or Continental grip to handle these difficult shots.
The player does not hit the ball with enough power with a Western grip, resulting in a short return.	Because the Western grip provides a great deal of topspin, if the ball is not hit with power, it will have a lot of spin and very little depth. These balls land short in the court and are relatively easy for the opponent to return from an advantageous court position. Make sure your players generate good racket head speed when using a Western grip to generate the power necessary to hit the ball deep in the court.
Using the Western grip, the player's ball has low net clearance and thus lands very short on the opponent's side of the court.	This error is similar to the preceding error. The Western grip gives lots of topspin, and a low ball will drop quickly and short in the court resulting in an easy return from the opponent. Make sure your players using a Western grip hit with ample net clearance so the ball lands deeper in the court. The higher the net clearance and the deeper the shot, the higher and longer the ball will bounce on the opponent's side of the court.

The Continental grip is sometimes called the hammer grip because the hand is in the same position as when holding a hammer. It is also called the universal grip because it is between an Eastern forehand and an Eastern backhand grip.

For the Continental grip, the base knuckle of the index finger is positioned over the small bevel just to the right of the top flat surface of the handle. The palm is halfway between the top and the side of the handle (see figure 3.17).

KEY POINTS

The Continental grip is used in the following situations:

- Defensive forehand groundstrokes
- Forehand and backhand volleys
- Serves
- Overheads

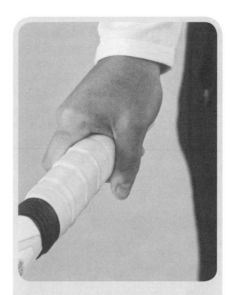

Figure 3.17 Continental grip.

DEFENSIVE FOREHAND GROUNDSTROKES

The Continental grip opens the racket face equally on both the forehand and backhand sides. It is effective for defensive shots and for shots hit with slice or backspin. It works best for balls contacted low or close to the court. It is very difficult to drive groundstrokes with topspin on balls at waist level or above, because the racket face is open and the hitter would have to roll the racket face to make it perpendicular to the court on contact.

FOREHAND AND BACKHAND VOLLEYS

The Continental grip is frequently used for both forehand and backhand volleys. It is ideal when there is no time to change the grip at the net. The Continental grip slightly opens the racket face on both the forehand and backhand sides. This open racket face produces a volley hit with backspin so the ball is hit with better control but will stay low after the bounce. No grip change is necessary to create this open racket face when using the Continental grip.

(continued)

SERVES

The Continental grip is also very good as a service grip, because the server can easily hit with both topspin and sidespin. The Continental grip allows the racket face to hit up on the ball to generate a topspin serve or around the ball to create sidespin. The topspin will curve a ball down in the court, and the sidespin will curve it from side to side either into or away from the receiver.

OVERHEADS

Once a player is at the net, he needs only one grip for volleys and overheads, the Continental grip. As stated earlier, this universal grip can be used equally well on both forehand and backhand volleys. Overheads with the Continental grip will have some spin for control, which will curve the ball into the court. No grip change is needed, and the overhead can be hit like a serve using the same grip.

Common Errors

Following are several common errors you may run into when teaching your athletes the Continental grip:

Error	Error correction
The player attempts to hit groundstrokes with topspin using a Continental grip.	When a player uses the Continental grip, the racket face is slightly open on contact when the ball is at waist level. The higher the ball is hit in the contact zone, the more the racket face will open, thus making a topspin drive very difficult to execute. Because the wrist has to roll and timing has to be perfect to hit topspin groundstrokes, this grip should only be used on very low or very wide balls that need to be hit with backspin.
The player swings too hard when using the Continental grip for groundstrokes.	When using the Continental grip for defensive groundstrokes that are very low or very wide, the player should swing slowly and short because the ball will tend to fly. This grip will open the racket face and make the trajectory of the ball high, and the open racket face will put backspin on the ball that will also cause the ball to go long.
The player's volleys go long when hit with a Continental grip.	If the racket moves forward on the volley, the ball will tend to travel long. It is best to have the racket move slightly high to low on the volley. The open racket face and high-to-low path imparts backspin that takes speed off the ball and gives the player better control when hitting the volley.

The Eastern backhand grip is the best grip for one-handed backhands because it places the racket head in a vertical position, with the wrist and hand in a strong position. With this grip, the player can hit the ball flat, with topspin, or with backspin.

To use the Eastern backhand grip, the player has to change from the ready position, in which the grip is generally held in a forehand position. The change from the forehand to backhand grip is made when the upper body turns to the backhand side. The nondominant hand, cradling the racket at the throat, turns the racket face so it is perpendicular or slightly closed when the racket points at the back fence. The dominant hand regrips when the racket is in the backswing position.

For the Eastern backhand grip, the palm of the hand is placed on top of the handle and the base knuckle of the index finger is on top of the flat portion of the handle (see figure 3.18). Once the hand is on top of the handle, the thumb must be strong and the wrist firm for the forward stroke. The thumb braces the racket from behind, and the wrist must be firm so the racket head does not drop and drag through the contact zone. This creates a strong hand and wrist position, and there will be a straight line from the elbow, wrist, and racket when the hand is in the proper Eastern backhand grip.

KEY POINTS

The Eastern backhand grip is used in the following situations:

- One-handed backhand groundstrokes
- High backhand volleys
- Serves

ONE-HANDED BACKHAND GROUNDSTROKES

The Eastern backhand grip is ideal for a one-handed backhand groundstroke, as mentioned previously. Players can hit the ball flat or with either topspin or backspin when hitting backhand groundstrokes with this grip. The hand is in a very strong position on top of the handle and the thumb is solidly behind the handle, so it is a strong grip and places the racket face perpendicular to the court. Spin is generated by the path of the swing—low to high for topspin, level for flat, and high to level for backspin.

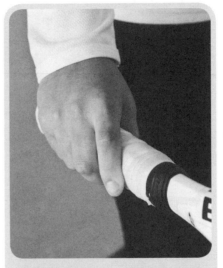

Figure 3.18 Eastern backhand grip.

HIGH BACKHAND VOLLEYS

The Eastern backhand is a strong grip for high backhand volleys. Hitting a high volley with a Continental grip causes the racket face to open. Changing to an Eastern backhand grip flattens out the racket face and allows the player to hit the volley flatter, preventing the ball from popping up off the strings. However, this grip is more challenging on low volleys, because the wrist must be adjusted to open the racket face.

(continued)

At a Glance

The following parts of the text offer additional information on the Eastern backhand grip:

One-Handed Backhand Groundstroke	73
Two-Handed Backhand Groundstroke	80
Lob	126
Groundstroke From Deep in the Court	134

SERVES

The Eastern backhand grip is perfect for applying extra spin when used as a service grip. It will create maximum topspin and sidespin. Because so much spin is generated by this grip, the server must hit the ball hard or it will have so much spin that it will either drop short in the court or hit the net.

Common Errors

Following are several common errors you may run into when teaching your athletes the Eastern backhand grip:

Error	Error correction
The player's palm does not get on top of the handle.	This is a very common error. Many players change the grip but not enough so that the racket face is vertical at the point of contact. If the hand has not made it all the way to the top of the racket, the racket face will be open and all the player can do is hit a slice or backspin backhand. Look to see that the palm is on top of the handle and the base knuckle of the index finger is directly over the top flat surface of the racket handle.
The player's thumb is placed directly along the back of the handle, creating a 90-degree angle between the racket and the arm; this results in a backhand swing that is a punching motion caused by a bent to straight position at the elbow.	When the palm is on top of the racket and the base knuckle of the index finger is on the top flat surface of the handle, the shoulder, elbow, wrist, and racket head should be in a straight line. The hand must be in a diagonal position on top of the handle for everything to be in a straight line. The swing pivots from the shoulder rather than the elbow.
The player lets the racket head drop and drag behind the hand through the contact zone.	Once the player assumes the Eastern backhand position, the racket head should be level with the hand at the completion of the backswing. If the grip and wrist are weak and loose, the racket will drop and drag through the hitting zone during the swing. The player can imagine that the racket is a flashlight and should not allow the flashlight beam to point to the ground. This will keep the racket head up and the wrist firm so the racket head can drive through the contact zone.

The two-handed backhand grip has gained popularity over the past several years. Players of every age and level of the game now use this grip. Several variations can be used, depending on which hand provides the most strength during the stroke.

The most preferred and flexible grip for the two-handed backhand grip is with the top hand in a semi-Western grip and the bottom hand in a Continental grip (see figure 3.19). The swing should look like a left-handed forehand, and the left hand should be in the stronger position. This will allow the player to hit strong two-handed backhands when the ball is in a comfortable hitting zone and a solid defensive shot when forced to reach and play the backhand with only one hand.

The two-handed backhand grip allows players to drive the ball when the contact point is in a comfortable position. It also should provide some flexibility when they must drop the top hand off the racket when they need extra reach or are at the net to hit volleys. Players using an Eastern, semi-Western or Western forehand grip will have to change grips. They must make this change quickly and during the backswing before hitting either a backhand groundstroke or volley.

KEY POINTS

The two-handed backhand grip is used in the following situations:

- Two-handed backhand groundstrokes
- Backhand volleys
- Switching to the Continental grip

TWO-HANDED BACKHAND GROUNDSTROKES

The two-handed backhand grip is used for the two-handed backhand groundstroke. Because it is strong and quick, it is great for groundstrokes and serve returns. The two-handed grip gives additional strength to the backhand groundstroke. It is especially strong for balls hit at waist level and above. Because this grip can be the starting grip in the ready position, the backhand can be hit quickly and with power given that no grip change is necessary when hitting groundstrokes on the backhand side.

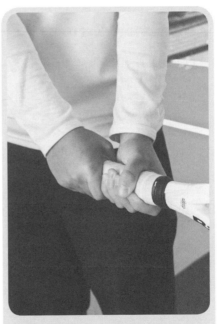

Figure 3.19 Two-handed backhand grip.

BACKHAND VOLLEYS

The two-handed grip can also be used for backhand volleys. It is effective for high backhand volleys, but it does not put the racket in the best position for low volleys or for backhand volleys when the ball is hit at the body. Although a two-handed grip does not give the player as much reach as a one-handed grip, the use of two hands makes the volley a very strong and quick shot. Many players who hit two-handed backhand groundstrokes feel more comfortable at the net when allowed to volley with two hands. This grip is especially strong when hitting a high backhand volley, a shot that is universally weak when hit with one hand.

(continued)

At a Glance

The following parts of the text offer additional information on the two-handed backhand grip:

Serve Return	95
Passing Shot	131

SWITCHING TO THE CONTINENTAL GRIP

The two-handed backhand grip is used for very wide and very low balls. For drop shots and volleys, the left hand can release giving the hitter a strong Continental grip with the right hand and a slightly open racket face.

Common Errors

Following are several common errors you may run into when teaching your athletes the two-handed backhand grip:

Error	Error correction
The player's grip is perfect, with the top hand in a semi-Western grip and the bottom hand in a Continental grip, but at contact the racket face is open and the ball flies off the racket with backspin.	Although the grip is correct, the strength is coming from the wrong hand. When the player has the correct grip, the power should be coming from the left arm and hand. If the right hand is the stronger hand, the racket face will open and the ball will be hit high and with backspin. Either have the player use more strength with the left hand and arm, or change the right hand all the way over to an Eastern backhand grip.
The player uses a semi-Western grip for the top hand but does not change from the semi-Western or Eastern grip with the bottom hand.	The two-handed backhand grip works only for balls that can be hit firmly with a very strong left hand. As soon as the player is forced to reach and drop the left hand off the racket on either low or wide balls, or for volleys, the racket face is open. When this happens, it is very difficult to play firm shots on the backhand side with a forehand grip of any type. Teach the player to move the right hand to a Continental grip so when he does have to release the top hand, he can still hit effectively with the Continental grip.
The player hits backhand volleys with a two-handed grip.	Backhand volleys can be hit with a two-handed grip, and some top players have been very effective with two hands on the backhand side at the net. This grip is very quick and gives volleys extra strength, especially high backhand volleys. However, wide balls and balls hit directly at the body must be played with one hand, so work with your player to make that change for those volleys.

Topspin is essential to pull or curve the ball down into the court on hard-hit groundstrokes. It gives balls ample net clearance and a long, high bounce after hitting the court. It makes the ball drop as it passes over the net and causes the net player to volley the ball up defensively rather than hard and down. Topspin also pulls the ball down on sharp-angled shots. Topspin gives players more margin of error both over the net and inside the baseline.

KEY POINTS

Following are the most important components of applying topspin:

- Starting position of the racket
- Swing pattern
- Racket angle at contact
- Follow-through and finish point

STARTING POSITION OF THE RACKET

To apply topspin, the racket must start below the contact point. The lower the racket starts below the contact point, the more topspin will be imparted on the ball. From the ready position, the player turns and drops the racket below the contact point at the backswing for topspin. If the racket goes to this low position directly, it is called a *straight back backswing,* as shown in figure 3.20. Many players turn and take the racket back high and let it drop before the forward swing, as shown in figure 3.21. This is a *loop backswing* and generates more racket head speed because the racket does not stop at the backswing position.

Figure 3.20 Straight back backswing.

a

b

Figure 3.21 Loop backswing.

(continued)

SWING PATTERN

From the ready position, and when the racket is in the backswing position, the racket must be below the point of contact so that it moves from below contact to above contact on the follow-through (see figure 3.22). The low-to-high racket path spins the ball as necessary for topspin. A more acute racket path will result in more spin.

a   b   c

Figure 3.22 **Applying topspin using a low-to-high swing pattern.**

RACKET ANGLE AT CONTACT

At contact the racket should be parallel with the net for most drives (see figure 3.23a) and open for a topspin lob (see figure 3.23b). Remember that the angle of the racket controls the height; rolling the racket over the ball will only direct the ball down into the net.

a   b

Figure 3.23 **Racket angle: (a) parallel for drives and (b) open for topspin lobs.**

FOLLOW-THROUGH AND FINISH POINT

There are many variations for the follow-through and finish point when applying topspin. Much is dictated by the angle of the racket path, the speed of the oncoming ball, and the type of shot. In a moderate topspin drive, as shown in figure 3.24a, the racket begins a foot below the contact point and the hand finishes at eye level height with the racket above the hand on the follow-through. If the player has good acceleration through the contact point, the follow-through will likely finish with the hand continuing up and over the opposite shoulder. For a topspin lob, because the swing is almost vertical, the hand and racket could finish straight up with the arm staying on the right side of the body (see figure 3.24b).

Another common finish point is with the arm across the body and the hand at shoulder height (see figure 3.24c). This is common with the attacking groundstroke because there is so much racket acceleration and body rotation and not as much of a low-to-high racket swing pattern. This is very common in aggressive baseline players who hit hard and without excessive topspin.

At a Glance

The following parts of the text offer additional information on applying topspin:

Forehand Groundstroke	66
One-Handed Backhand Groundstroke	73
Two-Handed Backhand Groundstroke	80
Lob	126
Approach Shot	100
Swinging Midcourt Volley	110

Figure 3.24 Finish point for *(a)* a moderate topspin drive, *(b)* a topspin lob, and *(c)* an attacking groundstroke.

(continued)

Common Errors

Following are several common errors that you might run into when teaching your athletes how to apply topspin:

Error	Error correction
The player rolls the racket over the ball to hit with topspin.	Spin is created by having the racket start below the contact point and finish above the contact point. In essence, the racket brushes up the back of the ball. For the ball to get up and over the net, the racket face must be vertical or slightly open at contact. When the racket rolls over the top of the ball, the ball will not clear the net, even though it will have topspin.
The player hits with too much topspin, taking speed off the ball and making it drop short in the court.	When the racket begins well below the contact point and the swing is at a sharp. upward angle, the ball will have excessive spin. The energy of the swing will go into spinning the ball, which will reduce the speed of the shot. When a player needs to hit with more power and depth, only moderate topspin is necessary. Have the player start the racket below the contact point and swing up and through the ball to reduce topspin and increase power.
The player hits topspin on very low or very wide balls.	When the player is pulled out of position, he must remember that he is no longer in the best position for playing offensive shots. Topspin is the power spin, but when the player cannot generate good racket head speed that goes low to high, attempts to hit topspin will result in very weak returns. The best spin when playing defensively is backspin, because the ball will get up and over the net as it is hit with an open racket face and travel deeper in the court.

Backspin makes the ball float and carries it deeper into the court. It gives a shot depth when a player cannot hit with much power but makes the ball fly long if the swing speed is too fast. It is used for defensive shots or shots that are hit with a low trajectory over the net, creating a low bounce.

STARTING POSITION OF THE RACKET

To create backspin in the ball, the racket must be above the contact point on the backswing so the player can hit down on the ball (see figure 3.25). The higher the racket starts, the more backspin will be imparted on the ball. From the ready position, the racket is prepared higher than the contact point at the backswing for the backspin shot.

SWING PATTERN

The path of the swing begins above the contact point and is down to and through the contact point (see figure 3.26). Rather than chopping down using a high-to-low swing pattern, players should swing from high to level and finish out and through the contact point. This level follow-through will increase the depth and provide a better feel to the shot.

KEY POINTS

The most important components of applying backspin are as follows:

- Starting position of the racket
- Swing pattern
- Racket angle at contact
- Follow-through and finish point

Figure 3.25 Starting position of the racket to apply backspin.

a   b   c

Figure 3.26 Applying backspin using a high-to-level swing pattern.

(continued)

At a Glance

The following parts of the text offer additional information on applying backspin:

Approach Shot	100
Volley	105
Drop Shot	118
Groundstroke From Deep in the Court	134

RACKET ANGLE AT CONTACT

For players to apply backspin, the racket angle must be slightly open at contact. This gives the ball the height necessary to clear the net. The racket angle can increase when the swing becomes shorter for controlled and touch shots. For example, there will be very little forward swing on a low volley, so the angle is fixed. The ball can be hit up and over the net, but not hit with the racket open so much as to make the ball pop up. On a drop shot or drop volley, the angle opens even more, and there is even less forward swing. The racket opens and the hand and grip are relaxed at contact to absorb the shock at impact for a very soft shot.

FOLLOW-THROUGH AND FINISH POINT

The backspin finish point varies depending on how hard the player hits the ball; there is a relationship between the length of the follow-through and the backswing. With a groundstroke, the racket travels in a high-to-level follow-through position and finishes with the hand fully extended in front of the body (see figure 3.27a). With a low volley, the racket finishes slightly out in front and at least level with the contact point (see figure 3.27b). The drop shot and drop volley have almost no follow-through after the contact point, and the hand faces up on the follow-through (see figure 3.27c).

Figure 3.27 Finish point for *(a)* a groundstroke, *(b)* a low volley, *(c)* a drop shot and drop volley, and *(d)* a chip return of serve.

Another shot that is hit with backspin is the chip return of serve. This is a very short but firm swing, and the racket finishes slightly ahead of and level with the contact point (see figure 3.27*d*). The intent is to hit the ball short and with backspin, so the stroke must be compact and controlled.

Common Errors

Following are several common errors that you might run into when teaching your athletes how to apply backspin:

Error	Error correction
The player hits the ball too hard with backspin and the ball tends to fly long over the baseline.	Remember that a backspin shot does not dip into the court like a topspin shot and cannot be hit at the same speed. Backspin makes the ball float in the air longer, and it travels longer before bouncing on the court. The player must realize this and slow the swing down by shortening the backswing and slowing the racket head speed through the contact point.
A ball hit with backspin consistently goes down and many errors occur in the net.	Backspin results when the racket goes from above the contact point down to the ball with an open racket face. The follow-through should finish level with the contact point. Balls will go down if the racket goes from a high-to-low pattern like a chopping motion. The player must keep the follow-through long, level, and toward the net rather than down to the court.
When the player imparts backspin, the ball pops up with little speed, thus making it an easy ball for the opponent to attack.	If the racket face opens up too much, the ball will pop up in the air. It will have backspin, but because it pops up in the air, it will generally land short and bounce high. To correct this, the player should flatten out the shot by hitting the ball with a more vertical racket face and a firm hand and wrist at contact. A weak grip and open racket face will only result in a weak backspin return.

To apply sidespin, the racket hits across the ball rather than directly behind the ball. A ball hit with sidespin stays low and bounces to the side after contacting the court. Sidespin can be used for groundstrokes, volleys, and the serve. It adds variation to groundstrokes and should be used only when in a comfortable hitting zone.

KEY POINTS

The most important components of applying sidespin are as follows:

o Starting position of the racket
o Swing pattern
o Racket angle at contact
o Finish point

To apply sidespin, the racket hits across the ball rather than directly behind the ball. A ball hit with sidespin stays low and bounces to the side after contacting the court. Sidespin can be used for groundstrokes, volleys, and the serve. It adds variation to groundstrokes and should be used only when in a comfortable hitting zone.

STARTING POSITION OF THE RACKET

To apply sidespin, the racket starts in a similar position as in any groundstroke, but at the forward swing the hand leads and the racket head is behind the hand so the racket makes contact on the inside portion of the ball (see figure 3.28).

For the serve, the racket starts from a position off center so it is hitting across the ball at contact. This is easily accomplished when the toss is farther from the body and toward the sideline.

Figure 3.28 Contact point for a sidespin forehand.

a   b

Figure 3.29 Racket path when applying sidespin: (a) groundstrokes and volleys and (b) serves.

SWING PATTERN

For the player to apply sidespin, the racket path starts outside the contact point and finishes inside the contact point for groundstrokes and volleys (see figure 3.29a). For serves, the racket starts inside and goes up and across and finishes outside the point of contact (see figure 3.29b).

RACKET ANGLE AT CONTACT

The racket angle on contact is vertical or slightly open on groundstrokes and volleys. The sidespin is created when the hand is in front of the racket face, allowing the racket face to brush across the ball at contact (see figure 3.30).

For a right-handed serve, when applying sidespin, the racket hits the ball and moves to the outside of the ball for the sidespin (see figure 3.31). The same is true for the left-handed serve. The left-hander also hits with the racket moving across the ball, but the spin goes in the opposite direction.

FINISH POINT

The finish for a groundstroke or volley with sidespin will look very similar to the finish for a groundstroke and volley with backspin (see page 51). It will be more level than the topspin shot and shorter because there is not as much racket head acceleration through the hit. Because the spin will not curve the ball in the court when hit hard, the follow-through can be shorter.

At a Glance

The following parts of the text offer additional information on applying sidespin:

Forehand Groundstroke	66
One-Handed Backhand Groundstroke	73
Two-Handed Backhand Groundstroke	80
Approach Shot	100

Figure 3.30 **Applying sidespin when contacting the ball.**

Figure 3.31 **Applying sidespin to a serve.**

(continued)

On the serve, the racket hits across the ball during the swing, and the arm and racket finish across the opposite hip and leg to complete the natural throwing motion and follow-through. If the hand finishes higher, the ball will have plenty of sidespin but very little power.

Common Errors

Following are several common errors you might run into when teaching your athletes how to apply sidespin:

Error	Error correction
The player hits groundstrokes with sidespin that are weak and have more backspin than sidespin.	If the ball pops up with more backspin than topspin, the grip was probably too loose and weak, and the racket went more under the ball than across the ball at contact. When a player is hitting a groundstroke with sidespin, the wrist lays back to allow the hand to be in front of the racket face, but the wrist must remain firm. If it is weak and loose, and the stroke is short and decelerating through the contact point, the racket will open and the ball will pop up with backspin.
Sidespin serves curve but lack speed and depth.	When a player is hitting a sidespin serve, the racket face must hit across the ball to make it spin. Many players exaggerate this and try to hit across and around the ball. This circular motion provides spin, but the racket still must be hit through the ball for the necessary power and depth.
Volleys hit with sidespin and at an angle are hit too long and go over the sideline.	Players must remember that a sharply angled volley with sidespin is not hit into a large court area. The sharper the angle, the less court the player has to work with. Players must remember that the sidespin only makes the ball curve; it does not bring the ball down. For this reason, the shot must be hit with soft hands and with little racket speed at the contact point. The sidespin angled volley allows the player to hit with an even greater angle, but the hands should be soft and the racket pattern should be very short and slow from backswing to follow-through.

Moving an opponent from side to side to hit or create openings, hitting shots to an opponent's weaker side, and hitting into an open court are all fundamentals of tennis. Being able to direct the ball side to side enables players to develop points rather than just wait until someone makes an error.

Controlling the shot angle is one of the five controls all players must master to be complete players. It is generally the first control learned after getting the ball back in play. The others are controlling shot height, depth, spin, and speed.

KEY POINTS

The most important components of controlling shot angle are as follows:

- Racket angle at contact
- Path of the swing
- Contact point on the ball

RACKET ANGLE AT CONTACT

Quite simply, the ball goes where the racket faces at contact. Because the palm of the hand is in the same plane as the racket face, the ball goes where the palm is facing at contact. The longer the racket face can face the target, the more frequently the player will hit the intended target. Even if the contact is slightly early or late, as long as the racket face is directed at the target, the ball will be directed toward the intended target.

PATH OF THE SWING

If the path of a swing is circular, timing has to be perfect to hit balls to the desired location in the court. Therefore, players who can lengthen the hitting zone by extending *through* the contact point will consistently hit accurate shots (see figure 3.32). To do this, they need to keep the palm of the hand in line with the target for as long as possible. This directs the racket face toward the target for a longer period of time.

a b

Figure 3.32 **Lengthening the hitting zone by extending through the contact point.**

(continued)

At a Glance

The following parts of the text offer additional information on controlling shot angle:

Forehand Groundstroke	66
One-Handed Backhand Groundstroke	73
Two-Handed Backhand Groundstroke	80
Volley	105
Overhead	113
Lob	126
Passing Shot	131

CONTACT POINT ON THE BALL

Two other factors help with the direction of the shot. For a crosscourt forehand, the player should make contact on the outside of the ball (see Forehand Groundstroke on page 66 of chapter 4 for more information). Conversely, contact on the inside of the ball directs the shot down the line. Hitting the ball on the outside is easier if the player hits it out in front of the body. Hitting the inside is more comfortable when the player makes contact farther back in the stroke.

Common Errors

Following are several common errors that you might run into when teaching your athletes how to control shot angle:

Error	Error correction
The player attempts to hit sharp-angled groundstrokes when he is deep and in the center of the court.	The player must understand that the closer he is to the net, the better he will be able to hit sharp angles. He can hit the most acute angles when he is very close to the net. He will have much more difficulty hitting a ball that will force the opponent off the court when he is positioned behind the baseline, especially if he is behind the baseline and in the center or the court.
The player tries to change the angle of an oncoming ball hit with power.	Any time the player changes the angle of the shot, there is more risk involved. It is much easier to return the ball along the same path as the incoming shot. When the angle is changed, the racket face must be directed at the target, but the ball will also tend to drift wide because when it hits the racket face, the angle of incidence will equal the angle of reflection. When the player changes the angle, she must hit firmly, so it is easier to change the angle on a slower ball.
The player is not hitting with enough topspin to pull the ball down into the court when hitting sharp-angled groundstrokes.	Shots that land in the court and travel over the sideline travel a shorter distance than those that hit the court and travel over the baseline. Therefore, extra topspin must be applied to the shot to drop it in the court. Along with directing the racket face at the target for the angle of the shot, the player must also use a sharp low-to-high swing path for extra topspin to pull the ball into the court. This is because there is less court to hit than when the ball is directed deep in the court.

Controlling the height of the shot is the second fundamental control. Being able to control the height of the shot allows players to hit offensive and defensive shots and to change from a defensive position to a neutral or even offensive position.

Just getting the ball back in play will only work if the opponent is less skilled. Changing direction moves the opponent side to side, but by being able to hit high and low, a player can hit balls that will be out of the opponent's comfort zone. A player can force an opponent in a good position at the net to volley the ball up defensively, or drive an opponent off the net with a well-placed lob. A player can also determine at what height the opponent likes to hit shots, and then keep that opponent from hitting the ball in that comfortable zone by keeping the ball higher or lower.

KEY POINTS

The most important components of controlling shot height are as follows:

- Racket angle at contact
- Path of the swing
- Speed of the swing

RACKET ANGLE AT CONTACT

The height of the shot is determined by the angle of the racket face at contact. When the racket is tilted back and the strings face the sky, this is considered an open racket face, and the ball will go high (see figure 3.33a). When the racket face is tilted down and the strings face the ground, this is considered a closed racket face, and the ball will go down (see figure 3.33b).

Figure 3.33 **Positioning of an (a) open and (b) closed racket face.**

(continued)

PATH OF THE SWING

The path of the racket swing will determine the amount of spin on the ball. For example, if the racket face is open and the swing is low to high, the player will hit a topspin lob. If the racket face is open and the swing is level, the player will hit a backspin lob.

For maximum control, the path of the racket should mirror the angle of the racket and the intended line of flight. For example, for a player to hit a lob, the racket face must be open and the path of the swing should be low to high and at the same angle as the open racket face.

SPEED OF THE SWING

The faster the swing, the farther the ball will travel. When the racket face is open, the ball will go high (a high lob). Conversely, if the swing is very slow and compact, the ball will be hit much softer (a drop shot).

Common Errors

Following are several common errors that you might run into when teaching your athletes how to control shot height:

Error	Error correction
The player is not hitting high shots with enough height.	If the player intends to hit a lob that will go over the opponent positioned at the net, he should make sure the apex of the shot is over the opponent, not over the net. If it is over the net, the ball will descend as it approaches the opponent, making for an easy overhead smash.
The player is hitting low balls flat, or without spin.	When the player is hitting the ball low, she is generally aiming the ball just over the net so the opponent will be forced to hit the next shot up. If the ball is hit flat, it will have little margin of error over the net. By adding some topspin, the player can hit a ball that will drop after clearing the net, making the low shot even more effective. A ball hit with backspin will tend to die after hitting the court, making the low shot stay even lower after it clears the net and bounces.
The player does not recognize when to hit the ball high and low.	Many players get into a pattern of hitting balls at a comfortable rally speed with similar height and spin on every shot. This might be effective when the opponent is at the baseline, but makes for an easy return if the opponent is at the net. Rather than try to overpower the return with a sharp angle when the opponent is at the net, the player should recognize that he can completely neutralize the opponent if he can make him retreat by lobbing a high ball over his head and deep in the court, or he can play a low shot that will make the opponent volley the ball up.

The speed of the shot is determined by the racket head speed at the point of contact. The faster the racket head is, the faster the shot will travel. When most players think about controlling shot speed, they think about power. Although it is fun to hit the ball hard, the complete player must be able to hit with power and also know when to take speed off the ball and play softer or more controlled shots. The best players use a variety of speeds depending on their court position, the opponent's court position, the type of shot being hit, the court opening, and the speed necessary to hit a successful shot.

KEY POINTS

The most important components of controlling shot speed are as follows:

- Path of the swing
- Speed of the swing

PATH OF THE SWING

There are a few ways to generate racket head speed. One is by lengthening the swing, as shown in figure 3.34. A long backswing will give the player time to generate speed before the hit. This applies especially to linear strokes.

In addition, angular momentum is created by body rotation. The hitter can generate racket head speed by quickly rotating the hips, trunk, and shoulders so the arm and racket accelerate through the contact zone after the body rotation toward the net (see figure 3.35).

Figure 3.34 Generating racket speed by lengthening the swing.

Figure 3.35 Generating racket speed using body rotation.

(continued)

At a Glance

The following parts of the text offer additional information on controlling shot speed:

Forehand Groundstroke	66
One-Handed Backhand Groundstroke	73
Two-Handed Backhand Groundstroke	80
Serve Return	95
Approach Shot	100
Volley	105
Drop Shot	118
Lob	126
Passing Shot	131

SPEED OF THE SWING

Using the opponent's speed is another way of generating speed. The faster the opponent hits the shot, the faster the player can return the ball, providing that the contact is solid, firm, and out in front of the body. If an incoming shot is hit with a lot of pace, the returning shot should be hit with a more compact backswing. Because the player has less time to prepare, he should shorten the backswing to take advantage of his opponent's speed.

Quite simply, the faster the racket head goes through the ball, the faster the ball will travel. The ball will not go as fast if the contact is not direct, such as when a swing goes low to high or high to low. In this case, spin is imparted and some of the energy used for power will be used to apply spin.

Common Errors

Following are several common errors that you might run into when teaching your athletes how to control shot speed:

Error	Error correction
The player tries to hit the ball too hard, resulting in too many unforced errors.	Everybody likes to hit the ball hard. However, hitting the ball hard usually results in too many unforced errors. The player must determine a comfortable rally speed and increase the speed only when she has a favorable court position, a comfortable contact point, and plenty of open court.
The player tries to match or exceed the pace of the opponent.	Players often try to return a hard-hit shot with even more power. This generally happens when the opponent can play a strong offensive shot with plenty of pace. Players tend to get excited and try to return these powerful shots with even more power, making too many errors. Players must be able to control these returns by taking speed off the oncoming shot. They must hit shots such as serve returns with short backswings so they don't generate extra power and can control the return.
The player chooses to make easy shots when the opportunity arises to hit with power and end the point.	When the player gets tight, he may be hesitant and cautious and not take opportunities to end the point. For example, if the opponent hits a weak return and is out of position, the player may move forward, be on balance, and have the ball in an ideal contact zone, but ends up pushing the ball back in the court so the opponent can make an easy return. Encourage the player to hit with more power when he has an opening and is in a good position. Have him determine the target area and focus on a quick setup and a strong swing. When he is set and has a large court opening to hit, errors will be at a minimum, and hitting winners will give him the confidence to try to end the point.

The depth of any shot is determined by two factors—the speed of the shot and the trajectory of the shot. Many inexperienced tennis players concentrate only on speed to hit the ball deep enough in the court to keep their opponent behind the baseline. Unfortunately, the harder the ball is hit, the closer to the net it must travel, and the closer to the net the ball travels, the greater the chance it has of hitting the net.

Experienced players hit at a speed they can control in a rally and increase the height at which they hit the ball over the net to achieve the best results. The higher net clearance has the added benefit of a longer and higher bounce that will keep the opponent in the backcourt and unable to attack by moving forward in the court.

KEY POINTS

The most important components of controlling shot depth are as follows:

- Speed of the ball
- Trajectory of the ball

SPEED OF THE BALL

The speed of the ball is created by the speed of the racket head before and through the contact point. A long and full backswing creates more time to generate racket head speed. Also, a quick body rotation from sideways to the net to facing the net accelerates the arm and racket through the contact point.

Conversely, when intending to hit short, such as a drop shot, the player uses a short backswing and slow racket head speed during the stroke and comes almost to a full stop at the contact point.

TRAJECTORY OF THE BALL

The trajectory of the ball is determined by the angle of the racket face at the point of contact with the ball. If the racket is held vertical to the court, the ball will not fly upward off the strings. The more the racket opens (strings facing the sky), the higher the trajectory of the ball off the racket face (see section on racket angle at contact on page 59).

At a Glance

The following parts of the text offer additional information on controlling shot depth:

Forehand Groundstroke	66
One-Handed Backhand Groundstroke	73
Two-Handed Backhand Groundstroke	80
First Serve	86
Serve Return	95
Approach Shot	100
Volley	105
Drop Shot	118
Forehand as a Weapon	122
Lob	126
Passing Shot	131

(continued)

Common Errors

Following are several common errors that you might run into when teaching your athletes how to control shot depth:

Error	Error correction
The player hits the ball hard and close to the net to achieve depth but makes many errors in the net.	Although this tactic works, the risk of hitting the ball into the net is too great. Have the player slow down the speed of the shot and increase the safety margin over the top of the net by hitting higher over the net.
The player hits balls intended to go short with too much depth.	When hitting a shot such as a drop shot, the depth should be very short in the court. The racket face must be open enough to achieve net clearance, but the speed of the swing must be slow so little power is generated at the hit. This can be accomplished by using a very short or abbreviated backswing.
The player hits with plenty of net clearance but balls still land short in the court.	The player should keep the same net clearance by keeping the same trajectory of the ball off the racket face, but swing faster at contact. If the player has very little backswing because he is nervous and plays cautiously, he will do little more than block the ball back in the court. Have him lengthen his backswing and finish with a full and complete follow-through.

chapter 4

Strokes and Shots

This chapter covers the strokes and shots players must know to be successful. In this chapter, you will find the following:

Forehand Groundstroke

KEY POINTS

The most important components of the forehand are as follows:

- Preparation
- Grip
- Stance
- Backswing
- Contact point
- Spin
- Follow-through

Most tennis players use the forehand groundstroke more than any other stroke in the game. For them, it is the weapon of choice from the baseline, and in most situations it is stronger than the backhand. Players are most comfortable hitting the forehand, and most rallies are hit with this stroke. All players should develop a forehand that allows them to hit accurately, deeply, and consistently from any place in the court. They should look for and hit as many forehands as they can from their preferred side.

PREPARATION

From the ready position used for all strokes at the baseline, the player turns the entire body so it faces the sideline while preparing the racket at the same time (see figure 4.1). This "unit turn" should be consistent on all shots hit to the forehand side. From this turn and racket position, the player is ready for the immediate forward swing on a hard-hit ball, or able to run to get in position on a wide or short ball.

Figure 4.1 Preparing for a forehand ground stroke: *(a)* ready position and *(b)* turn to the sideline.

GRIP

Most players wait in the ready position with the forehand grip (see page 35). This makes the forehand easy because the player simply has to prepare the racket and body and swing without having to worry about moving the hands into the correct grip.

When the player must change the grip, this should be done during the unit turn stage. For example, a ball that will be contacted high in the hitting zone would be better played with a Western grip (see page 39). Conversely, when the ball is contacted close to the ground, the Eastern grip will provide a more suitable and stronger hand position at the contact point.

STANCE

The stance is determined by the position of the oncoming ball, the speed of the ball, and the player's preference. When a player has time, he should use a square or open stance, depending on which is most comfortable (see figure 4.2). If the ball is hit directly at the player, typically the player uses a simple side step, as shown in figure 4.3 on page 68, and plays an open stance forehand. However, when the player has to cover a lot of court to return an opponent's shot, the closed stance might be the only option because the last step before contact could be the front foot stepping toward the sideline (see figure 4.4 on page 68).

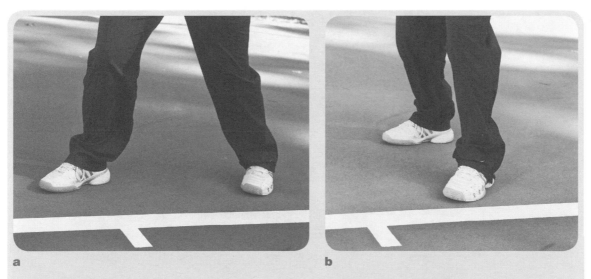

a

b

Figure 4.2 **Stances for a forehand groundstroke:** *(a)* **open or** *(b)* **square.**

(continued)

a   b   c

Figure 4.3   Side step for a forehand groundstroke.

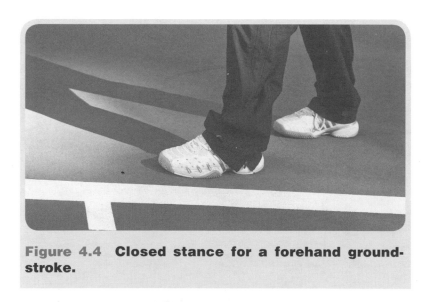

Figure 4.4   Closed stance for a forehand ground-stroke.

Another type of forehand groundstroke that has been made more popular by the speed of the game is one that is used for a wide ball. For this shot, the player assumes an open stance, hits the ball defensively with backspin (see figure 4.5a), and then pushes on the outside foot to recover quickly back into the court (see figure 4.5b).

Figure 4.5 Defensive open stance for a forehand groundstroke.

BACKSWING

For the hard-hit ball, or very short ball, the unit turn is the only backswing necessary; it enables the player to contact the ball even with the front hip. If the player has time, she can take a longer backswing. As a general rule, the longer the backswing is, the greater the speed of the racket at contact point will be.

The height of the backswing determines the type and the amount of spin on the shot. The lower the racket starts below the contact point, the more topspin will be generated. If the racket is at the same height at the backswing as the contact point, the ball will be hit flat. A high backswing causing a high-to-low racket path will generate backspin and must be hit with an open racket face.

CONTACT POINT

The contact point varies depending on the grip and the stance. A player hitting with a semi-Western grip (see page 37) prefer to have the ball about even with the body and high in the "strike zone" (see figure 4.6a on page 70). The player hitting with an Eastern grip and a square stance prefers the ball at about waist level and even with the front hip (see figure 4.6b on page 70).

The key is to create a constant contact point based on the player's preferred stance and grip. The more a player can play the ball in the ideal contact area, the more control and power he will have for each shot. The same thinking holds true for golfers and baseball players. Golfers hit best when they are balanced, their footing is level, and the swing is long and with plenty of body rotation. Baseball players have the best results when they hit balls in the middle of the strike zone.

(continued)

Figure 4.6 Contact point for a forehand groundstroke using *(a)* a semi-Western grip and *(b)* an Eastern grip.

SPIN

Spin is determined by the racket angle at the contact point and the path of the swing as illustrated by the following:

- A low-to-high swing path with a vertical racket face will produce topspin. The lower the racket starts and the higher it finishes, the more topspin will be produced.
- When the racket starts and finishes at the same level as the contact point, the ball will be hit flat.
- A high-to-low swing pattern with a slightly open racket face will produce backspin.

All hard-hit forehands must be hit with topspin to keep the ball in the court. A flat shot hit at the same speed and trajectory will travel farther through the air before bouncing. The ball hit with backspin will travel farthest before bouncing and stay low. Although this shot cannot be hit hard, a backspin shot with a low trajectory tends to skid on the court. This shot is effective against players who like a fast-paced, higher ball to return.

FOLLOW-THROUGH

There are several types of follow-throughs, depending on the grip and the length and height of the backswing. The follow-through should be a full and natural continuation of the stroke. If a player uses a long, low backswing, the follow-through will be long and high. If the follow-through is short, the racket will decelerate through the contact zone.

To make sure the racket is accelerating through the contact zone, the player should have a follow-through that is as long as or longer than the backswing (see figure 4.7a). If a player wants to take speed off the ball, the follow-through should be shorter than the backswing (see figure 4.7b). An example would be when a player has to move forward and play a low ball. The combination of hitting up with a full swing into a shorter court will likely cause the ball to travel over the baseline. A short backswing and follow-through are necessary to take speed off the ball and keep it in the court.

a   b

Figure 4.7 Follow-through for a forehand groundstroke: (a) long and high and (b) short.

(continued)

Common Errors

Following are several common errors you may run into when teaching your athletes a proper forehand groundstroke:

Error	Error correction
The player does not hit every shot with a purpose.	Every forehand groundstroke should either be a high-percentage shot with a quick and efficient recovery or a shot to the opponent's weakness. When a player is in a neutral position on the court and rallying the ball with the forehand, the crosscourt forehand will give her the most court to hit, the lowest net to clear, and the shortest distance to move to the perfect recovery position. When in doubt, she should play solid crosscourt forehands. The alternative would be to hit to the opponent's weaker side to break it down and force a weak return.
The forehand is the player's stronger side, but he does not play as many shots as possible with the forehand.	As simple as this sounds, if the player is slow or tired, he may end up playing lazy or weak backhands just because he doesn't move quickly enough to set up for a forehand. In most situations all that is needed is a step or two to get into perfect position, so teach him to always be ready to move quickly and into position to play his stronger forehand groundstroke.
The player doesn't know when to transition from neutral to offense or from neutral to defense on the forehand side.	When the player gets a shorter ball, she should be ready to turn up the heat and play more offensively with either an attacking forehand groundstroke or an approach shot. She must also realize that when she is in trouble by being very deep or wide in the court, she will have to be much more cautious and hit the ball with less speed, more net clearance, and good depth. Teach her to recognize where she is on the court so she can hit the best shot from that position.

The one-handed backhand groundstroke is generally weaker than the forehand groundstroke for most players. It is the side that is attacked by opponents from the backcourt with aggressive groundstrokes, from the midcourt with approach shots, and at the net with volleys and overheads.

Your athletes will need to determine which backhand will be more efficient for them, the one-handed or two-handed backhand. The one-hander has better reach and can generally impart backspin more easily than the two-hander. The contact point is farther out in front and the body stays more sideways to the net through the stroke. The one-hander will need to change his grip because the Eastern, semi-Western, and Western forehand grips are not efficient for a one-handed backhand.

The player using the two-handed backhand, as described on page 80, generally has more success hitting with topspin and can handle higher balls with less difficulty. However, two-handers have limited reach, and many have difficulty with low balls. At the net, many two-handers are uncomfortable transitioning to a one-handed backhand volley, a shot that is necessary for wide volleys.

KEY POINTS

The most important components of the one-handed backhand groundstroke are as follows:

- Preparation
- Grip
- Stance
- Backswing
- Contact point
- Spin
- Follow-through

PREPARATION

From the ready position, the player turns the entire body so it faces the sideline (see figure 4.8). Both hands prepare the racket during the backswing. The player changes to the Eastern backhand grip by turning the racket into position with the nondominant hand.

a   b

Figure 4.8   Preparing for a one-handed backhand groundstroke: *(a)* ready position and *(b)* turn to the sideline.

(continued)

GRIP

To ensure a perpendicular racket face on contact, the player must change the grip from the forehand grip to the Eastern backhand grip, as mentioned previously. The dominant hand moves to the top of the handle by turning the racket with the nondominant hand held at the throat of the racket. The nondominant hand turns the racket, and the dominant hand regrips the handle after the turn so the hand is in an Eastern backhand grip position.

STANCE

The stance for the one-handed backhand should be balanced, and the feet should be square (stepping directly at the net) or semiclosed by stepping slightly toward the sideline (see figure 4.9). In both cases, the back foot should be planted so that the forward foot can step into the shot. The back foot should be parallel with the baseline. The front foot should step forward and open to a 45-degree angle before contact. A large step, slightly wider than the shoulders, will give the player a wide, well-balanced stance and allow for maximum weight transfer.

With the weight on the back foot, the body is fully loaded, and the hips, shoulders, legs, and back are ready for the forward swing. The weight transfers from the back foot to the front foot as the racket moves from the backswing through the contact point and on to the follow-through.

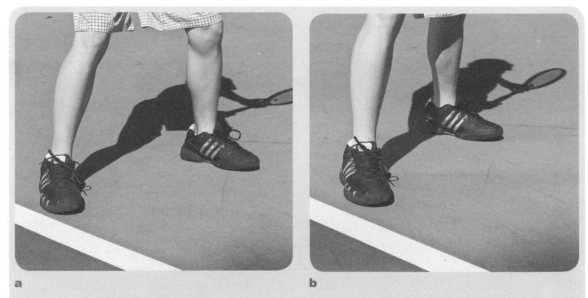

a   b

Figure 4.9 **Stance for a one-handed backhand groundstroke: *(a)* square or *(b)* semiclosed.**

BACKSWING

The backswing for the one-handed backhand groundstroke is easy and controlled when the body turns toward the sideline and both hands are on the racket. The nondominant hand positions the racket to the full backswing position and turns the racket so the dominant hand can regrip with an Eastern backhand grip.

To hit a flat backhand, the backswing (see figure 4.10), contact, and follow-through are level. For a backhand with backspin, the racket starts high and finishes level with an open racket face (see figure 4.11). For a backhand hit with topspin, the racket must be prepared below the point of contact during the backswing. At the turn, if the racket preparation is high, the racket should drop below the contact point before the forward swing, which is called a loop backswing (see figure 4.12 on page 76). The racket can also be taken back and prepared below the contact point directly from the ready position, which is called a straight backswing (see figure 4.13 on page 77). Both are acceptable, but the loop backswing provides a continuous motion through the entire swing, whereas the straight backswing stops at the full backswing position.

Figure 4.10 **Backswing for a flat one-handed backhand groundstroke.**

a   b

Figure 4.11 **Backswing for a one-handed backhand groundstroke with backspin.**

(continued)

Figure 4.12 Loop backswing for a one-handed backhand groundstroke with topspin.

Figure 4.13 **Straight backswing for a one-handed backhand groundstroke with top-spin.**

CONTACT POINT

The contact point for the one-handed backhand groundstroke is in front of the dominant shoulder and farther from the body because the hitting arm is in a comfortably straight position. Ideally, the contact point will be at waist level (see figure 4.14).

SPIN

Spin is determined by the racket angle at the contact point and the path of the swing.

○ A low-to-high swing with a vertical racket face will produce topspin. The lower the racket starts and the higher it finishes, the more topspin will be produced.

○ When the racket starts and finishes at the same level as the contact point with a vertical racket face, the ball will be hit with no spin, which is called a flat shot.

Figure 4.14 **Ideal contact point for a one-handed backhand groundstroke.**

(continued)

○ A high-to-level swing with a slightly open racket face produces backspin.

All hard-hit backhands must be hit with topspin to keep the ball in the court. A flat shot at the same speed and trajectory will travel farther through the air before bouncing. The ball hit with backspin will travel farthest before bouncing and stay low after the bounce. Although this shot cannot be hit hard, the shot is effective against an opponent who likes a fast pace and a ball higher in the contact zone. The backspin backhand hit with a low trajectory tends to skid on the court and stay low after the bounce.

FOLLOW-THROUGH

A topspin backhand finishes with the classic long and high follow-through that ends with the arm straight and the racket head pointed at the sky (see figure 4.15). The weight will be on the front foot, and the nondominant arm will reach toward the back fence for balance. The follow-through for both the flat and backspin backhand is forward and level with the contact point with the arm fully extended toward the net and the weight on the front foot (see figure 4.16).

Figure 4.15 Follow-through for a one-handed backhand hit with topspin.

Figure 4.16 Follow-through for a one-handed backhand hit flat or with backspin.

Common Errors

Following are several common errors you may run into when teaching your athletes the one-handed backhand groundstroke:

Error	Error correction
The player doesn't change his grip from his regular forehand grip to a backhand grip, so the stroke is weak and ineffective.	The player must change his grip from a forehand to a backhand grip quickly before making contact. The hand should go from being in back of the handle to being on top of the handle, and the thumb should be in a strong position in back of the handle. The grip change occurs as the player turns the upper body and prepares the racket in the backswing position. Teach your players to make the grip change by turning the racket during the body turn with the nondominant hand and regripping with the dominant hand before making the swing.
The player has difficulty hitting a solid one-handed backhand groundstroke down the line.	One-handed backhand groundstrokes are hit with much less upper-body turn than forehands or two-handed backhands. When the hips and shoulders rotate so they face the net, the racket goes across the body and results in a crosscourt shot. To correct this, the player must stay more sideways through the shot with the weight moving from the back foot to the forward foot. Have the player set up and drive through the ball with the legs, and have the nondominant hand reach back toward the back fence at the contact point. This will delay the body rotation until after the ball is off the strings and allow the player to hit the ball down the line by hitting through rather than across the ball.
The player has a weak backhand, with a short swing leading with the elbow.	The correction begins when the player prepares the racket. The body should be turned and facing the sideline. The hitting arm should be straight at the end of the backswing and across the body. Before the forward swing, the dominant hand should be in front of the right thigh for right-handed players. When the racket is in this position, the swing leads with the shoulder rather than the elbow. The arm swings forward and high with a firm wrist, the racket head is above the wrist at contact, and the elbow is straight. The follow-through finishes with the hitting hand at eye level.

Two-Handed Backhand Groundstroke

There are two ways to play a backhand groundstroke. The more traditional way is to hit with one hand, as we learned on page 73. This involves a grip change, and the contact point is forward and out in front of the body.

The two-handed backhand groundstroke, however, is probably used by more players at all levels than the one-handed version. In most situations, players can hit the ball harder with two hands and can generate more racket head speed using a shorter backswing. The grip change is minimal, and the stroke is easier to disguise. Because the two-handed backhand groundstroke is played much like a forehand on the nondominant side, there are many similarities between the two, including backswing position, contact point, body rotation, and follow-through.

PREPARATION

The two-handed backhand groundstroke has many variations. Grips, stances, backswings, and follow-through positions all vary depending on the player. In all two-handed backhands, the first movement is the preparation phase, in which the body turns toward the sideline and the racket is taken to the backswing position (see figure 4.17). One thing all players using this stoke have in common is early preparation and good balance when the weight loads on the back foot.

a   b

Figure 4.17 **Preparing for a two-handed backhand groundstroke:** *(a)* **ready position and** *(b)* **turn to the sideline.**

GRIP

The two-handed backhand grip has several variations. When the nondominant hand does most of the work on the forward swing (such as when a right-hander hits a left-handed forehand), the player uses a semi-Western grip (see page 37) on both hands. The player makes little or no grip change and can hit from the forehand or backhand side.

Another grip variation is with the nondominant hand in a semi-Western grip and the dominant hand in a Continental grip (see page 45). This grip is strong with both hands and arms working together on the forward swing. If the player is forced to reach and hit with only one hand, the Continental grip, with a slightly open racket face, is good for defensive shots.

The third grip variation is with the dominant hand in an Eastern backhand grip (see page 43) and the nondominant hand in a semi-Western forehand grip (see page 37). This is a strong grip because both hands and arms are used equally in the forward swing.

STANCE

Because players using the two-handed backhand groundstroke hit with a full body, trunk, and shoulder rotation, they can hit with a slightly closed stance, such as in the one-handed backhand as shown in figure 4.8b on page 73, a square stance (see figure 4.18a), or an open stance (see figure 4.18b).

The slightly open and square stances can be used when the dominant hand is in the Continental grip or Eastern backhand grip position. The contact point is played farther

a   b

Figure 4.18 **Stance for a two-handed backhand groundstroke:** *(a)* **open or** *(b)* **square.**

(continued)

in front because the dominant hand and arm do more work, so the contact point must be farther forward.

Players hitting with a lot of body rotation and primarily with the nondominant hand (such as in a left-handed forehand) do well with the open stance. The hips and shoulders begin by facing the sideline and rotate so they face the net on contact, but the stance is open, allowing the player to hit and recover quickly back into the court.

BACKSWING

The backswing for a two-handed backhand groundstroke has three variations, depending on the racket head position at the end of the backswing. The first is the loop backswing, in which the racket head is cocked up before dropping below the contact point and swinging forward (see figure 4.19a). The second backswing variation is with the racket parallel to the ground (see figure 4.19b), and the third is the low, straight backswing that positions the racket below the contact point immediately during the backswing (see figure 4.19c). All three variations are acceptable and determined by the preference of the player. The loop backswing generates the most power because the racket picks up speed when it drops below the ball and moves forward without pausing at the end of the backswing.

a   b   c

Figure 4.19 **Backswing for a two-handed backhand:** *(a)* loop, *(b)* parallel, and *(c)* straight.

CONTACT POINT

The contact point for the two-handed backhand groundstroke varies depending on the grip of the nondominant hand. With all grips, the player should contact the ball at waist level.

- When the dominant hand is in a semi-Western grip, the stroke is hit like a left-handed forehand (for a right-hander). The contact point is at waist level, even with the front hips, and the elbow has a slight bend close to the body (see figure 4.20a).

- When the dominant hand is in a Continental grip position, the contact point is more forward and farther from the body, but still at waist height (see figure 4.20b).

- When the dominant hand is in the Eastern backhand grip, the contact point is even with the front foot, at waist level, and a straight arm length from the body, similar to a one-handed backhand contact point (see figure 4.20c).

a   b   c

Figure 4.20 Contact point *(a)* when the dominant hand is in a semi-Western grip, *(b)* when the dominant hand is in a Continental grip, and *(c)* when the dominant hand is in an Eastern backhand grip.

(continued)

SPIN

The two-handed backhand groundstroke is usually very efficient for hitting with topspin. When both hands are on the racket, it is easy to drop the racket head on the backswing and accelerate the racket head up and through the contact point for topspin. With all the grips mentioned earlier, the racket face is perpendicular to the ground at the contact with the low-to-high swing path producing the topspin.

To hit with backspin, the swing goes from a high to a level position and the racket is slightly open on contact. This is easily achieved when the nondominant hand relaxes. The swing resembles that of a one-handed backspin backhand.

FOLLOW-THROUGH

Although the stances, grips, and contact points for the two-handed backhand groundstroke have variations, the follow-through is fairly consistent in all cases. The hips and shoulders have turned from facing the sideline to facing the net, and the player's weight finishes on the front foot. The swing finishes with the racket head pointing to the sky with the hands over the opposite shoulder (see figure 4.21).

Figure 4.21 Follow-through for a two-handed backhand groundstroke.

Common Errors

Following are several common errors you may run into when teaching your athletes a proper two-handed backhand groundstroke:

Error	Error correction
The player is not able to hit with topspin with the two-handed backhand groundstroke because the racket face is slightly open on contact with the ball.	In most situations, the inability to generate topspin starts with a grip problem and hitting most strongly with the dominant arm and hand. If a right-hander hitting a two-handed backhand has the most strength coming from the right arm and hand, and the right hand is not in an Eastern backhand grip, the racket face will be open and all shots will be hit with backspin and generally go high as well. To correct this, the player must hit harder with the left arm and hand. The left arm will drive the racket through the ball rather than having the right hand pull the racket into the ball. When the left arm is dominant, the left hand should be in an Eastern or semi-Western grip; this will put the racket face vertical upon contact. The low-to-high swing will give the stroke the topspin necessary to drive the ball and keep it in the court.
The player has to drop the left hand and play a weak one-handed shot because of slow feet and a poor starting position.	To hit the two-handed backhand effectively, the ball must be in a comfortable hitting position. When the ball is too far away from the body, the player could reach the ball with a one-handed backhand but not with two hands. For that reason, when using the two-handed backhand, a player must work harder and move quicker to get into a proper hitting position so she can drive the ball. If the feet are slow or she is tired or lazy, she will be quick to drop the left hand and play weak one-handed backhands at full reach.
The player has difficulty with low balls because he lacks the ability to get below the ball, open the racket face, and hit the ball with backspin.	The correction here is with the body position and changing the stronger arm and hand. First, the player must get down by bending from the knees and not from the waist, like sitting in a chair. The racket must get below the ball on the backswing so the player can make contact with an open racket face. This is much easier if the nondominant hand relaxes so the dominant hand supplies most of the strength in this shot. The dominant hand in a Continental grip is ideal to create the open racket face necessary for returning the very low ball.

KEY POINTS

The most important components of the first serve are as follows:

- Preparation
- Grip
- Stance
- Backswing
- Toss
- Contact point
- Spin
- Follow-through
- Recovery

The serve is the only shot in the game that the player can totally control. It is the most important stroke in the game because every point begins with the serve. The server is in a position to control the speed, spin, and placement of the serve. The server also controls the pace of the game and can either speed up or slow down the game by changing the pace of service between points.

The first serve is the most important shot and, when hit effectively, gives the server outright winners or forces either errors or weak returns from the opponent. These weak returns allow the server to dictate play during the point by holding the offensive advantage and best court position.

PREPARATION

Before addressing the starting position, let's look at the pre-serve ritual. Because the serve is the only shot in the game that the player has complete control over, she has the opportunity to be totally prepared. Rituals prepare the player physically, mentally, and emotionally. They help her establish a comfortable starting point so she can be totally focused on each serve.

Rituals are evident in basketball players on the free throw line and baseball players stepping into the batter's box. In tennis, taking a few seconds to do the same thing before each serve delivery prevents the server from rushing and establishes a point of focus. Although rituals vary with each individual, those commonly used are deep breathing, bouncing the ball, relaxing or shaking out the hitting arm, or adjusting a cap or wrist band. The key is to encourage the player to establish a ritual before each serve and to do it every time before putting the ball in play.

After performing the ritual, the server should get in a relaxed position at the baseline. The front foot should be at a 45-degree angle to the baseline, and the back foot should be parallel to the baseline. There are several variations, just as there are for batting stances. The key is to have the feet in the same position, relax the serving arm and hand, and focus on the intended target.

GRIP

To achieve the spin necessary to pull the ball down into the court on a hard-hit serve, a player needs to use the Continental grip. Some players use an Eastern backhand grip for additional spin, but this is covered more in the Second Serve section beginning on page 92.

It is important that the hand be in a relaxed Continental grip (page 41). A tightly held grip will inhibit the hand, wrist, and forearm flexibility necessary for an effective and powerful serve. The server should relax the hand and grip the handle with the fingers, rather than locking the handle into the palm with a vice grip.

STANCE

The server should assume a starting position by facing the sideline. The front foot should be at a 45-degree angle to the baseline, and the back foot should be parallel to the baseline (see figure 4.22a). Some players prefer a shoulder-width stance (see figure 4.22b), and others like the feet closer together.

a   b

Figure 4.22 **Stance for the serve:** *(a)* **front foot at a 45-degree angle and back foot parallel to the baseline and** *(b)* **feet shoulder-width apart.**

BACKSWING

Two types of backswings are used for a first serve. In the more traditional backswing the racket drops down and swings back so the hitting arm points to the back fence before the elbow bends and the racket drops to make contact over the server's head (see figure 4.23 on page 88). The second backswing is more abbreviated; the server rotates the upper body and cocks the hitting arm in a throwing motion (see figure 4.24 on page 88). In both cases, however, the body rotates away from the net and coils. The weight is loaded on the back foot, and the knees are flexed in preparation for a push up from the ground.

(continued)

Figure 4.23 Traditional backswing for the first serve.

Figure 4.24 Abbreviated backswing for the first serve.

TOSS

While the racket is swung into position and the body rotates and coils, the nonracket arm tosses the ball into the contact zone (see figure 4.25). The arm should reach to full extension, and the ball should be released from the fingers without any wrist action. The player can imagine the toss as reaching up to a high shelf and just letting the ball release from the fingers without any spin. The ball is lifted to the contact point 12 inches in front of the baseline at full arm extension, and even with the right shoulder.

Note that players will vary the toss slightly for different types of serves. It is easier to hit a slice serve when the toss is more to the right. And, the topspin serve is easier when the ball is not as far in front. If the player is moving to the net after the serve, he will most likely prefer a toss that is farther in front of the baseline.

Figure 4.25 Toss for the serve.

CONTACT POINT

After the toss and backswing, energy is transferred from the legs, hips, trunk, shoulder, arm, wrist, and racket head. The legs drive up and the body rotates so the hips and shoulders are parallel with the baseline (see figure 4.26).

At contact, the weight has driven up and out from the front foot, the body has turned so it faces the net, the hitting arm has reached maximum elevation, and the nonhitting arm is tucked close to the chest. During this rotation of the upper body and drive-up stage with the legs, the racket drops behind the back and the elbow leads the forward motion toward the net, followed by the forearm, wrist, and racket.

Figure 4.26 Contact point for the serve.

(continued)

At a Glance

The following parts of the text offer additional information on the first serve:

Eastern Forehand Grip	35
Continental Grip	41
Serve-and-Volley	166

SPIN

At the contact point, the racket should be swinging upward to create topspin and around to create sidespin. Sidespin will make the ball curve, whereas topspin will make the ball drop into the court. The more the racket head hits up, the more topspin will be generated. The faster the swing is, the faster the ball will rotate. The server should feel as though he is brushing up and over the ball, thus creating a spinning action.

FOLLOW-THROUGH

The drive-up with the legs, as well as the reaching up with the serving arm for contact, should lift the body off the ground. The weight lands on the front foot inside the court, and the racket follows through across the body and past the front leg (see figure 4.27).

RECOVERY

Because the force and rotation of the body moves the server into the court, she has to use a split step in preparation for the return at the baseline, or move forward for the first volley if she must go to the net to hit a weak return. To return to the baseline, the server must hop or step back quickly after the follow-through so she is prepared for the return. The follow-through and forward weight transfer will cause the server to land inside the baseline. She will either split step for balance and recover to behind the baseline and prepare for a groundstroke, or land and move toward the net to volley.

Figure 4.27   Follow-through for the serve.

Common Errors

Following are several common errors you may run into when teaching your athletes a proper first serve:

Error	Error correction
The server hits the ball too hard on the first serve.	Hitting a low percentage of first serves in the court gives the opponent the opportunity to set up for better returns. Every player should attempt to get a high percentage of first serves in the court. The most effective serves are hit with good depth, direction, and spin. If the player is simply hitting the ball hard to try to win points with the serve, have him hit with more spin for a greater margin of error over the net. Also work on having him serve to the three targets: A (alley), B (body), or C (center). Hitting with spin to curve the ball in the court and to target areas will make the first serve much more effective and should give the server a huge offensive advantage.
The server just puts the ball in play, putting little or no pressure on the opponent.	A player without the ability or strength to win points with a hard serve often resorts to just putting the ball in play. Explain to the player that a fast serve is not necessary for an effective serve; in fact, a well-placed first serve can be very effective. Have the player develop consistent serves to the three target areas and learn to change spins and even the speed of the serve. The unpredictability of these serves will keep the opponent off balance.
The player serves without recognizing the strengths and weaknesses of the opponent, hitting a strong serve right into the strength of the opponent, rather than a well-placed, easier ball right at the opponent's weakness.	Make sure the player is aware of the strengths and weaknesses of the opponent. Once she identifies the weakness, she must be relentless and hit as many serves as possible to that weakness. Encourage her to keep on pounding that weakness until the opponent begins to change position to cover up the weakness. When this happens, the server has the opportunity to win easy points by hitting the serve into a big opening created by the opponent's moving to cover up a weakness.

Second Serve

When hitting the second serve, the player wants to be accurate with more margin of error over the net and inside the service court lines without losing too much speed. What the server wants to avoid is a big first serve that misses, followed by a very safe and very soft second serve. It has been said that a player is only as good as his second serve.

Nearly everything that was discussed in the section on the first serve applies to the second serve. However, there are a few differences in the path of swing, contact point, and spin.

PREPARATION

As discussed in the First Serve section beginning on page 86, the preparation is the same for both the first and second serve. The server is in a balanced position, the hands are relaxed, the eyes search for and locate the target, and the breathing is slow. The same ritual should be used before both the first and second serve. Be sure to stress that players should not rush to hit the second serve. After missing a first serve, the player is not immediately ready to hit a second serve with purpose. He should take time to survey the situation and fully prepare his body to hit an effective serve. A server who rushes to hit a second serve would not notice, for example, that the opponent moved forward or a step or two to the side to favor his more powerful side.

GRIP, SWING, AND SPIN

To get the ball in play with more net clearance, yet still dropping in the court, the server needs to impart additional topspin on the second serve. Changing the grip, the path of the racket, and the contact point will help her do this.

The grip should be a Continental grip (page 41) or even closer to an Eastern backhand grip (page 43) to provide flexibility in the wrist and impart more topspin on the ball. The path of the swing should be more upward so the server can hit the ball up and over the net. To hit more up

Figure 4.28 Toss for the second serve.

on the ball, the server should toss the ball more over the head, rather than over the right shoulder and in front of the baseline (see figure 4.28). One thing to note on the second serve is that the racket head speed is as great on the second serve as it is on the first serve. The difference is that because there is more spin, the second serve will be slower.

As mentioned, the server is forced to hit up rather than out when the contact point is above the head. The server must adapt to this toss by arching the back on the backswing (see figure 4.29a) before the wrist snaps the racket head up the back of the ball at the contact point (see figure 4.29b). The more the server hits the ball up, the more topspin she will impart, and the ball will drop into the court after clearing the net. Not only will the ball drop into the court, but it will also bounce high and long after it hits the court making it more difficult for the returner to move forward to play an offensive serve return.

At a Glance

The following parts of the text offer additional information on the second serve:

Continental Grip	41
First Serve	86
Serve-and-Volley	166

a   b

Figure 4.29 **Backswing and contact point for the second serve.**

(continued)

Common Errors

Following are several common errors you may run into when teaching your players to hit second serves:

Error	Error correction
The player does not hit the second serve with enough spin, so the ball doesn't have adequate net clearance and spin to drop into the court.	Make sure the player is serving with the correct Continental grip or even a grip closer to the Eastern backhand grip. This will help her hit up on the serve to create the topspin necessary to pull the ball into the court after it clears the net. She will also need to generate good racket head speed at contact to get the necessary spin.
The player does not give himself an extra margin of error on the second serve.	To increase his margin of error, the player should, first, not hit hard and flat with little net clearance. Second, he should not risk aiming the second serve too close to the lines. Encourage the player to give himself a little cushion both over the net and inside the lines so he doesn't make unnecessary errors.
The player misses the first serve and immediately puts the second serve in play.	Make sure your players go through the same ritual they perform for a first serve before hitting a second serve. This means that they should take time to position themselves, take note of where the opponent is standing, aim the serve, and visualize the serve going to the correct spot in the service court. Just getting the ball in play, even with a second serve, is not acceptable. They should at least take the time to hit the serve to the opponent's weaker side.

Although the serve is the most important shot in the game because every point begins with the serve, the return would rank a very close second. Knowing that the server has the advantage, the returner should be thinking first about getting the ball back in play. Weak serves can be hit aggressively with a large swing and from a good court position.

Only when the returner can develop some consistency in making the server play another shot should she think about putting pressure on the server by hitting to a weakness or with more depth, speed, or spin. However, if the serve is ineffective, the returner should immediately take that opportunity and play a more offensive or forcing return. This is usually accomplished by stepping inside the baseline and hitting a more aggressive return from her preferred side to put pressure on the server.

KEY POINTS

The most important components of the return of serve are as follows:

- Preparation
- Grip
- Positioning and movement
- Backswing
- Contact point

PREPARATION

The returner should be in a low ready position with a wide base and weight forward (see figure 4.30). He should be focused on the server and contact point so he can recognize quickly if the serve is going to the forehand or backhand. Some returners are comfortable standing a step deeper so they can move forward to a split step just before the serve is hit (this will be explained in more detail in the Positioning and Movement section on page 96).

GRIP

When in the ready position for the serve return, the player can choose whether to wait with a forehand or backhand grip. The body is in a ready position facing directly at the server with the hands in either a forehand or backhand grip (pages 35 and 43).

For a two-handed serve return, the

Figure 4.30 Ready position for the serve return.

player can wait with the two-handed grip and be perfectly prepared for both the forehand and backhand return. The player only needs to turn and release the nondominant hand for the forehand return.

(continued)

For a one-handed serve return, the grip must change, depending on the side (forehand or backhand) the serve comes to. For example, if the returner is waiting with a forehand grip and the serve is hit to the backhand, the returner must turn the upper body to prepare the racket. Because both hands are on the racket in the ready position, the returner also needs to use the nondominant hand to quickly turn the racket face at the throat into the backhand grip position. The dominant hand regrips the racket before the forward swing is made. If the returner is waiting with a backhand grip, he must change to the forehand grip before the backswing because the nondominant hand will not be in contact with the racket after the upper body turns and the racket is in the backswing position.

POSITIONING AND MOVEMENT

The serve returner should position himself along a straight line from the server through the middle of the service court. This will give him an equal amount of court to cover on both the forehand and backhand sides. The returner should be on the baseline, but this can be adjusted based on the speed of the serve. The starting position could be a step or two behind the baseline when returning a fast serve and inside the baseline when returning a slow serve.

The returner should be in a ready position with eyes, feet, and shoulders facing directly at the server. The returner must recognize the direction of the serve and begin movement at contact—not waiting until the ball crosses the net. If a serve is hit hard, there might only be time to turn the hips and shoulders before making a swing. From the ready position the returner should make a slight hop into a split step position just prior to contact by the server so the returner's weight is forward with the knees flexed and he is ready to move forward or to either side.

All movement with the feet will be forward. If the ball is served wide, the returner will turn and step forward and across to make contact (see figure 4.31). This will allow the returner to cut the ball off before it gets too wide. If the returner turns and moves parallel with the baseline, she will make contact (if she makes contact at all) from a position wide in the court and will open up the opposite side of the court for the server's next shot.

Figure 4.31 **Getting into position for the serve return using a forward movement.**

BACKSWING

Because the ball is coming quickly in a serve, there is little time for a backswing. The returner should concentrate on an abbreviated backswing so she can make contact in the front of the body. Also, because the ball is coming at a high rate of speed, the backswing should be shorter. Hitting an effective serve return with heavy spin is difficult. Mild topspin will be created if the racket path is low to high, but this will not be an acute low-to-high angle. The flat return swing pattern starts and finishes level with the ground. The backspin return swing pattern is high to level with a slightly open racket face.

CONTACT POINT

It is vital that the contact point be in front of the body on the serve return. Balls that get behind the front hip on either forehand or backhand returns are very difficult to control. The upper-body turn, short backswing, and step across and forward, as described previously, will keep the ball in front of the body for the best control and power.

Topspin will allow for a firm return that will drop in the court. The swing pattern is low to high, as shown in figure 4.32, but the angle will not be as acute as that of the topspin groundstroke, for which the player has more time for the stroke. The flat return is safe and simple. The racket path is level, from backswing to contact point (see figure 4.33). The backspin return racket path is high to level, as shown in figure 4.34, with a slightly open racket face. Because the ball has backspin, it will float long if hit high over the net, so it must stay down and close to the net. The backspin will take speed off the serve, and the return will stay low after making contact with the court and force the server to hit up on the next shot. The backspin chip return is especially effective against the server closing on the net to volley and is hit with a very short backswing and follow-through.

At a Glance

The following parts of the text offer additional information on the serve return:

Semi-Western Grip	37
Applying Topspin	47
Controlling Shot Angle	57
Controlling Shot Speed	61

a   b

Figure 4.32   Backswing and contact point for the topspin return.

(continued)

a   b

Figure 4.33   **Backswing and contact point for the flat return.**

a   b

Figure 4.34   **Backswing and contact point for the backspin return.**

Also, be aware that the contact point is generally higher in the "strike zone." This is because the serve is hit from the highest reach of the server, so the ball will bounce high. After making the return, the returner must quickly shuffle to the center of the court for the next shot, or move quickly to the net if attacking the net after the return.

Common Errors

Following are several common errors you may run into when teaching your athletes the serve return:

Error	Error correction
The player is making too many errors because of the speed of the serve.	This is the most common error. The easiest correction is to shorten the backswing. Because the ball is coming quickly, the player will not have time for a normal backswing, nor does she need that big of a swing because the ball is coming in at a higher rate of speed. Encourage the player to shorten the backswing so she can make solid contact in front of the body.
The player is having difficulty because of the high speed and high bounce of the serve.	Encourage the player to give himself a little more time by moving back a step or two to make the return. He will have more time to read and react to the ball, and moving back will allow the ball to drop into a more comfortable hitting position.
The player can't make returns on serves hit wide to either the forehand or backhand side.	If the player can't get into position for the wide serves, she should move forward so she can hit the serve before it gets too far away. If she is starting too far behind the baseline, she may not be able to move far enough right or left because of a well-placed angled serve to the center or alley side. Her best solution is to move in and cut the ball off before it gets too wide.

Approach Shot

The approach shot is a transition shot that takes a player from the baseline position to an offensive net position. An effective approach shot allows the player to move to the net so he is in an ideal volley position by the time the opponent can make contact with the next shot, and in the best possible position to end the point with his next shot, either a winning volley or an overhead. To get into an ideal volley position, the player must hit the approach shot from a ball landing short in the court; he should be moving toward the net through the hit.

KEY POINTS

The most important components of the approach shot are as follows:

- Preparation and stance
- Grip
- Approach
- Contact point
- Backswing
- Spin
- Follow-through
- Recovery

PREPARATION AND STANCE

To get a good forward start on the ball, a player should recognize when her opponent is in trouble and most likely to hit a short return. She can move a step or two forward in the ready position so she can react and move as soon as she recognizes that the ball will land short in the court. As a general rule, balls landing in the service court are short enough to return with an approach shot.

GRIP

The grip for the approach shot will vary depending on a couple of variables. One is the height of the ball at the contact point, and the other is the type of approach shot being hit. If the ball will be contacted low or close to the court, a backspin, or slice, approach shot is the most appropriate. This shot is hit over the net at a low trajectory and stays low after the bounce. This forces the opponent to hit up on the return, thus making for an easy volley or overhead. The best grip is an Eastern forehand grip for a forehand approach shot (page 35), an Eastern backhand grip for a backhand approach shot (page 43), or a Continental grip for either a forehand or a backhand approach shot (page 41). These grips allow the player to hit with a firm wrist and a slightly open racket face.

A second type of approach shot is hit hard with topspin. The intention of this shot is to force a weak or hurried return. It is best hit when the contact point is at waist level or above. This aggressive approach shot sets up an easy volley or overhead. The topspin approach shot is hit with the same grips used for topspin forehand and backhand groundstrokes—a semi-Western forehand grip (page 37) or an Eastern backhand grip (page 43). Even though the ball will bounce higher because of the trajectory, it can be hit hard and deep to force a weak return.

Extra topspin can be used to hit a looping topspin approach shot. This is an extremely effective approach shot if the opponent has difficulty returning high-bouncing balls. The high-bouncing ball is very difficult to drive with a one-handed backhand and will usually generate a very weak return when a looping topspin approach shot is hit high to the backhand side. The grips for this type of approach shot are the Eastern backhand grip (page 43) on the backhand side and a semi-Western grip (page 37) or full Western grip (page 39) on the forehand side.

APPROACH

While moving toward the net, the player should position himself on the same side of the court the ball lands on. The volley position should be halfway between the service line and the net, and about 3 feet (1 m) from the center on the side on which the ball lands.

It is more advantageous to hit approach shots up the line rather than crosscourt because doing so reduces the distance the player must run to be in the perfect volley position. Of course, there are always exceptions to the rule. If the opponent is out of position, the best shot might be to the open court. A second exception is if the opponent has a weak side, either forehand or backhand, and the approach shot can result in a defensive return simply by hitting to the weaker side.

CONTACT POINT

On both types of approach shots (the backspin and the topspin), the contact point is even with the front hip. The backspin approach shot is hit when balls are below waist level, and the topspin approach shot is hit when balls are hit at waist level and above.

The backspin approach shot is hit by moving through the ball at contact, as shown in figure 4.35. Although the movement is forward, the body is facing the sideline through the hit. The feet slow down so they are facing the sideline for a stride or two before the body turns forward to the net after the hit. The backhand is hit as the right leg crosses in back of the left leg as the player moves through the ball before attacking the net.

Figure 4.35 **Contacting the ball using a backspin approach shot.**

(continued)

Contact with the ball when using the topspin approach shot is different from contact using the backspin approach shot. This is because the player must bend the knee and thrust up at the contact point because the racket must go from below the contact point to above it to apply the topspin. The player must load just prior to hitting the ball and drive off the back leg through the contact zone for maximum lift and power (see figure 4.36). The position of the stance is determined by the direction of the final step prior to contact and can be open, semiopen, or square on the forehand side and square on the backhand side.

It is important to note that the topspin approach shot is hit harder than the backspin approach shot, so the player has less time to move into the ideal volley position before the opponent can make the return. Combine this with the fact that the player must stop and load, rather than move through the ball at contact, and you can understand why the player has more difficulty getting into a proper volleying position when hitting a topspin approach shot. Considering these two factors, the player is best served by hitting the topspin approach shot on very short balls to avoid getting caught in a defensive volley position.

a   b

Figure 4.36   Contacting the ball using a topspin approach shot.

BACKSWING

On both types of approach shots—topspin and backspin—the backswing is shorter than a shot hit from the baseline. Remember, the backswing is like the accelerator on a car—the farther you push it down, the faster the car can go. The same can be said about the backswing. The longer the backswing is, the faster the racket head will be moving through the contact zone. Given that the approach shot is hit well inside the baseline, the backswing must be shorter or the ball will sail long. This is especially true when hitting and moving forward through the backspin approach shot.

The swing path for the backspin approach is a high backswing that moves down to the contact point with a slightly open racket face and a level follow-through. The racket head drops below the contact point on the backswing for the topspin approach shot, either with a loop or straight-back backswing.

SPIN

The spin on the low backspin approach shot is generated by the high-to-level path of the swing and the slightly open angle of the racket. This is necessary to get net clearance on the ball contacted below the top of the net. The ball with backspin stays in the air longer and will therefore go deeper in the court. It also tends to skid on the court and will stay low because of the trajectory of the shot.

The topspin approach shot is hit with a low-to-high swing path with the racket angle perpendicular to the court. The spin will drop the ball quickly into the court, and the ball will bounce higher after hitting the court. To hit a looping topspin approach shot, which forces the opponent to hit a high-bouncing ball, the player must apply more spin by using a lower backswing and higher follow-through.

FOLLOW-THROUGH

The follow-through on the backspin approach shot is level and out toward the target. The follow-through is long, smooth, and controlled. Players should be careful not to let the racket head finish low, because it will drive the ball into the net. Also, the racket face should remain slightly open, but if it opens too much, the ball will pop up with little pace making for a much easier passing shot from the opponent.

The topspin approach shot follow-through should be high, but short. A long follow-through with a lot of body rotation will impede the forward movement to the net.

RECOVERY

Recovery is critical for an effective approach shot. The player must accelerate to the net after the shot so she can be in the ideal volley position (a split step) before the opponent makes contact. The split step is when the player goes from running forward to standing with both feet parallel to the net (see figure 4.37). The player should be balanced with the weight forward, knees flexed, and body directly facing the opponent. From this position the player can move right or left, forward or back. From this position at the net, the player should be able to move in a step or two for a volley or back two or three steps for an overhead.

At a Glance

The following parts of the text offer additional information on approach shots:

Applying Topspin	47
Applying Backspin	51
Controlling Shot Speed	61

(continued)

a　　　　　　　　　　　　　　　　　　　**b**

Figure 4.37　Split step when recovering after an approach shot.

Common Errors

Following are several common errors you may run into when teaching your athletes the approach shot:

Error	Error correction
After playing the approach shot, the player is not in a good position at the net, set and ready for either a volley or overhead.	In most cases, the correction is to train your player to keep moving forward as he plays the approach shot. If he moves to the short ball and stops before playing the approach shot, he will lose momentum and not make it to the net before the opponent makes the return. Other corrections would be to hit the approach shot deeper on a shorter ball and run to the net faster or hit the approach shot slower.
When the player hits the approach shot, it bounces into the ideal contact point for the opponent and gives her an opportunity to drive the ball with both speed and spin.	Ideally the player should be able to hit the ball and keep it low so the opponent will have to lift rather than drive the ball. Hitting the ball with a low-to-high swing on the approach shot will result in a topspin shot that will bounce high and long. Teach the player to hit the approach shot with a high-to-level swing and a slightly open racket face. The trajectory of the ball will be much flatter, and the ball will have backspin and stay low after it makes contact with the court.
The player moves to the net so quickly after hitting the approach shot that he is unable to split step and be ready for a volley or overhead.	Players must be able to move to the net under control, so they are in an ideal volley position (a split step) just before the opponent makes contact with the ball. If the player is running too fast, the split step may not occur. When this happens, the opponent easily hits the ball right or left, and the player is not able to react quickly enough to make the volley. Also, if he is moving forward too quickly, it is difficult to stop and move back for an overhead. Teach the player to hit the approach shot, move in quickly, but always split step and be ready for the next shot, even if he is not in an ideal volley position. He can move across and in to intercept the passing shot for a volley, or turn quickly and move back for the overhead. As in all sports, teach players to move quickly but not to rush.

Players have the opportunity to hit point-ending shots with the volley. Because they are at the net when they hit volleys, they can hit sharp angles, firm shots to the open court, or even delicate drop volleys that die after hitting the court. Once at the net, players need to be able to hit all of these volleys depending on their position in relationship to the net, the position of the opponent on the court, the speed of the ball from the opponent, and the height of the ball at contact (either above or below the top of the net), using both forehand and backhand volleys to end the point.

PREPARATION

The player at the net has less than half the amount of time to hit the ball compared to when the player is in the backcourt. Because of this, preparation for the volley is very important. Players must be prepared to move aggressively forward and side to side for the volley or back for an overhead from the same starting position.

Ideally, the player should be positioned in the service court halfway between the net and the service line with the weight forward and the feet at least shoulder-width apart. The knees should be flexed and ready to make an aggressive move to the ball. The body should be well balanced with the back straight; head up; and feet, hips, and shoulders facing the net. The player should hold the racket at about chest level. The racket should be close to the body and pointed toward the backhand side. The elbows should be wider than the shoulders. With the racket closer to the body, the player can turn the body and prepare the racket quickly. By keeping the elbows away from the body, the player can keep the racket from getting behind the body when turning it to either the forehand or backhand side. The player's eyes should be focused on the opponent so she can see, even before the ball is hit, where the ball might be directed, either right or left or a high lob. The opponent's body position, racket angle, and swing pattern will provide cues on where the ball will be hit, which will enable a player at the net to get a quick start to the ball.

GRIP

When volleying, players should use a Continental grip (page 41). It allows the player to hit both the backhand and the forehand volley. The Continental grip slightly opens the racket face on both sides so volleys are hit with moderate backspin for control. This grip produces an open racket face with the wrist in a strong position for a low volley. For sharp volleys, the player should have a firm grip on the handle. Touch volleys, such as low volleys and soft-angle volleys, must be hit with "soft hands" and a much looser grip on the racket. Even players using a two-handed backhand grip will need to hit with one hand on balls that are very low or wide. The Continental grip is the best grip in both of these situations.

KEY POINTS

The most important components of the volley are as follows:

- Preparation
- Grip
- Moving to the ball
- Backswing
- Contact point
- Spin
- Follow-through
- Recovery

(continued)

MOVING TO THE BALL

Movement at the net will be across to reach the ball and forward to get the ball early. The closer the player is to the net, the more likely she will be to hit the ball above the top of the net and so be able to hit aggressively down into the court. Also, the closer the player is to the net, the more the angle of the volley can be increased. If the player does not move forward, but instead waits for the ball to come to her, the ball could drop below the top of the net and force her to hit up to get the ball over the net. This volley cannot be hit hard, because the open racket face will make the ball go up to clear the net. If hit hard, the ball will travel long.

Because the ball is traveling so quickly at the net, all movement must be quick and efficient. The first movement should be to prepare the racket face, followed by the shoulder turn, hip turn, and step forward and across. Depending on the speed of the oncoming ball, the player can take additional steps forward and across once the racket is in position and the body is turned. Any extra forward movement will give the volleyer a better chance of playing the ball above the top of the net for an offensive and aggressive volley, either with speed and power or with a sharp angle away from the opponent.

BACKSWING

Because the ball is moving quickly at the net, there is no need to take a backswing to generate power on the volley, nor is there time. In most situations, it is best to prepare the racket so the strings face the target (see figure 4.38). The speed of the oncoming ball and the movement of the body forward will supply all the power necessary for the volley.

When the ball is coming in slowly, many players tend to wait for it and use more swing. Encourage them to keep the backswing to a minimum and attack these weaker shots moving forward. The power for the volley is generated by the forward body movement rather than the swing of the racket. If a player at the net gets a very slow ball, moves forward, and still has time for a slight backswing, this is acceptable and will permit the player to hit with additional power.

Figure 4.38 **Preparing the racket for the volley.**

CONTACT POINT

The classic forehand volley contact is made with the racket head above the wrist, the elbow bent and tucked in, and the ball in front of the body (see figure 4.39a). The backhand volley contact point is farther out in front with a straight elbow (see figure 4.39b). A ball hit directly at the body is played in front of the body with the backhand side of the racket.

a   b

Figure 4.39   **Contact point for (a) a forehand volley and (b) a backhand volley.**

SPIN

With the exception of the swinging midcourt volley (for more information, see page 169), which is hit with topspin, and the very high volley, which is hit flat, volleys are played with backspin. The spin is generated as the racket moves forward through the ball with a slightly open racket face.

Because the backspin takes pace off the ball, a soft-angle volley or drop volley should be hit with more backspin. This is accomplished by using a more open racket face and a relaxed and soft grip at contact. If a ball is hit very hard at the net player, many times this player can only get the racket facing the ball before contact. This "reflex" volley will be hit flat, without any spin, and with no backswing or follow-through.

(continued)

FOLLOW-THROUGH

Because the volley requires little backswing, the follow-through is short and compact. Terms such as *punch* and *catch* are used for the volley and describe the shortness of the stroke. To prevent too much swing on the volley, the player should finish the volley with the racket face directed at the target. The racket head should not drop below the top of the net, even though the path of the racket is slightly high to level to produce backspin. For solid volleys contacted below the top of the net and close to the court, the racket face should be open to get the ball up, and the swing should be short and level for a firm hit.

There is a tendency for the swing pattern to go high to low in a chopping manner. Because the racket face is open, the player feels the need to hit down on the ball to keep it in the court. The high-to-low chopping motion is not only difficult to time, but will hit the ball into the net if the racket face does not open enough, or pop the ball up weakly if the racket face opens too much.

RECOVERY

Hopefully the volley will be the winning last shot of the point. However, this is not always the case, so the player must develop the habit of recovering into position after the forward and crossover steps. This will bring the player back to the original starting position with the weight forward and over a wide base, racket up and slightly shaded toward the backhand side, elbows wider than the shoulders, head up, eyes forward, and back straight.

The player must remember to shift to the right or left of the center service line so he is on the same side as where the ball lands in the opponent's court. He must do this very rapidly because the ball will come back quickly if the opponent returns the volley. This is especially true in doubles, in which more volleys are returned because there are two opponents on the other side of the net and less space in which to hit a clean volley winner.

Also note that it is important to recover first with the racket, even before the body and feet can recover, so the player is ready to hit any ball that might be returned. This is especially useful when playing doubles because the action can be very quick due to the possibility of all four players at the net volleying from very close proximity. When at the net, all great volleyers move quickly to hit the volley and recover just as quickly so they are ready if the ball is returned.

Common Errors

Following are several common errors you may run into when teaching your athletes the volley:

Error	Error correction
The player uses too much swing and can mis-hit or hit with too much power.	Teach your players to think of the volley as a placement shot rather than a power shot. In almost all situations an opening is available when playing at the net. Players should concentrate on making contact out in front of the body, and to do this they need to take little or no backswing. Teach them to use the speed of the opponent's shot to generate all the speed necessary for the volley.
The player gets a very easy return and waits for the ball. It drops below the top of the net before she makes the volley.	Explain to the player that she can play offensive sharp angles and firmly hit shots into the open court only if she can play the ball down into the court. To do this, the contact point must be above the net level. Explain that when the ball is returned hard by her opponent, the ball stays up and the volley is easy. However, when the return is weak, it is easy to wait for the ball, but it might drop before she can make contact above the top of the net. Encourage her to move in a step or two before making contact. By getting closer to the net, she will have an easier time hitting a volley firmly to the open court or soft and with a sharp angle.
The player is forced to hit from below the top of the net with a volley, making hitting the ball with topspin almost impossible.	Explain to the player that when playing a low volley he must hit the ball up to clear the net, but he shouldn't hit it too hard or it will sail long. The racket face has to be open to get the net clearance. The open racket face will also create backspin, which will take speed off the ball and allow him to keep the ball in the court. Teach your players to hit volleys with a Continental grip so that the racket face is open on both the forehand and backhand sides. Although the semi-Western and Western grips might be good for topspin groundstrokes, they are very limiting at the net. The low-to-high swing is very difficult to time, and the low ball is almost impossible to lift over the net with these grips.

One of the newer shots in the game is the swinging midcourt volley. This shot is very effective against the opponent's looping groundstroke that is hit high over the net so it will bounce high and deep in the court. Rather than moving back and playing a groundstroke from deep in the court, the player quickly moves forward and hits a swinging topspin volley from the midcourt.

KEY POINTS

The most important components of the swinging midcourt volley are as follows:

- Preparation
- Grip
- Moving to the ball
- Backswing
- Contact point
- Follow-through
- Recovery

PREPARATION

Getting into the proper position to play this shot is critical for success. The player must recognize when the opponent will hit a ball with little speed and plenty of net clearance to get the ball back deep into the court and be ready to move forward quickly to play the shot from above the top of the net. Before hitting the shot, the player should move forward and be set and on balance, with the weight loaded on the back foot.

GRIP

This shot will resemble an aggressive topspin groundstroke. The exception, of course, is that the ball is hit in the air. The grip for a swinging midcourt volley should be the preferred grip used for a topspin groundstroke—usually a semi-Western forehand grip (page 37) because the ball will be contacted at waist level or above.

MOVING TO THE BALL

Being able to anticipate a high and soft return that will land deep in the court will help the player get an early start on this shot. The starting position can be on or slightly inside the baseline to reduce the distance the player must cover before hitting the shot. From this closer ready position, the player moves very quickly forward so she is stationary and loaded and has her racket back and ready for a full swing just prior to making contact.

BACKSWING

The backswing for the swinging midcourt volley looks like a groundstroke backswing and starts a foot below the contact point so the player can hit with topspin. To get the racket back and low, the player can either take it straight back or use a continuous loop backswing, as described on page 47.

CONTACT POINT

The contact point for this shot is similar to the contact point of a topspin ground-stroke, which is waist level or above and in front of the body (see figure 4.40). However, it is very important that the contact be made at least at waist level. To be effective, this shot must be hit sharply with some topspin to bring the ball into the court.

Because the ball is hit sharply, the player must impart topspin to pull this hard-hit shot into the court. Heavy topspin is not necessary because it will take speed away from the shot. However, more spin will be needed if the contact point is low.

Figure 4.40 Contact point for the swinging midcourt volley.

FOLLOW-THROUGH

A full follow-through in which the racket finishes up and over the opposite shoulder is needed for this shot (see figure 4.41). The racket must accelerate through the contact zone, so a full long and high follow-through is necessary.

a   b

Figure 4.41 Follow-through for the swinging midcourt volley.

(continued)

RECOVERY

Recovery after the swinging midcourt volley should resemble that of an approach shot, which is a down-the-line or the aggressive groundstroke hit forcefully to the open court. The player is trying to hit a winner with this shot, but if the opponent does return it, the player should be in a position to end the point with a winning volley at the net. The player must remember to move forward to the net quickly after playing the shot and position himself on the same side of the center service line as where the ball will land. If the opponent returns the shot, the next shot will be easy if the player is in the correct position at the net. If the player hesitates to admire his shot, he can be caught in the middle of the court and may be forced to play a defensive volley, which is a low volley hit below the top of the net from the midcourt.

At a Glance

The following parts of the text offer additional information on the swinging midcourt volley:

Continental Grip	41
Overhead	113

Common Errors

Following are several common errors you may run into when teaching your athletes the swinging midcourt volley:

Error	Error correction
The ball drops too low and forces the player to lift the ball to get the proper net clearance.	When the ball drops too low before it can be volleyed, the player must lift the ball for net clearance and hit with topspin to keep the ball in play. All of this takes away the advantage of playing the shot with power and depth by hitting the ball relatively flat from above the top of the net. The player must be selective on what ball to attack to make sure she will be able to move in quickly and get into position to play the ball above the net. The correction is to get the right ball and move in immediately when the opponent hits the floating return. Any hesitation will prevent the player from getting to the ball soon enough to be able to play it offensively.
The player hits the ball with too much topspin, making the ball land short without the power to run through the open court.	The swinging midcourt volley should be hit with only a slight amount of topspin for maximum power and depth. The player should use a full swing with a slight low-to-high racket path.
The player is out of position when the ball comes back.	The player should have a plan to put the finishing touches on the point if the swinging midcourt volley is not a clean winner. He must either move to the net to finish the point with a volley or an overhead, or drop back to the baseline and be ready for an aggressive groundstroke from the weak return. Make sure he is moving and in the right position after the shot and prepared to play another shot if the opponent makes the return.

The overhead, also known as the overhead smash, is the most potent point-ending shot a player can hit. Generally it is played inside the service line at a contact point above the head, so there are options to drive the ball hard into the court or angle the ball away from the opponent. When hit solidly and accurately, the overhead should not come back.

PREPARATION

The overhead shot is played when the opponent hits a lob while the player is at the net. The ready position is the same as the volley ready position at the net—halfway between the service line and the net. The feet, hips, and shoulders are facing the net, the knees are flexed, the racket is held at chest level, and elbows are slightly wider than shoulder width (see figure 4.42). In this position the player can move forward for a volley, or back for an overhead.

KEY POINTS

The most important components of an overhead are as follows:

- Preparation
- Grip
- Positioning
- Backswing
- Contact point
- Follow-through
- Recovery

Figure 4.42 Ready position for an overhead.

GRIP

In the ready position, the player should use a Continental grip (page 41), which is ideal for both forehand and backhand volleys as well as the overhead. The Continental grip gives the wrist the flexibility needed for the overhead, and will produce some spin for control.

(continued)

POSITIONING

From the ready position, when the opponent hits a lob, the player turns the hips and shoulders sideways to the net and prepares the racket with the arm in a throwing position (see figure 4.43). With the body sideways to the net and the racket up, the player moves to get in the proper position for the overhead.

If the ball is slightly behind the player, he will need to take a few side shuffle steps. If the ball is farther over the player's head, he will need to take some crossover sideways steps to quickly retreat for the shot. If the ball is lobbed very high or if it is windy, it is best to let the ball bounce and play the overhead after the bounce. In this situation, the player must retreat well beyond the bounce so he can make contact with his body weight moving forward.

Lobs that are well hit and over the head of the player at the net require a quick turn and two or three crossover side steps so the weight is loaded on the back leg. The player can then jump, make the overhead, and land on the front leg, as shown in figure 4.44. This is possible because the overhead motion rotates the body in the air so the back leg swings forward. This is called the scissor kick overhead.

In all cases, however, the player will want to be in a position so he can make his swing with the contact point at the same point as the serving contact point. This position is as high as the player can reach, slightly in front of the body, and even with the hitting shoulder. Your players should move quickly into position so their weight can be transferred forward and their body can turn toward the net before the overhead, resembling the weight transfer, body rotation, and contact of the serve.

Figure 4.43 **Preparing for the overhead by turning the body sideways to the net.**

a
b

Figure 4.44   Scissor kick overhead.

BACKSWING

When the racket is in the full backswing position, the upper arm is parallel with the court and pointing at the back fence (see figure 4.45). The elbow is bent and the wrist is relaxed so that the racket is laid back. The opposite arm is extended up on the net side of the body for balance. The opposite hand can shield the ball from the sun or help track the ball into the hitting zone.

Figure 4.45   Backswing for the overhead.

(continued)

CONTACT POINT

The contact point for the overhead is the same as the serve contact point—as high as the racket can reach, over the right shoulder, and a foot in front of the body (see figure 4.46). If the player contacts the ball behind this point, he will need a stronger wrist snap to bring the ball into the court.

The overhead is intended to be hit for an outright winner. It is generally hit firmly with only a slight amount of spin for control. The farther back in the court the overhead is hit, the more spin will be needed to keep the ball in the court. The overhead can be hit hard and flat when the ball is hit close to the net. It can be directed into the open court or forcefully smashed into the court and bounced over the opponent's head.

Figure 4.46 **Contact point for the overhead.**

FOLLOW-THROUGH

After the player hits an overhead, the wrist continues to snap and the arm swings down and across the body (see figure 4.47). The weight transfers from the back leg to the forward leg. The left arm pulls into to the chest at the hit to assist in body rotation, and the racket finishes across the body and on the outside of the opposite leg.

Figure 4.47 **Follow-through for the overhead.**

RECOVERY

The overhead is usually a point-winning shot, but the player must be able to hit and recover to the ideal volley position, halfway between the net and service line, after the shot. The opponent might return the ball, and because the shot is hit hard, it will come back quickly. It is important for the player to hit the overhead with the weight moving forward so he can recover toward the net quickly.

The exception is the overhead played after the bounce and close to the baseline. In this case the player should return to the normal baseline position and be ready for the opponent's return.

At a Glance

The following parts of the text offer additional information on the overhead:

Continental Grip	41
Volley	105

Common Errors

Following are several common errors you may run into when teaching your athletes the overhead:

Error	Error correction
The player is in a good starting position but fails to move back quickly enough to keep the ball in front and play an effective overhead.	As soon as the lob goes up in the air, the player should turn quickly with the racket up and be ready to hit and move sideways and back so the ball stays in front of her. She should be able to set and hit a strong shot with her body moving forward. Watch to see if she reacts too slowly, or backpedals to get in position. Moving back without getting sideways to the net is slow, and the player could stumble and fall backward.
The player has a wide-open court and easy lob, but he overhits and misses the overhead.	Encourage the player to know where the opponent is and how much court he has to work with for the shot placement. Many players get excited, overhit, and miss this easy shot.
The player does not let the ball bounce on the very high lob, especially if it is close to the net or if the wind is blowing the ball around.	When the lob is hit high in the air, it is best to let the ball bounce and play the overhead after the bounce. Because the ball has bounced, the wind will not blow it around as much. It is much easier to time the swing on a ball that is falling from a lower height. Make sure the player does not let the ball bounce and go behind her, but rather that she positions herself a step or two deeper so she can move forward after the bounce if necessary. Remind her that she has time because the ball is a high lob.

Drop Shot

KEY POINTS

The most important components of the drop shot are as follows:

- Preparation
- Grip
- Backswing
- Contact point
- Trajectory
- Follow-through
- Recovery

The drop shot is a softly hit shot with backspin that falls onto the court just after clearing the net. It can be hit as an outright winner or to force an opponent to the net. This tactic is effective if the opponent is vulnerable at the net, or slow or out of condition.

PREPARATION

The drop shot must be played from a short ball and should be hit from well inside the baseline. The player should be prepared in the normal ready position—at the baseline with the body facing directly at the net, the weight forward with the knees slightly flexed, and the racket held up and in front of the body (see figure 4.48).

The choices with the short ball are an approach shot, an aggressive groundstroke, or a drop shot. Disguise is an important factor because it freezes the opponent at the baseline until the shot is hit. With that in mind, when hitting a drop shot, the player should prepare the body and the racket as if he were going to hit an approach shot or an aggressive groundstroke.

GRIP

Because he will hit the ball with backspin, the player must be able to hit with an open racket face. An Eastern (page 35) or Continental grip (page 41) works well on the forehand side because it makes it easy to open the racket face to get the height necessary to get the ball up and over the net and to create backspin. When the player is hitting on the backhand side, a Continental grip is best because the racket face is open, which gives the shot the necessary elevation to get up and over the net with backspin.

Figure 4.48 **Ready position for a drop shot.**

BACKSWING

The backswing for the drop shot begins high, like a loop backswing. Just before contact, the racket path goes from high to level and the racket is open to create backspin (see figure 4.49). The best drop shots are played with a backswing that is the same as a backswing for an aggressive groundstroke. This "disguise" prevents the opponent from anticipating the short drop shot, forcing her to prepare in the backcourt and move forward only after the shot is hit.

a   b

Figure 4.49 **Backswing for a drop shot.**

CONTACT POINT

The swing for the drop shot is slow and soft, and contact is made even with the front hip at waist level. The racket arm has a slight bend at the elbow. At the contact point, the racket swing pattern will be a high to level with an open racket face. This provides the elevation needed to get the ball up and over the net as well as the backspin needed to make the ball hit and stay low without a long bounce.

The high-to-level swing and the open racket face create backspin on drop shots. The backspin takes speed off the ball and prevents the ball from hitting and bouncing long after making contact with the court. A soft drop shot with backspin should bounce three times before reaching the service line.

(continued)

TRAJECTORY

The trajectory of the drop shot is up off the racket face, and the ball should be traveling down as it crosses over the net. It is important that the trajectory is more up and down, rather than out, because it should bounce close to the net. The ball should bounce close to the net so the opponent has to run all the way to the net to retrieve this shot. If the player hits the ball with a flatter arc, the ball will have a longer bounce, which makes it easier for the opponent to reach for a return.

FOLLOW-THROUGH

The follow-through for the drop shot is slow and controlled. The racket moves forward toward the target and the racket face is open (see figure 4.50). The follow-through is short because the ball is hit only a short distance and with just enough speed to get the ball over the net. The racket face finishes open to create enough trajectory to get the ball up and over the net and to give the ball backspin. The drop shot is the best example of a player taking speed off an oncoming shot. The softer and slower the ball is hit, the better the result of the drop shot. There should be little or no forward weight transfer or body rotation and only a short follow-through when hitting the perfect drop shot.

a   b

Figure 4.50   Follow-through for a drop shot.

RECOVERY

The recovery after the drop shot varies depending on the situation. If the opponent is fully extended and forced to simply pop the ball up to get it over the net, she should be at the net and ready for a volley.

If the opponent has better play on the drop shot, the recovery should be at the baseline. The opponent will be at the net after playing the drop shot, and so the return shot will be a passing shot into the open court or a lob over the opponent's head.

As you can see, the drop shot does not have to be a perfect winner to be effective. Because the opponent has to run quickly and cover a lot of court to keep the ball in play, the player has some openings in the court for the next shot.

At a Glance

The following parts of the text offer additional information on the drop shot:

Continental Grip	41
Applying Backspin	51
Controlling Shot Height	59
Controlling Shot Speed	61

Common Errors

Following are several common errors you may run into when teaching your athletes the drop shot:

Error	Error correction
The player tries to hit the perfect drop shot from too deep in the court.	If the ball is played from or behind the baseline, the ball has to travel much too far to be able to hit the court and not bounce too far forward, which is what makes the opponent have to run to the net. The correction is to make sure the player hits drop shots only when he is inside the baseline. The farther inside the baseline the player is, the more effective the shot will be because the ball will be in the air for a shorter time. The player will have an easier time hitting the ball and stopping it from bouncing long if he hits it softer and with more backspin.
The player hits the drop shot too firmly, causing it to travel too deep in the court and bounce long.	To correct the ball that travels too far, the player needs to take speed off the ball and hit with a short stroke and soft hands. The shot requires little or no backswing, and the hands should be very soft and relaxed on the handle at the hit. The short swing coupled with the soft, shock-absorbing grip will give the player soft, short drop shots.
The player hits the ball so it bounces too far after making contact with the court, becoming a short ball to the opponent.	The drop shot must be hit with backspin so the ball bounces up rather than long after hitting the court. Teach your players to hit soft drop shots with backspin by having them turn the hand from facing forward to facing up during the stroke. When the racket turns under the ball, it creates backspin as it moves forward through the contact point. Players should be careful that the racket does not chop down on the ball. Doing so will impart backspin, but will also make the trajectory of the shot down and into the net rather up and over the net.

Forehand as a Weapon

KEY POINTS

The most important components of the forehand as a weapon are as follows:

- Preparation
- Grip
- Backswing
- Contact point
- Follow-through
- Recovery

The modern game emphasizes aggressive groundstrokes and developing a weapon. All baseline players should develop a shot they can use offensively when they get a shorter ball. This is generally the forehand, and here is how players can make it a weapon.

PREPARATION

When hitting an aggressive shot into an open court or trying to force an opponent to make a weak return, a player must execute several things perfectly. Preparation is the first. Once the player recognizes that his opponent has hit a weak shot, he must react quickly to put himself in a perfect position for his next shot. He is looking for a shot inside the baseline that he can play in his strike zone. He has to move to the ball quickly so he is in a perfect position—wide base with weight loaded on the back foot, body balanced, head steady and racket back and prepared to hit (see figure 4.51). The stance should be his preferred stance, either square, semiopen, or open. The important factor is that the body is coiled and facing the sideline and the weight is loaded on the back leg.

GRIP

The grip for the forehand as a weapon should be the preferred grip ranging from an Eastern forehand grip (page 35) to a Western forehand grip (page 39). In most cases, the semi-Western grip (page 37) is best because the ball can be hit with moderate topspin. The Eastern grip gives the player a flatter shot with less topspin, which has less margin of error over the net and inside the baseline. The Western grip gives players excessive topspin and makes the ball bounce high after hitting the court rather than through the court after the bounce.

Figure 4.51 Loading position when hitting a forehand as a weapon.

BACKSWING

The backswing will be a full backswing with the body coiled and the racket back as shown in figure 4.52. This is because the player has time to set up and will want maximum racket head acceleration through the hitting zone. The racket pattern for the backswing is low to high, but not so pronounced as to give the player too much topspin and less speed to drive the ball through the court.

Figure 4.52 **Backswing when using the forehand as a weapon.**

CONTACT POINT

The ideal contact point for the forehand as a weapon is at least waist level and even with the front foot, with the elbow bent on contact (see figure 4.53). Players should make sure the contact point is in the middle of the strike zone so they can be on balance and generate as much power as possible with the swing. Swinging fast on balls that are not in the ideal contact point will make it very difficult to stay on balance and hit with control.

Players hitting the forehand as a weapon should avoid excessive topspin,

Figure 4.53 **Contact point when hitting a forehand as a weapon.**

which takes speed away from the shot and causes the ball to loop into the court rather than penetrate through the court after the bounce. In other words, the attacking forehand should have topspin, but it should be hit flatter than a neutral topspin groundstroke played from the baseline. The low-to-high racket path will not be as excessive because the player wants less spin and more power.

(continued)

FOLLOW-THROUGH

The follow-through goes through the ball and across the body rather than high over the head or even behind the head (see figure 4.54). This shot will have topspin but only enough to keep the ball in the court. A very high follow-through will produce more topspin and less power on the shot.

This shot is the best example of hitting a ball with power. All of the energy of the player's body rotation and swing should be directed at the contact point for maximum racket head speed. This means that the player's body must be allowed to continue on with a full rotation and the racket will have a long and complete follow-through across the body.

Figure 4.54 **Follow-through when hitting a forehand as a weapon.**

At a Glance

The following parts of the text offer additional information on using the forehand as a weapon:

RECOVERY

This shot may not be the one-punch knockout, but if hit firmly and deep into the court, it should put the opponent in a more defensive court position and often results in a weak return. Players must be ready for the follow-up second shot by getting into position quickly so they can play their next offensive shot into the open court.

Players should recover back toward the center of the court but anticipate a weak return in response to a well-played forehand. Players should be ready to move into position very quickly so they can follow up with yet another aggressive forehand, hitting either a winning shot or, at the very least, keeping the opponent in a defensive position deep in the court.

Common Errors

Following are several common errors you may run into when teaching your athletes the forehand as a weapon:

Error	Error correction
The player hits too aggressively from deep in the court, which does not put pressure on the opponent and causes too many unforced errors.	Hitting the ball hard is fun, but players should make sure they are in the right position to hit this aggressive groundstroke. Players should be inside the baseline, on balance, and have a ball that is in a comfortable hitting position before hitting this aggressive forehand.
The player hits this shot with too much topspin, so it lacks the speed and depth to be an offensive weapon.	Too much topspin makes the ball drop short in the court. The ball bounces up and high rather than forward after it hits the court. The player should use only moderate spin so the shot has more speed and depth. This is easily accomplished by starting the racket slightly higher on the backswing and finishing slightly lower than a normal topspin drive. In other words, the low-to-high swing should be more level for maximum speed and depth.
When the ball drops into a low contact point, the player lifts the ball up and hits with more topspin to pull the ball into the court, which does not allow him to drive the ball hard and keep it in the court.	This error relates to the preceding two errors. The correction is to move in quickly so the contact point is at least at waist level and then to flatten out the stroke for maximum power. If the player is slow or tired, it will not be easy to move forward far enough to get the ball higher in the contact zone, and he will be forced to hit up rather than through on a ball he wants to play aggressively.

Lob

The lob is a shot that is needed when the player is out of position and must neutralize the opponent's offensive position and gain time to recover. It can also be used offensively when the player is in a better court position as an alternative to a passing shot. In this case the player hits the lob over the opponent at the net and into the open backcourt. The lob can be used to change the pace of the game and provides variety to every player's arsenal of shots. Being able to hit defensive, neutral, and offensive lobs is essential for every complete player.

PREPARATION

The preparation for a lob is from the same position as a typical groundstroke ready position; however, a few factors determine what type of lob the player will hit.

One factor is the position of the opponent. If the opponent is in an ideal volley position—halfway between the service line and the net and ready to play a volley—and the player is out of position, a defensive lob is the player's best option. This lob is hit high and deep to give the player time to return and force the opponent from the offensive net position to a position deep in the court.

A more neutral lob can be hit when the opponent is in the ideal volley position and the player is balanced and in position to play a lob from a more normal groundstroke position. The intent is to turn the tables and take an offensive position at the net as a result of a lob hit over the opponent at the net and into the backcourt. While the opponent retreats to hit the lob that will bounce in the backcourt, the player moves forward to an offensive volley position for the next shot.

The player hits an offensive lob when he is in a good position at or inside the baseline and the opponent is not completely set in the ideal volley position or has moved close to the net, anticipating closing out the point with a winning volley. The offensive lob is hit lower, just over the opponent's racket and with topspin so the ball hits the court and has a long bounce that runs toward the back fence.

In all situations, the player hitting the lob must be prepared quickly so he will have options. When there is an opponent at the net, he will generally have control of the point. No matter what happens, if the player's preparation is poor or slow, he will only have the option to hit a defensive lob because he will be out of position and will not be able to use the full swing necessary for an offensive topspin lob. The player may find it helpful to be in a ready position a few steps behind the baseline, especially if the opponent is attacking with a powerful approach shot, an approach volley, or an overhead smash.

MOVEMENT TO THE BALL

For both the neutral and the offensive lob, the player must move quickly so he is totally prepared for the shot, with the body in a balanced position and the racket back and low so he can hit the ball in a comfortable contact position (see figure 4.55). The player should have enough time to hit with the intended height, depth, and direction.

When hitting a defensive lob, the player will most likely be out of position, either very wide or deep in the court, and quite possibly on the move. The player's goal is to get the ball up in the air so it is high enough to give him time to recover, and deep enough to make the opponent retreat for the next shot.

Figure 4.55 **Player prepared to hit a neutral or offensive lob.**

BACKSWING

For all lobs, the backswing starts well below the contact point so the racket is moving up and forward at the contact point (see figure 4.56). The racket face is open to give the ball a high trajectory over the net. The combination of racket angle and swing pattern starting low and finishing high gives the ball height and spin.

Figure 4.56 **Backswing for the lob.**

(continued)

CONTACT POINT

The offensive and neutral lobs have the same contact point as the typical groundstroke—at waist level and even with the front hip with the elbow slightly bent (see figure 4.57). For a defensive lob, however, the player may have little choice. Often, the only option is to open the racket face and swing up and forward regardless of the contact point. In this case the player is just trying to keep the ball in play and recover to a better position for the next shot.

Lifting the ball with an open racket face imparts very little spin. This is most effective with a neutral lob. For the offensive lob, the player applies topspin by swinging almost vertically low to high, with a slightly open racket face for the proper trajectory. The spin will make the ball drop sharply after going over the opponent's outstretched racket and hit the court with a long, forward bounce over the baseline. This long bounce makes it very difficult for the opponent to retrieve the shot after it hits the court.

Backspin is applied when the racket face is open and the racket moves forward into the ball. This occurs when the player is running and reaching the ball at full extension. The backspin is a defensive spin that causes the ball to hit and bounce up rather than long if the opponent selects to play it after it bounces.

Figure 4.57 **Contact point for an offensive or neutral lob.**

TRAJECTORY

All lobs are high, arching shots that are hit over the head and racket of the opponent at the net. The defensive lob is hit the highest to give the player more time to recover. The neutral lob is medium in height. Players should be sure to give themselves plenty of margin of error both over their opponents and inside the baseline. The offensive lob should have the lowest trajectory and the most topspin so the bounce will be longer, making the ball very difficult to run down after making contact with the court.

FOLLOW-THROUGH

The follow-through for the neutral lob finishes with the arm and racket at head level and the racket face open and directed at the target (see figure 4.58*a*). The offensive lob finishes with the arm and racket up and behind the head (see figure 4.58*b*). The swing pattern is almost vertical from the backswing through the contact point to the follow-through. The defensive lob follow-through is very compact with an open racket face (see figure 4.58*c*).

a

b

c

Figure 4.58 Follow-through for *(a)* a neutral lob, *(b)* an offensive lob, and *(c)* a defensive lob.

(continued)

RECOVERY

If the player hits an offensive lob accurately, it will be an outright winner, but the player should be recovering to an offensive position to play a winning volley or overhead if the opponent returns the ball. For the neutral lob, recovery is at the net. The player has now changed positions with the opponent and is in the offensive net position; the opponent is in the defensive position at the baseline.

Recovery for the defensive lob is back in the center of the court and several steps behind the baseline. The player needs to be prepared for an overhead smash, so she will want to give herself as much time and distance as possible to run down the next shot.

Common Errors

Following are several common errors you may run into when teaching your athletes lobs:

Error	Error correction
The player hits the lob too short and too low.	Remind the player that the reason he is hitting a lob is to give himself time to get back in a good court position and to drive the opponent away from an offensive net position. If he tries to be too perfect by hitting the lob just high enough to get over his opponent and just deep enough to get behind him, he runs the risk of hitting short or low. Encourage him to give himself plenty of margin of error and to hit the lob high with the apex of the lob over the opponent. This will give him time to get into a good court position and prepare for the return.
The player fails to get ready for the next shot by retreating deep in the court to return the overhead or moving to the net to hit a volley or smash.	Encourage the player to always be ready to play the next shot after the lob. If the lob is short or low, she must get back deep in the court and ready for the opponent's smash. She might have to gamble and cover the open court, forcing the opponent to hit harder or closer to the lines. If she hits a lob high and deep and her opponent has to turn and retreat to run it down, she should take advantage of this opportunity to move quickly to the net so she is in an ideal volley position and ready to play a point-ending volley or overhead smash.
The player doesn't lob the ball over the weak side.	The player should make sure he knows his opponent's weak side so that when he has enough time to line his lob up, he can direct the lob over the weak side shoulder. Explain that very few people can hurt you with a backhand overhead, so even if the player's lob is short or low, his opponent will have difficulty ending the point with the weak backhand overhead.

The passing shot is hit when the opponent is at the net and the player is in the backcourt. Because the net player has the advantage to win the point in this situation, the player in the backcourt must hit a passing shot with both speed and accuracy. To do this, the player must quickly read the situation, get into position, determine the target, play the passing shot, and recover so she is in the best position to return the next shot if necessary.

KEY POINTS

The most important components of the passing shot are as follows:

- Preparation
- Court positioning
- Backswing
- Contact point
- Speed
- Follow-through

PREPARATION

To hit a quality passing shot, the player must move quickly so he is in a position in which he is steady and on balance so he can take a full swing. While moving into position, the player must pick out the target for the passing shot based on the position of the opponent at the net while keeping in mind the opponent's strengths and weaknesses. The goal is to move to the ball so he can make contact at or above waist level and drive forward off the back foot. Before the hit, the player must determine the direction of the shot along with the speed and spin necessary to hit to the selected target area.

COURT POSITIONING

Players must be in a position to hit the ball quickly on either side or directly at the opponent positioned at the net. The passing shot is easier when the player is closer to the net, providing he hits the ball high enough in the contact zone so he does not have to lift it to get it over the net. Players should learn to move forward and inside the baseline before hitting the passing shot. This reduces the distance the ball must travel to get past the opponent and limits the time they have to move to play a volley. When the player is well behind the baseline, the lob is the best option because it is very difficult to hit a ball with enough speed, accuracy, and spin when an opponent is at the net.

BACKSWING

In most situations the passing shot is hit with more speed than a typical groundstroke when both players are rallying from the baseline. For this reason, a full backswing is necessary to generate enough power for the passing shot. However, if the player is forced to hit the ball quickly from a hard-hit approach shot or volley, she will have to use a quicker, shorter, and more compact backswing.

(continued)

CONTACT POINT

To hit an effective passing shot, the player must hit the ball at the ideal contact point—waist height and even with the front foot; the arm should be a comfortable distance from the body (see figure 4.59). Generating power is difficult when the player is reaching wide to play the ball. It is also difficult to hit with power and topspin when the ball is hit close to the court. Also, the lower the player strikes the ball, the more he must lift it to get it over the net, which makes the volley easier for the opponent.

The best passing shots are hit with topspin. Because topspin pulls the ball down in the court, the passing shot can be hit with good speed and still land in the court. Topspin also makes the ball dip as it crosses over the net so the opponent is forced to hit a volley soft and up rather than hard and down. This soft volley often leads to another passing shot from a slow and possibly short ball.

Figure 4.59   Ideal contact point for a passing shot.

At a Glance

The following parts of the text offer additional information on the passing shot:

Applying Topspin	47
Controlling Shot Angle	57
Controlling Shot Speed	61

SPEED

The speed of passing shots is greater than the typical rally speed when both players are at the baseline. Hitting the ball harder gives the opponent less time to move for a return volley, whether it goes right, left, or even directly at the opponent at the net. However, players should be careful never to sacrifice accuracy for speed. It does not matter how hard the ball is hit if it does not land in the court. Players would be better served by making the opponent play an additional shot that might give them an easier ball in return or open more court for the next passing shot.

FOLLOW-THROUGH

The passing shot follow-through is high because of the low-to-high swing pattern; consequently, the racket finishes above the head (see figure 4.60). The follow-through should be compact because the player needs to move quickly after hitting a passing shot to get back into position if the opponent volleys.

Figure 4.60 **Follow-through for a passing shot.**

Common Errors

Following are several common errors you may run into when teaching your athletes how to hit passing shots:

Error	Error correction
The player hits too hard and makes too many errors.	The player should concentrate on a comfortable contact zone and a solid hit. He should try to hit with power only when he is set and on balance before starting the forward swing. Wild and fast swings made when out of position result in far too many errors.
The player hits passing shots from too far behind the baseline.	Teach your player to move forward before contact. Hitting the ball from inside the baseline gives the opponent much less time to hit a volley. If the player must hit a ball from behind the baseline, she should lob rather than try to hit a passing shot.
The player hits passing shots without enough topspin.	Because topspin is necessary to keep a hard-hit passing shot in the court, the ball must be contacted so that the racket can make a low-to-high swing pattern. It is difficult to hit with enough topspin to keep a hard-hit ball in the court when the contact point is low. When the contact point is too low, the player must hit the ball up to get it over the net. When this happens, additional topspin is necessary to keep the ball in the court.

KEY POINTS

The most important components of deep groundstrokes are as follows:

- Preparation
- Grip
- Backswing
- Contact point
- Follow-through

Often in the course of a match a player must hit a groundstroke, either forehand or backhand, from deep in the court. This is necessary when the opponent has hit a high shot that lands deep in the court. One solution is for the player to develop the skill to take this ball on the rise and play it aggressively without giving up court position. The other alternative, which is easier and safer, is for the player to move back and give herself plenty of time to play the ball in a comfortable hitting position.

PREPARATION

When hitting groundstrokes from deep in the court, the player must be in a balanced position behind the baseline prior to contact and set so he can transfer his weight and rotate his body as he hits the shot. The player's stance will need to be either square (see figure 4.61a) or slightly open (see figure 4.61b) so the weight can shift forward and the body can rotate into the shot. Be careful that the player does not become lazy and hit from an extremely open stance with the weight falling backward on the hit because it will be difficult to hit through the ball for a solid and deep return. If the stance is closed, the player will not be able to rotate into the ball and will hit the shot with only the arm and without the advantage of the forward weight transfer and rotation of the body.

Figure 4.61 Body positioning for groundstrokes from deep in the court: *(a)* square stance and *(b)* slightly open stance.

GRIP

For a groundstroke from deep in the court, the grips, for both forehands and backhands, should be similar to those used when hitting shots from the baseline. The grips range from the Eastern (page 35), semi-Western, and Western forehand grips (pages 37 and 39); the Eastern backhand grip for a one-handed backhand (page 43); and the two-handed backhand grip with the top hand in a semi-Western and the bottom in either a Continental or an Eastern grip (pages 37 and 45). However, if the player has moved back and is still forced to hit a ball high in the contact zone, the grips need a slight adjustment to maintain a vertical racket face at the contact point. This means that the player will need to position the hand more behind the handle for a high forehand grip (see figure 4.62a) and around toward the top of the handle for a high backhand grip (see figure 4.62b). In both cases, the hand and wrist should be in a neutral and strong position at contact.

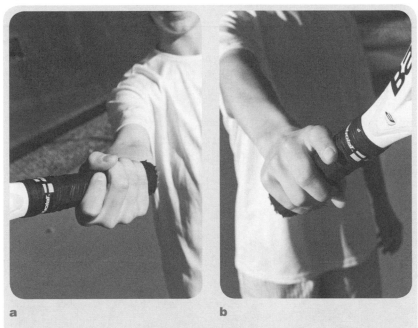

a   b

Figure 4.62 **Grips for balls hit higher in the contact zone:** *(a)* **forehand and** *(b)* **backhand.**

(continued)

BACKSWING

Players will never have more time to prepare for a shot than on deep groundstrokes. They will also need a complete backswing to generate the power necessary to return the ball back deep in the court. The backswing should be long and point at the back fence and be positioned at least a foot below the contact point (see figure 4.63). The weight should be loaded on the back foot when the racket is in the full backswing position.

CONTACT POINT

Ideally, the contact point for a deep groundstroke should be the same as that for the conventional forehand and backhand hit from the baseline. However, if the contact point is high, the backswing should start higher and be positioned a foot below the contact

Figure 4.63 Backswing for a groundstroke from deep in the court.

point. At contact, the weight transfers forward and the body rotates so the hips and shoulders are facing the net when hitting with a forehand, as shown in figure 4.64*a*, or a two-handed backhand, as shown in figure 4.64*b*. For the one-handed backhand, the weight transfers to the forward foot and the racket drives from the forward shoulder with more weight transfer than body rotation so it won't hit across the ball.

a   b

Figure 4.64 Contact point for groundstrokes deep in the court: *(a)* **forehand and** *(b)* **two-handed backhand.**

Because the deep groundstroke is hit with the swing pattern beginning low and finishing high, the shot imparts topspin. If the racket path is too vertical, there will be too much topspin and the ball will drop short in the court. If the grip is not positioned so the racket face is vertical at the contact point with the high ball, the racket face will be open and cause the ball to be hit with backspin. The ideal shot is hit with moderate topspin so the ball travels deep in the court and takes a high and long bounce. This forces the opponent to play a shot from deep behind the baseline.

Also note that from the ready position, the player will have to retreat quickly so he won't hit with the weight on the back foot while falling away from the shot. Remember, because your player is well behind the baseline, he will have to hit the ball higher over the net and with more force than if he were hitting from the baseline. If he can't set up and drive through this ball, he will probably hit a weak and short return that is ideal for his opponent to play aggressively on the next shot.

FOLLOW-THROUGH

Because the deep groundstroke begins with a full backswing, the follow-through is long and high. The racket travels in a low-to-high swing pattern, and the follow-through finishes with the hand at least at head level and over the opposite shoulder for the forehand and two-handed backhand (see figure 4.65a). The one-handed backhand should finish with the hand at head level, the arm all the way through and pointing over the net, and the racket head directed at the sky (see figure 4.65b). The best follow-through for a groundstroke hit from deep in the court will be one with a complete forward

a   b

Figure 4.65 **Follow-through for a groundstroke from deep in the court:** *(a)* **two-handed backhand and** *(b)* **one-handed backhand.**

(continued)

weight transfer and a full body rotation so that the hips and shoulders are facing the net. The racket must also have a complete, unrestricted swing and a high follow-through so the ball can be hit high enough that it lands deep on the opponent's end of the court.

Common Errors

Following are several common errors you may run into when teaching your athletes groundstrokes from deep in the court:

Error	Error correction
The player does not get far enough behind the baseline to set up and drive forward for the shot.	One of two things may be causing this error. The player may be failing to get back far enough for the shot. She moves back, but the high-bouncing deep shot causes her to hit off the back foot with the weight falling away from the net. A player with this problem needs to retreat quickly and all the way back so she can set and load on the back leg and drive forward at the hit. If, however, the player is late getting to the ball because she reacts too late or moves back too slowly, she needs to improve on her reaction time and speed. It is easy to get lazy on this shot because there seems to be plenty of time to get back and set up. However, this must be done quickly so the weight is not moving back when the ball arrives.
The player hits the ball with too much topspin, and the ball lands short in the court.	It is easy to hit this shot with too much topspin, especially if the player is leaning back at the hit. This lean away from the net causes the player to have a much more acute low-to-high swing pattern, which results in too much topspin. The additional topspin causes the ball to drop either in the net or short in the court, giving the opponent an easy ball to attack. The player should make sure he is well balanced and that his racket goes from a low backswing that begins 1 foot below the contact point to a high follow-through with the hand at head level.
The player's shot falls short in the court, making it easy for the opponent to attack.	In this case the ball lands short in the court because it is not hit high enough or hard enough. Have the player use a full swing and aim the shot higher over the net for consistently deep returns from a position deep in the court.

PART III

Teaching Tactical Skills

Tactical skills get at the heart of tennis. Without a proper understanding and execution of tactical skills, your players will often commit basic errors in match situations. You can empower them by teaching them how to read situations, apply the appropriate knowledge, and make the correct decisions.

Chapters 5, 6, and 7 focus on the basic and intermediate tactical skills in tennis, showing you how to teach your athletes to make good decisions. These skills include offensive tactical skills such as keeping the ball in play, identifying and hitting to the opponent's weakness, playing to one's own strengths, and moving the opponent to create openings in the court. This part also covers styles of play and how to help each player determine his most appropriate style based on his skills, size, speed, physical condition, and temperament.

THINKING TACTICALLY

Throughout the presentation of tactical skills in this part, we will often refer to what is called the game situation. As described in Rainer Marten's *Successful Coaching, Third Edition*, the game situation includes shot selection, the position of the players on the court, and the recovery after each shot. In other words, your players need to know specific information when they face specific situations. For example, when serving at 30-40, the player should ask herself whether her opponent is winning points by hitting powerful and accurate shots or as a result of her own serving errors. If she decides that she herself is making unforced errors, she may elect to hit a safer first serve to her opponent's weak side rather than go for a hard serve hit close to a line to see if she can force an error on the return.

You and your players must know key information to make the best decisions. Following are a few questions that you and your team should ask yourselves when facing tactical situations during a match:

- What is your strategy?
- How does your game plan affect your strategy?
- How does the game situation (the score, the strengths and weaknesses of the players, the physical playing conditions, and so on) affect your game plan?

For each skill in this part, we first present an overview that paints a picture or puts your athletes into a specific scenario in the match in which you would be likely to use the particular tactical skill. The Watch Out! section highlights distractions that may affect your athletes' ability to make appropriate decisions and provides insights into what to look for. The Reading the Situation section offers important cues that your athletes need to be able to read to make the appropriate decisions for the situation. The sections under Acquiring the Appropriate Knowledge provide the information your athletes need to make the proper decision and successfully execute the skills, as presented in the overview. Finally, as in the technical skills chapters, the At a Glance section refers you to the other important tools in the book that will help you teach the skill.

chapter 5

Singles and Doubles Tactics

Singles and doubles are two distinct games played on the tennis court that require different skills and tactics. There are some obvious distinctions between the singles and doubles games.

The first distinction between singles and doubles games is the total size of the playing area. When playing singles, players must hit every shot that is returned on their side of the court, which is 27 feet wide and 39 feet deep for a total of 1,053 square feet. A doubles team must return all balls from a larger doubles court measuring 36 feet wide and 39 feet deep for a total of 1,404 square feet. Because two players cover this larger area, theoretically each player is responsible for only 702 square feet of court, a considerable difference compared to the singles court. Because both courts have the same depth, another way of looking at the court is that the singles player must cover a 27-foot court in width, and each player on a doubles team must cover 18 feet, or half of the 36-foot court width.

The second distinction between the singles game and the doubles game is the increased width of the doubles court. Each doubles alley is 4 feet 6 inches in width, so the doubles court is 9 feet wider (36 feet total) than the singles court (27 feet total). The doubles alleys come into play especially with shots that are directed away from opponents such as the serve return and passing shot. The wider court gives players more space to hit the ball in the court and thus allows greater angles on all returns.

This greater angle is even more pronounced when shots are played at the net. When using the wider court, players can hit volleys and overheads with more angle compared to hitting deep or down the middle. Even if an opponent can get to and return a sharply angled volley or overhead, he will be well off the court, which will create large openings. It is very difficult for the remaining doubles player to cover the entire 36-foot court.

Finally, doubles tennis has the increased complexity of two players having to coordinate their actions while playing against two opponents. A winning doubles team must have a clear understanding of game strategy and the ability to communicate and work together on the court.

Tactical Differences Between Singles and Doubles Play

These and other differences mean that singles and doubles players need different skills and tactics. Let's begin by taking a look at the main tactical differences between singles and doubles play.

Singles

Singles players must keep the ball in play, hit to the open court, play to the opponent's weakness, and play to their own strength, which we will learn more about in the section Singles Tactics on page 145. Before learning tactics for singles play, however, players should choose a style of play that can help them understand how to develop individual play tactics. The styles of play for singles fall into the following categories:

- Counterpunch
- Serve-and-volley
- Aggressive baseline play
- All-court play

A counterpunch player succeeds by moving well and keeping pressure on the opponent by simply getting to and returning every shot that is hit back in the court. This "keep the ball in play" tactic is especially effective if the player can move quickly around the court and is in superior physical condition. Most shots from counterpunchers fall in the neutral category because they rarely take risks by trying to hit hard and close to the lines to end points quickly. Neutral shots are played when both players are in the backcourt and neither has the advantage or opportunity to hit a point-ending shot.

The serve-and-volley style of play is the fastest way to hit to the open court by getting the player to the net quickly after a serve for a well-placed volley or overhead. The serve-and-volley style of play puts a singles player in a position at the net quickly so she can play an offensive volley or overhead very early in the point. This style favors the player with a strong serve and aggressive play at the net.

The aggressive baseline style of play uses the strength of the baseline player to put pressure on the opponent by creating openings in the court. He hits to the opponent's weakness and uses spin, power, and angles to hit openings in the court, generally with a series of shots. Similarly, the all-court player has the same attributes at the baseline but with the additional skill of moving to the net when the opportunity arises to end the point with a well-placed volley or overhead.

Doubles

Doubles is a game of positioning in which two players work as a team to create and hit openings on the opponents' side of the court. Singles players use many neutral shots (neither offensive nor defensive) and more rally-type shots. Doubles play has a much clearer differentiation between offense and defense.

It is fair to say that coaches work much more on net play with doubles teams than they do with singles players. Learning how to play the net effectively is important in doubles, given that each player on the team covers only an 18-foot court rather than the 27-foot court that singles players must defend.

Doubles tactics, which you will learn more about in the section Doubles Tactics on page 147, include keeping the ball in play, hitting to the weaker player, isolating the opponent at the net, hitting to the middle, taking control at the net, hitting the correct shot, and working as a team. Shot selection and court positioning are also essential for successful doubles play. Teamwork is critical, requiring that each player either move to the best possible position to end the point or defend against the attacking team.

Formations

In doubles play, the formations the team uses determine the tactics it uses. Possible formations include both players at the net, both players in the backcourt, and one player at the net and one in the backcourt.

Both Players at the Net   Because there is less court to defend in doubles, the most favorable offensive formation is both players at the net. From that position the team can execute several tactics by hitting to the weaker player, isolating the opponent at the net, and hitting between the opponents. A team with both players at the net is definitely in an offensive position, and both players should be trying to end points as quickly as possible with well-placed volleys and overheads. The opposing team will be forced to play defensive tennis by hitting over their heads or by making them hit neutral shots by keeping the ball below the top of the net when the opponents make contact in the net position. The opposing team will have very little time to react and return shots when two players are at the net.

An aggressive doubles team with both players at the net should be in the best position to win points, games, and matches. This formation is generally the most successful, providing both players have solid volley and overhead skills at the net. Because players must develop these skills, practice time should be devoted to volley technique, working as a team, positioning, and quick movement while at the net. In addition, the team should practice overheads so that both players can hit point-ending shots from inside the service line with either power or direction. The players also need to master neutral overheads on shots hit behind the service line along with recovery and positioning at the net when they are forced back from the net by an opponent's lob.

Both Players in the Backcourt   When both players are in the backcourt, they are in a defensive mode and have to rely on different tactics to win points. When both opponents are at the net, the two backcourt players can hit to the weaker player, hit to the middle, or drive the offensive team away from the net by lobbing over their heads. Because hitting offensive shots successfully from the two-backcourt position is difficult, the team in this position should use a series of shots to create openings on the court and opportunities to win the point.

One Player at the Net and One Player at the Baseline   The one player at the net and one player at the baseline (one-up, one-back) formation combines both offensive and defensive positions on the same team. The tactics the team uses will depend on where the players hitting the shot are positioned and where the opponents are on the opposite side of the net. When hitting neutral or defensive shots, the deep player has the options of keeping the ball in play by hitting to the deep player on the opposite side of the court, hitting to the weaker player, and taking control of the net by moving forward to hit a short ball and joining her partner at the net. The player at the net should think more offensively than the deep player, with tactics such as hitting to the weaker player, isolating the opponent closer to the net, and hitting between the opponents.

Choosing a Doubles Formation

When selecting a doubles formation, you must look at several variables. Consider whether your team is the serving or receiving team, whether they are hitting or returning a first or second serve, and their individual playing styles.

Most high school tennis players use the one-up, one-back formation. This works well because this is how the serving team is positioned before beginning the point so the players are already in their positions and the shot selection is very simple.

The serving team has the option of either staying in the one-up, one-back formation or moving to the two players at the net formation. The serving team has the advantage because it can make the first strike by hitting an offensive serve. The server can move forward to the net immediately after the serve or wait for the first short ball to move forward to join his partner at the net. The aggressive doubles team will do this at the first opportunity to get both players at the net.

If the server is not comfortable at the net, the team could decide to play in the one-up, one-back formation after the serve and most likely throughout the point. The player already at the net has to think only about hitting volleys and overheads because she is in a good starting position, and the backcourt player can focus on directing shots to the opposite backcourt player or over the player at the net by hitting a lob.

CHOOSING DOUBLES PAIRINGS WISELY

The dynamic of selecting the right players to play singles and doubles has many variables. Choosing a doubles team is easy if you have two aggressive players who get along well and have good skills and movement at the net. Other, less obvious pairings can also work.

If your doubles team will be playing predominantly in the one-up, one-back formation, you could select one aggressive net player and one backcourt retriever. This team might consist of a tall player who loves to be at the net and a small player who likes the backcourt, moves quickly, and is willing to run down any shot that gets over or past the player at the net.

Coaching a one-up, one-back team involves ensuring each player understands his role. The backcourt player should be consistent and give the partner at the net opportunities to hit shots that will end points from the net position. The backcourt player should not hit risky shots but be content to play errorless tennis and let the partner at the net hit the winning shots.

Another team formation is two players with good skills from the baseline. The two players at the baseline should use good groundstrokes, lobs, and court positioning to force opponents to hit many shots from either the baseline or the net. Two-back teams try to win points by forcing opponents to make unforced errors.

Regardless of the formation of a pairing, you must consider how well these players communicate and get along. If the partners like each other, they will be a better team. They will compete hard, work together to create openings and win points, and encourage and support each other when their opponents have the momentum.

The receiving team has three options. The first is to remain in its starting position and play the one-up, one-back formation. This gives the team the opportunity to have the net player hit winning shots at the net from a good volley position, while the backcourt player plays groundstrokes to the other backcourt player or lobs over the player at the net.

After the serve return, the aggressive returner can get to the net so the team is in the two-up formation. The goal is to beat the serving team to the net so either player at the net can win the point quickly. The backcourt player can move forward after returning a weak serve or on the first short ball.

Finally, the receiving team might start with the two players in the backcourt. It might do this because the server is very effective and the returns create easy volleys or overheads as a result of the serving team attacking the net. By moving back, the receiver's partner avoids being the target of the player closer to the net. This also gives more defensive-minded teams, or teams that are content to keep the ball in play, additional time to react to and run down all shots returned to their courts.

Singles and Doubles Tactics

Now that you've had an overview of the differences between singles and doubles play, let's look at each of the tactics for singles and doubles in more depth. We have discussed the styles of play for singles players and the formations of doubles teams. The next section explains the various tactics used by both singles players and doubles teams. These tactics are explained from the simplest to the more complex. All of these tactics build on the information covered earlier on singles players' styles of play and doubles teams' formations.

Singles Tactics

Singles play puts one individual against another individual. The player with the best serve or forehand does not always win the match. Singles players who can keep the ball in play and hit the ball from side to side and short and deep will be able to set the stage to win points by either causing the opponent to make errors or creating and hitting open areas of the court to end points. In singles, the tactics are as follows:

- Keeping the ball in play
- Hitting to the open court
- Playing to the opponent's weakness
- Playing to one's strength

Keeping the Ball in Play

One of the most fundamental singles tactics is to keep the ball in play. A player who can keep every ball returned in play will never lose. This tactic forces the opponent to hit winning shots to end points. By keeping the ball in play and eliminating errors, players can be very successful at almost all levels of play.

The advantages of keeping the ball in play are quite simple. First, it is an easy tactic to follow and execute. Second, it puts all of the pressure on the opponent to hit winning shots to end points.

Players use this tactic when they determine that they can win more points than they lose just by keeping the ball in play. If a player can win points simply by getting balls back in the court so the opponent makes errors, there is no need to even think about any other tactic. Keeping the ball in play requires hitting shots with very little risk of an error; that is, not hitting hard or close to the lines.

Keeping the ball in play is helpful when the opponent is off balance and therefore cannot hit with a good stroke, or is not in good court position. Players should understand that they are in trouble and at risk of making an error when they are out of position or off balance. Just getting the ball back in play at these times will simplify their shot selection and help reduce errors.

The best way to keep the ball in play is to use solid and consistent groundstrokes. Players who move well and are patient enough to let their opponent make errors are very comfortable with this tactic. Court positioning is also important in executing this tactic. The more a player is out of position, the closer to the middle of the court and higher over the net she should be aiming. Players keeping the ball in play should always select the highest-percentage shots that will give them the most court to hit and the lowest net to clear, and that will place them in the best possible recovery position.

Hitting to the Open Court

When just getting the ball back in the court is not effective because the player makes more errors than the opponent, or the opponent hits more winning shots than errors, the player must be more aggressive to create openings and then hit to those openings. A player uses this tactic to move the opponent and force him to hit a variety of shots from different areas of the court. This movement will eventually wear down the opponent, and as he becomes tired, the openings will become larger.

The closer a player is to the net, the faster she can hit the ball to an opening and the less time the opponent will have to react for the return. Creating openings from the backcourt generally takes a series of shots directed side to side or short and deep. The intent is to keep the opponent on the move until she is out of position and her return is weak so the player can hit a strong shot from an offensive position inside the baseline.

Playing aggressive shots from side to side from the baseline can create openings. Another way to create an opening is to hit to the opponent's weakness. The opponent will either make a weak return or run around the weakness thus opening up the court. Getting to the net will allow the player to hit a winning shot to the open court with either a volley or overhead. A player should hit the first ball that lands short in the court in a rally and move forward with an approach shot that will enable him to move to the net position. Similarly, if the opponent hits soft, high, and deep, the player can move forward and hit the ball out of the air and follow that shot so he is in the net position and ready for the next shot, either a volley or an overhead.

Playing to the Opponent's Weakness

The reason for this tactic is to break down the opponent by forcing her to hit her weakest shot or by hitting balls that place her in her weakest position. This not only affects her confidence and rhythm but also makes her hit from her weakest side or position.

A player should direct shots to an opponent's weakness any time there is an opportunity. Once he has determined the weakness, the players should be relentless in playing as many shots as possible to that weakness. The thinking player will hit to the weakness regardless of the situation. For example, if a player is in a defensive position deep in the court and the opponent is in a strong offensive position at the net, a defensive lob might be the best shot. Keeping in mind the weaker side, the player could direct a lob over the backhand shoulder of the player at the net so he will be unable to hit an overhead.

Neutral shots such as groundstrokes when both players are at the baseline can easily be directed to the weaker side. Offensive shots such as aggressive groundstrokes from inside the baseline, volleys, and overheads should be directed at the weaker side with more pace, giving the opponent less time to prepare or move around the weak side to play the shot on the strong side. A player can exploit an opponent's weaker side by first hitting to the stronger side to create an opening on the weak side. This is effective if the opponent tries to cover up her weakness by moving closer to her weak side, thus making it more difficult to hit the ball there. Hitting to the strength forces the opponent to the stronger side and opens up the weakness for the next shot. Players should always take advantage of any short or easy ball and play their best or favorite shot to the opponent's weaker side. A player hitting her best shot to the opponent's weaker side will have a definite advantage.

Playing to One's Strengths

Once a player has determined his favorite shots, it makes sense that he should try to play those shots as much as possible. This is also the case for the player's favorite style of play. If a player likes to hit volleys and play short points, he should try to get to the net at the earliest opportunity and should definitely be using the serve-and-volley style.

Playing their favorite style and best shots puts players in a comfortable playing condition. When they are comfortable, they have an easier time playing at their own pace and rhythm. The game is easier and more fun when players can play their best shots, especially when they can hit their best against an opponent's worst. Players should play their best shots from their favorite areas of the court at every opportunity. This is easier if their opponents have not determined their strengths and weaknesses. Players should always be looking for weak returns and be ready to move quickly so they can play those returns with their best shots. Players can anticipate opponents' weak returns any time their opponents are in trouble because they are hitting from a deep or wide position on the court, they are rushed or off balance, or they are playing a shot on their weaker side.

To play to her strengths, the player should be ready to move so she can play her best shot from her favorite position on every shot possible. If the opponent is doing her best to hit to the player's weakness, the player should look for an opportunity to be in a position to play her best shot. When the player has done her work and has moved into a good position so she can hit her best shot, she should go for it. This is not the time to play defensively or tentatively. This is when the player should relax and hit with more pace and closer to the lines.

Doubles Tactics

Doubles matches one pair of players against another pair of players. The team that plays well by creating and hitting openings and preventing the opposing team from exploiting openings will beat the team that does not understand the strengths and weaknesses of both players and the formation of the doubles team. A team that thinks, communicates, and plays as a unit, rather than two individuals, will have success using some or all of the tactics explained in this section. In doubles, the tactics are as follows:

- Keeping the ball in play
- Hitting to the weaker player
- Isolating the opponent at the net
- Taking control at the net
- Hitting to the middle
- Hitting the correct shot
- Working as a team

Keeping the Ball in Play

Just as in singles, keeping the ball in play is the most fundamental tactic for doubles. Even though doubles play provides more opportunities to hit point-ending shots, keeping the ball in play puts pressure on the opponents to hit more placements than errors. By not giving the opposing team any "free" points because of unforced errors, a team can frustrate its opponents because they have to win all of their points by hitting great shots.

A doubles team that can get balls back in play will win more points than it will lose. This happens when the opponents make errors, they become impatient or frustrated, or they get tired. Keeping the ball in play also is an excellent tactic to use in adverse playing conditions. In windy conditions, for example, executing a more complex tactic can be difficult; getting the ball back in play will be very effective.

The doubles team using this tactic will need a great deal of patience and consistency. The key is to get to and return every shot and not make errors by trying to hit too hard, too close to the net, or too close to the lines. Players should hit high-percentage shots to the largest areas of the court and over the lowest part of the net. It is also important that the players work as a team so they are in good court positions. That way they will be set and on balance when hitting shots rather than having to react and lunge to retrieve balls returned to their sides of the court.

Hitting to the Weaker Player

Hitting to the weaker player is a tactic that works especially well if there is a discernable difference in skill level between the players on the opposing team. The tactic is to put tremendous pressure on the weaker player. Because he is forced to play most of the shots, he is the one who will have to beat your team. Using this tactic also tends to frustrate the stronger player, who may try to cover more of the court or work too hard to end points, often resulting in errors.

A doubles team will want to identify the weaker player and hit in her direction at every opportunity. This tactic can be used as early as the serve return. All shots that can be hit offensively with more power and spin are especially effective. When players have time to set up and hit their best shots, they should have the opportunity to hit to the weaker side of the weaker player. Even when a team is out of position and it must hit a defensive return, directing the ball at the weaker player will still be the best tactic.

Executing this tactic requires that the team determine very early in the match, or even during the warm-up, which is the weaker player. In addition, they should know the weaker side of that player for when they have opportunities to hit there.

Isolating the Opponent at the Net

Isolating an opponent at the net is a good tactic to use when a team has one or two players at the net and the opponents have at least one player at the net. When a player or team is in the offensive position at the net, they want to take away the offensive position of the opponent by putting pressure on the player closer to the net. They hit hard and down toward that player. This reduces the time the net player has to react. Even if the player can return this shot, he must hit it up and soft. This sets up an even more aggressive shot from the opposing team or player at the net.

A player or team will use this tactic when they are in a good position at the net and can hit balls with a volley or overhead from above the top of the net. They can hit these high balls down firmly so even if the opponent can return them, the shots should result in another easy, high ball that they can hit with another aggressive volley or overhead.

The team or player using this tactic has to initially be in a good position, halfway from the service line to the net or closer. On the first high ball they can reach, they want to move and hit the ball down in the direction of the opponent at the net. Hitting firmly at the opponent in the backcourt is not effective because that player has much more time to react to and play the shot from the baseline.

Once a team or player can hit a volley or overhead down at the opposing net player, that team is in control of the point. All shots the opponent can play will have to be hit up. If the opponent hits up and hard, the ball will go long. If the opponent hits up and soft, the next shot can be another volley or overhead hit down, giving the opponent less time to react to and return this aggressive shot.

Taking Control at the Net

When a doubles team gets to the net, it is in a good position to hit volleys and overheads that will end the points quickly. These shots can be played into open areas of the court or at the closer opponent, forcing that player to play defensive shots with less reaction time.

To take control at the net, a team must first get to the net before the opposing team does. Getting to the net could occur when the server follows the serve to the net, the returner comes in after the serve return, or either player moves to the net following an approach shot or approach volley. Another way is to wait until the best opportunity to get to the net and not provide the opponents an opening to move forward by returning the ball deep in the court. A final way to take control of the net is with a well-placed lob when the opposing team is at the net. This forces the team at the net to retreat to the backcourt and gives the team that hit the lob an opportunity to move forward to a strong net position. The key to controlling the net is to get both players to the net before the opponents can take that offensive position.

Once at the net, a team can control the points by playing offensive volleys and overheads. Because these shots are played close to the net, they are hit quickly to the open areas of the court and opponents have less time to react. Players can hit volleys and overheads with greater angles because they are hitting them closer to the net.

Hitting to the Middle

When two opponents are at the net, a very basic tactic is to hit between them. This is a good tactic for several reasons. Hitting down the middle is definitely the highest-percentage shot. There is a large margin of error because if the player does not hit the shot well, it will probably land in the court because it is nowhere near the sidelines. The shot will travel over the lowest part of the net, because the net is lower in the center than at the net posts. Even though the opposing players are in a good position, they might be confused, resulting in neither player moving to get the ball. Conversely, they might move at the same time and clash rackets attempting to hit the ball. Lastly, if either player at the net volleys the ball, he will not be able to hit with much angle because he is playing the shot from the center of the court.

Hitting to the center is especially effective when both opposing players are in a good position at the net. When in the backcourt, a player must choose a low-risk shot. This is the perfect first shot to see who moves and how they recover after playing a volley. The drive down the middle is also the preferred shot if both players move back and hit overheads well. Finally, hitting to the middle is also effective when a doubles team is at the net and can play either a volley or overhead. Between the two opponents is generally a very good and safe target.

Hitting to the middle is probably not the best choice when the ball will be played very deep or wide in the court. Also, if one of the opposing players at the net has an obvious weakness or a definite weaker side, it is probably best to hit to the weaker player or weaker side rather than go down the middle.

Hitting down the middle should nearly always be the first option when playing a shot from the baseline against two players at the net. Players should set up early and hit their best shot, preferably with some topspin that will make the ball dip below the top of the net before the opponents can play it. If the opposing team volleys the ball back deep, a second or third down-the-middle shot is a good option. If the opponents volley short and wide, this will create more openings, depending on how they are positioned at the net.

Hitting the Correct Shot

Hitting the correct shot when playing doubles is challenging. This is made more difficult because of the combinations available—both at the net, one up and one back, or two in the backcourt. Each player is in a neutral, defensive, or offensive position and should hit the correct shot depending on that position. A player deep in the court should hit either neutral or defensive shots to the opponent deep in the court so she can stay in the point. A player at the net should be thinking more offensively and directing balls back sharply at the closer player.

Players should choose their shots based on the position of all players on the court. Hitting from deep in the court to the opposing deep player is an excellent starting shot. It will keep the team in the point and make the opponents play the next shot. The player at the net should hit a close-to-close shot to finish a point. This shot is hit to overpower the closer opponent, because she will have very little time to react. This tactic is especially important to use when both players on the opposing team are of equal ability and the player cannot exploit a weakness by directing shots at the weaker player. If opponents are of equal skill level, hitting the right shot becomes key to either staying in or ending the point.

Working as a Team

A doubles team has a choice of various tactics. All can be successful, but the most effective doubles teams are those that work together as a team. Players should be trying to set up their partners so they have easy shots, aggressively hit point-ending shots, or can conservatively hit shots to stay in the point. Players should always be moving to place themselves in the best possible position to put the ball away or to defend against openings on the court.

Doubles players must hit every shot with a purpose. They should move after every shot to cover any court openings as well as move before opponents can play to defend against any court openings. The best doubles players move together as a team and understand what shots their partners will play so they can anticipate the return. This is only possible if both players are executing the same plan. This requires constant communication so each player knows the plan and can concentrate on executing it. When partners work in sync, they can create a rhythm and flow that will get the momentum on their side.

Communication between partners should begin even before they take the court. Partners should discuss the formation they intend to play and under what conditions they would move from one formation to another. They should discuss who will serve first and on what side of the court they will return from, either the deuce court or ad court. They should also discuss the playing conditions and reinforce what each player will do if there are wind or sun considerations that day.

Another time to communicate is during the warm-up period. Both players should be looking for the weaknesses and preferences of the opposing team. Together they should determine the stronger and weaker player and the strongest and weakest positions. By helping each other with this analysis, they will be ready to attack the weaker player or position when play begins.

Good doubles teams communicate after every point. This could be in the form of an encouraging word, a high five, or specific instructions on what to do or where to go with the next return. Each player should determine the tendencies of the opposing players and share these observations with the partner. This might involve identifying the opposing team's poor court position or simply the frustration either player has with a certain shot.

Communication can even occur during play, when one player tells his partner what the opponents are doing during a point. For example, if both players are at the net and the opponents lob, as players go back to return the shot, the player not hitting can tell his partner whether the opponents are both moving to the net or are staying back. He can also warn his partner at the net to move back if he hits a short lob and thinks his partner will be a target for an opponent's overhead.

chapter 6

Offensive Tactical Skills

This chapter covers the offensive tactical skills players must know to be successful. In this chapter, you will find the following skills:

Aggressive Baseline Play (Singles)

Aggressive baseline play is one of the most common styles of play in the game today. The aggressive baseliner capitalizes on every opportunity to take the ball early from a position inside the baseline and hit forcing groundstrokes that put the opponent on the run. The aggressive baseliner puts pressure on the opponent by forcing him to hit the ball deep in the court consistently. The aggressive baseliner takes advantage of the first short ball and puts the opponent in a defensive position by hitting aggressive shots to the corners of the court.

 WATCH OUT!

The following tendencies in your athletes may cause poor play:

- Not being patient and waiting for the right ball to attack.

- Being overaggressive on shots. The intent is to keep the opponent on the run and create an opening, not to hit an outright winner on the first shot.

- Not getting to the right position on the court before attempting to hit a forcing groundstroke.

- Watching just the ball and not being aware of the opponent and the openings on the court.

READING THE SITUATION

Players should do the following to gain the best advantage by being aggressive and keeping the opponent on defense:

- Know their opponents' strengths and weaknesses.

- Recognize and react to the first short ball from the opponent.

- Play an aggressive shot only when they can make contact in a comfortable hitting position.

- Before hitting, decide whether the next shot will be a volley from the net or another aggressive groundstroke from the backcourt.

- Hit to the open court if the opponent is slow or tired. Hit behind the opponent if she is anticipating the shot and moving to the open court.

ACQUIRING THE APPROPRIATE KNOWLEDGE

To be aggressive baseliners, players must know about the following:

Physical Playing Conditions

The physical playing conditions can significantly affect the game. Thus, players should pay attention to the following conditions when playing aggressive baseline shots:

- Court speed. The smoother the court surface, the faster the game is because the ball will slide or skid on the court and move forward without losing much speed after the bounce. When the court is rougher or more textured (i.e., slow), the ball bounces up higher and loses speed on contact with the court. This upward bounce takes speed off the shot.

- Wind direction. Playing forceful groundstrokes is difficult when the wind is blowing directly from the opponent's end of the court.

REMINDER!

When trying to use aggressive baseline play, players must understand the match strategy and game plan. They should also consider the questions on page 140.

- Ball speed. Depending on the court surface and the amount of spin players use, the felt nap of the ball can either become fluffed up, which slows the ball down, or worn down, which causes the ball to travel through the air faster.

Strengths and Weaknesses of Opponents

Players must account for their opponents' strengths and weaknesses to know how to gain the best advantage when using aggressive groundstrokes. They should consider the following about their opponents:

- Does the opponent have a favorite side, either forehand or backhand? The player should determine this and direct her shots to the weaker side when possible.

- Is the opponent right or left handed? The player should think about who he is playing before automatically going to what he considers to be the weak side.

- Does the opponent prefer to hit the ball with angles, or does she keep the ball back in play down the center of the court? If the opponent likes to hit with angles, the player can look for more angled shots in return. It is more difficult for the opponent to create angles when the ball is hit deep and down the middle.

- Is the opponent slow or tired? If so, the player's shots can have a greater margin of error inside the lines and still be effective.

- Is the opponent predictable? If the opponent always plays a forehand crosscourt, or if she always hits the backhand with backspin, the player should be ready in advance for the specific return.

At a Glance

The following parts of the text offer additional information on aggressive baseline play:

Square Groundstroke Stance	22
Open Groundstroke Stance	25
Applying Topspin	47
Controlling Shot Angle	57
Controlling Shot Speed	61
Forehand Groundstroke	66
One-Handed Backhand Groundstroke	73
Two-Handed Backhand Groundstroke	80
Approach Shot	100
Forehand as a Weapon	122

Self-Knowledge

In addition to being aware of their opponents' strengths and weaknesses, players need to know their own abilities. When using aggressive groundstrokes, players should answer the following questions:

- Can you use your best shot? If the player has a favorite side, he should get into position quickly to play an aggressive shot. If not, he will have to be content to return the ball deep and safe on his less favorite side.

- Can you use topspin well? The player will need topspin to pull the harder-hit shot into the court. A ball hit hard with backspin will fly long. A flat shot is effective but has a low margin of error over the net and inside the baseline. Too much topspin takes speed off the ball, causing it to land short in the court.

- Do you understand the dimensions and geometry of the court? Wider balls give better opportunities for angled returns.

- What is your favorite shot? For example, if the player's favorite shot is a crosscourt forehand, she should set up the point so she hits this shot as much as possible.

Decision-Making Guidelines

When deciding whether to hit aggressive groundstrokes, players should be sure to consider the previous information. They should also consider the following guidelines:

(continued)

○ Recover into a good court position. If the player hits a hard shot, the opponent could use that speed to return the shot into the open court.

○ Pick on the weak side. Sometimes playing to the weak side is a better choice than playing the highest-percentage shot. Playing to the weak side will always produce more errors from the opponent. If there is a distinct difference between the strong and weak sides, hitting the lower-percentage down-the-line shots rather than the safer crosscourt shots could be the best option because doing so will create more errors from the opponent. Sometimes just hitting a firm shot to the opponent's weakness is all that is necessary to elicit an error.

○ Be able to shift from offense to either neutral or defense. If a player's attacking groundstrokes are returned aggressively, she may have to retreat and play a neutral or even defensive return. She must be patient on these shots and avoid the errors caused by trying to be offensive from a defensive area of the court.

○ Players need to play aggressively but also move the opponent around the court to create an opening before attempting the point-ending shot.

The drop shot is a great way to end a point when the player is in good position inside the baseline and the opponent is behind the baseline. A well-placed, softly hit drop shot is the most delicate of all shots and can be an outright winner. It can also bring the opponent to the net as a setup for a passing shot or lob to the open court.

The drop shot is hit with very little racket movement and requires soft hands and a great deal of touch. It definitely changes the pace of the point. Players who can hit the drop shot accurately and confidently show variety in shot making.

⚠ WATCH OUT!

The following tendencies in your athletes may cause poor play:

- Attempting the drop shot in tricky wind conditions.
- Having an extreme grip such as an extreme Western grip. This will impede players from opening the racket face enough to hit the drop shot.
- Not watching their positions. Players shouldn't attempt a drop shot if they are behind the baseline.
- Not being in a comfortable contact zone. Players should hit a drop shot only if the ball is in such a zone. The high ball is very difficult to control.

ACQUIRING THE APPROPRIATE KNOWLEDGE

To use the drop shot, players must know about the following:

Rules

Players need to know several main rules when hitting drop shots:

- Rules about hitting the ball before the second bounce
- Rules pertaining to touching the net with the racket, shoes, or anything one is wearing

Physical Playing Conditions

The physical playing conditions can significantly affect the game. Thus, players should pay attention to the following conditions when contemplating a drop shot:

- Wind direction. Players should rarely hit drop shots when the wind is at their backs. However, when the wind is blowing from the opponent's side of the net, drop shots are very effective. The wind prevents the ball from traveling too far once it clears the net and after the bounce.

READING THE SITUATION

Players should do the following to gain the best advantage by hitting soft drop shots:

- Recognize when the opponent is behind the baseline.
- Know when the opponent is slow or tired.
- Be inside the baseline to hit an effective drop shot.
- Be able to hit a drop shot from the same position as a forehand or backhand drive. Disguise is important.
- Grip the racket softly and apply backspin to make the ball die after hitting the court.

REMINDER!

When trying to decide whether to use a drop shot, players must understand the match strategy and game plan. They should also consider the questions on page 140.

(continued)

○ Court speed. Slow courts, or courts that are soft or have a lot of texture, are best for drop shots. Hard, smooth courts (i.e., fast courts) such as concrete courts don't grab the spin as well; plus, the ball will bounce higher.

Strengths and Weaknesses of Opponents

Players must account for their opponents' strengths and weaknesses to know how to gain the best advantage when using drop shots. They should consider the following about their opponents:

○ Does the opponent move forward well, or does he get a slow start because he is too comfortable at the baseline? Drop shots are very effective when the opponent prefers to stay back and hit groundstrokes. An opponent who is comfortable hitting groundstrokes at the baseline is less comfortable moving forward to play a short, low ball. The drop shot forces the opponent forward, pulling him out of his comfort position at the baseline playing higher-bouncing shots.

○ Is the opponent slow or tired? A slow or tired opponent will have trouble getting to a well-placed drop shot. Because the drop shot lands just over the net, the opponent will have to run a long way just to get to the ball. If she is slow, she may not reach the ball before it bounces twice on the court. If she is tired, she will have to spend a great deal of energy just to get to the ball. She might even decide it isn't worth the effort to run for the shot, giving the player an easy point. If the opponent does run all the way to the net to return the drop shot, she may play a weak or sloppy shot because she is hitting on the run and is not set to play her best shot.

○ Even if the opponent can run to and get the drop shot before it bounces twice on the court, can he hit shots well while running forward at full speed? The player should know whether his opponent can hit a counter drop shot or push the ball back deep in the court. If not, and he tends to hit the ball too firmly when running at full speed, the drop shot is an ideal shot to play.

○ If the opponent reacts well and moves forward quickly, is she agile enough to stop, recover, and assume a good court position to be ready for either a passing shot or lob? Many players run well but have a hard time stopping and setting up for the next shot.

○ Is the opponent uncomfortable at the net, or does he have a weak volley? If so, an average drop shot will do the job of bringing him into the net and exposing the weak volley or overhead. He has no chance to run forward to retrieve the drop shot and return to the baseline for a groundstroke.

Self-Knowledge

In addition to being aware of their opponents' strengths and weaknesses, players need to know their own abilities. When using the drop shot, players should answer the following questions:

○ Can you recognize a fairly easy ball? The player needs to have a fairly easy ball that she can play from inside the baseline to have an opportunity to hit a good drop shot. It is very difficult to hit an effective drop shot from behind the baseline or from a hard-hit shot. The player must look for a ball that is not hit hard and lands short in the court from the opponent because this will give her the best opportunity to hit an effective drop shot.

○ Can you take speed off the ball? Only players who can take pace off the ball and absorb the shot with soft hands will be able to hit the drop shot. The drop shot must be hit only hard enough to get over the net. This means that if the player strikes the ball firmly, it will have too much speed and will travel too far. The player must have soft hands to absorb the speed of the ball and return it gently back over the net and into the court.

- Do you have the right grip to be able to play the ball with an open racket face for some backspin? Western grips make drop shots very difficult to hit. The drop shot must be hit with an open racket face to get the necessary height over the net and backspin. Because the Western grip closes the racket face, a better grip would be a Continental or Eastern grip.

- Can you disguise a shot? Disguise plays a large part in hitting the drop shot effectively. The player must prepare for a drop shot with the same body position and preparation as he would with a ball he would drive.

- Do you know your favorite side for hitting a drop shot? If the player does not know her favorite side for the drop shot, she should figure it out. Most players prefer to hit the drop shot on one side or the other; they should hit most drop shots on the preferred side.

At a Glance

The following parts of the text offer additional information on the drop shot:

Square Groundstroke Stance	22
Eastern Forehand Grip	35
Eastern Backhand Grip	43
Applying Backspin	51
Controlling Shot Height	59
Controlling Shot Speed	61

Decision-Making Guidelines

When deciding whether to use the drop shot, players should be sure to consider the previous information. They should also consider the following guidelines:

- The player shouldn't even think of hitting a drop shot if the opponent is very fast, is on or inside the baseline, or prefers to be at the net, or if the wind is at the player's back. Chances of winning the point with a drop shot are slim to none in these situations.

- After hitting the drop shot, the player should return to a good position so if the opponent does reach the ball and get it back, the player is in position to hit either a passing shot or lob to the open court.

- If the player can't play an effective drop shot, or he is making too many errors trying to hit the shot, he shouldn't use the shot that day. Players should not play the drop shot if they are losing more points than they are winning with this shot.

- A player shouldn't use the drop shot if he is under pressure and his hands go from soft to firm. The drop shot might be an easy shot to play early in a match when there is no pressure, but it becomes very difficult when under pressure. The drop shot is probably not the best shot if the player is tight.

Keeping the Ball in Play (Singles)

Against many players, just getting the ball back over the net and into the court is all that is necessary. Tennis at most levels is a game of errors, and winners are often the players making the fewest errors. If a player always gets one more ball back than his opponent, he will never lose a point. That sounds very simple, but it requires skill, determination, good court awareness, recovery to the right area of the court, and the ability to hit the highest-percentage shot.

 WATCH OUT!

The following tendencies in your athletes may cause poor play:

○ Not thinking strategically. If the player is just not getting balls back, she should still be trying to dictate points by picking on the weaknesses of her opponent and setting up to her own strengths.

○ Being impatient and not letting the opponent make mistakes. Many players tend to go for too many winners, giving opponents easy points by making unforced errors.

○ Not focusing well because of errors. Everyone makes errors, but players must be careful not to let their errors discourage them so much that they change their style. They should find out what is working and continue to execute to the best of their abilities.

○ Not playing within one's own style. Players should not try shots that are not in their repertoires.

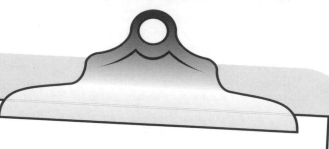

READING THE SITUATION

Players should do the following to gain the best advantage by keeping the ball in play:

- Remember that getting the ball back in play forces the opponent to take risks to win points.
- Use lower-risk shots with good net clearance that land well inside the lines such as crosscourt or down-the-center shots hit with moderate topspin. These shots have very low risk of an unforced error and force the opponent to hit one more shot. In addition, lobs when the opponent is at the net are less risky than passing shots.
- Add topspin for better net clearance and safety inside the baseline.
- Keep backswings compact and under control to avoid overhitting.
- Don't try to outslug an opponent who hits hard but makes lots of errors. Playing steady will win most points in this situation.

ACQUIRING THE APPROPRIATE KNOWLEDGE

To get more balls back than their opponents do, players must know about the following:

REMINDER!

When considering how to keep the ball in play, players must understand the match strategy and game plan. They should also consider the questions on page 140.

Physical Playing Conditions

The physical playing conditions can significantly affect the game. Thus, players should pay attention to the following conditions when keeping the ball in play:

- Court speed. The speed of the court can determine the length of the points being played. Slow courts make hitting winners difficult, so there are more chances to make errors. Winners are easier to hit on smooth fast courts, so players will want to keep opponents deep in the court and limit their offensive opportunities.
- Wind direction. A player can be more aggressive when the wind is at her back because the opponent will have a difficult time hitting winners into the wind. When the wind is in her face, though, she can, and must, hit through the ball to keep her shots deep in the court.
- Ball speed. Changing conditions can change the speed of the ball. If the ball fluffs up, it will be slow, and the points will be longer. If the ball wears down, it will speed up so players have to be careful not to overhit and to put more spin on the ball to keep it in the court.

Strengths and Weaknesses of Opponents

Players must account for their opponents' strengths and weaknesses to know how to gain the best advantage when keeping the ball in play. They should consider the following about their opponents:

- Does the opponent have a low shot threshold? Does she become impatient after a few balls and try to end the point regardless of the shot that must be hit and her court position? Players with low shot thresholds are easier to play because they generally make unforced errors just because they lack the patience for waiting for the right ball to attack.
- Is the opponent in poor physical condition? Is he slow or just out of shape? With this kind of opponent, the player should hit more balls to force him to make errors. He won't be able to hit well on the run, if he even tries to run down shots that require that extra effort.
- Does the opponent have a strong and weak side? It makes sense to hit as many balls as possible to the weaker side.
- Is the opponent uncomfortable at the net? The player doesn't have to hit great passing shots or lobs if the opponent can't put volleys or overheads away.
- Can the opponent do anything with the ball that is hit right down the center of the court? This is a player's safest shot. If the opponent cannot capitalize on this shot and eventually makes an unforced error by trying to hit too hard or create an angle that is a low-percentage shot, the player should just keep the ball going right to the opponent.

Self-Knowledge

In addition to being aware of their opponents' strengths and weaknesses, players need to know their own abilities. When keeping the ball in play, players should answer the following questions:

- Are you in good physical condition? Keeping the ball in play makes points last longer, so players must be in better physical condition than their opponents.
- Do you know how to position yourself on court and select shots? Court positioning and shot selection are critical so the player is always hitting the highest-percentage shot and then recovering into the best possible court position.
- Do you know your opponent's preferences? If the opponent has a favorite shot or area of the court in which he is most comfortable, the player shouldn't let him get into that position.
- Do you know how to find the opponent's weakness and exploit it? This does not mean trying to overpower the opponent. Sometimes the opponent will struggle with a high-bouncing ball. This

(continued)

is a perfect opportunity for a player to play very high percentage returns by giving herself more net clearance and playing right to the opponent's weakness.

○ If your opponent likes speed, can you take pace off the ball? Taking pace off the ball can be really frustrating to many players and will force them into early errors by trying to hit the ball too hard.

At a Glance

The following parts of the text offer additional information on keeping the ball in play:

Square Groundstroke Stance	22
Applying Topspin	47
Applying Backspin	51
Controlling Shot Angle	57
Controlling Shot Height	59
Controlling Shot Speed	61
Forehand Groundstroke	66
One-Handed Backhand Groundstroke	73
Two-Handed Backhand Groundstroke	80
Lob	126
Groundstroke From Deep in the Court	134

Decision-Making Guidelines

When deciding whether to keep the ball in play on every shot, players should be sure to consider the previous information. They should also consider the following guidelines:

○ Change court position to be better prepared for the opponent's most potent weapons. For example, if the opponent has a big first serve, the player should stand farther back to give himself more time to hit the return and then move into a good court position for the next shot.

○ Decide to hit very neutral shots when winning points. There is no need to try anything risky if the player is winning most of the points with very high percentage shots.

○ Take advantage of situations which can end points, but be in the right position in the court and have a ball that can be played comfortably in the hitting zone. Getting the ball back in play when the player has huge court openings is not the intent.

○ Let the opponent self-destruct if she is mentally fragile. If the opponent starts to make a series of errors and becomes angry, the player should just give her more of the same and let her completely fall apart. There is no need to try anything more risky if the opponent is giving the player a lot of easy points because she has lost her concentration or rhythm.

○ The best offense is a good defense when out of position. The player should hit defensive shots when off balance or in a poor court position. The goal is to get the ball back, recover to a good court position, and get ready for the next shot.

Even in doubles, in which points are more likely to be won than lost in comparison to singles, keeping the ball in play can be an effective tactic. No matter what formation either team is in, the team that gets the final shot back in the court always wins.

Many successful high school doubles players are determined to get to and return every shot that is hit to their side of the court. They may lack power and maybe even pinpoint placement, but they are very difficult to beat because they force their opponents to try to hit point-ending shots. Opponents are pressured into hitting with more pace or closer to the lines (or both), which increases the likelihood of an error.

 WATCH OUT!

The following tendencies in your athletes may cause poor play:

○ Not staying focused and determined to get every ball back in the court. The opposing team might hit several winning shots, but your team should keep the pressure on them to hit winners for the entire match.

○ Not keeping errors to a minimum. Errors happen, but your team can minimize them by hitting higher over the net and well inside the lines.

○ Not being prepared to play long points. Your players should get to and return every ball and make their opponents hit a lot of shots until they make an error.

○ Getting overly aggressive and trying for point-ending shots from the baseline. Team members should be at the net before they try a more offensive shot.

ACQUIRING THE APPROPRIATE KNOWLEDGE

To get more balls back than their opponents do, players must know about the following:

Physical Playing Conditions

The physical playing conditions can significantly affect the game. Thus, players should pay attention to the following conditions when keeping the ball in play:

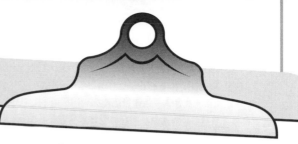

READING THE SITUATION

Players should do the following to gain the best advantage by keeping the ball in play:

- Keep the ball between the opponents. Hitting down the middle is the highest-percentage shot by a doubles team.

- Direct all balls played from the backcourt back to the backcourt player on the opposing team. If both opposing team players are at the net, the ball should be hit down the middle or lobbed over their heads.

- Use topspin to curve the ball down in the court for better safety inside the baseline. This also makes the volley more difficult to hit for the player at the net.

- If the opponents like to get to the net, the partners should move together to the baseline so the net team cannot overpower the player at the net.

- Lob any time they are in trouble. This will give both players time to get in the best possible position for the next shot.

REMINDER!

When considering how to keep the ball in play, doubles players must understand the match strategy and game plan. They should also consider the questions on page 140.

(continued)

○ Court speed. The speed of the court can determine the length of the points being played. Slow courts make it more difficult for opponents to hit winners so they have more chances to make errors. Opponents will hit more winners on smooth fast courts, so players must keep them deep in the court and away from the net where they will have more offensive opportunities.

○ Wind direction. Doubles teams should play the wind to their advantage. They can be more aggressive when the wind is at their backs because their opponents will have a difficult time hitting winners into the wind. When the wind is in their faces, they can and must hit through the ball to keep their shots deep in the court.

○ Ball speed. Changing conditions can change the speed of the ball. If the ball fluffs up, it will be slow and the points will be longer. If the ball wears down, it will speed up and players will have to be careful not to overhit and put more topspin on the ball to keep it in the court

Strengths and Weaknesses of Opponents

Players must account for their opponents' strengths and weaknesses to know how to gain the best advantage when keeping the ball in play. Doubles players should consider the following about their opponents:

○ Can your opponents end points at the net? If not, the players must wear them down by getting balls back until they make an error.

○ Are your opponents uncomfortable at the net but solid from the backcourt? Players can force opponents to the net by hitting short so they will have to move to the net and hit volleys and overheads. When opponents are at the net, players can also lob the ball over their heads.

○ Are your opponents hard hitters? If this is the case, players should be patient. The opponents might hit a winning shot or two, but if the players keep the pressure on, the hard hitters will eventually break down and make errors.

○ Are the opponents getting tired or frustrated? Keeping the ball in play should work well with tired or frustrated opponents.

Self-Knowledge

In addition to being aware of their opponents' strengths and weaknesses, doubles players need to know their own team's abilities. When keeping the ball in play, doubles players should answer the following questions:

○ Are you in good physical condition? Keeping the ball in play will make the points last longer so players must be in better physical condition than their opponents are for this tactic to work.

○ Do you know how to position yourselves on the court and how to select shots? Court positioning and shot selection are important so players can hit the highest-percentage shots and then recover to the best possible court positions.

○ Do you hit deep? Doubles players should keep out of harm's way as much as possible by hitting balls back to the player deep in the court. The player at the net has too many opportunities to end the point with an overhead or volley.

○ Do you know how to use topspin? Adding topspin to their groundstrokes allows players to hit higher over the net and gives them more safety inside the baseline. It also creates shots that are more difficult for the player at the net to volley.

○ Is there a weaker player on the opposing team? Players should direct most shots at opposing players who have difficulty putting shots away or who are more prone to errors.

Decision-Making Guidelines

When deciding whether to keep the ball in play on every shot, doubles players should be sure to consider the previous information. They should also consider the following guidelines:

- Players should position themselves a step or two deeper in the court. Players will have more time to prepare for the hard-hit shots if they take a step or two back. Also, the deeper position will give them time to move for all shots.

- Be patient and be willing to play neutral or defensive shots, especially when the opponents are on offense.

- Take easy shots at the net to end the points when there is very little risk. Even though doubles players should be thinking about keeping the ball in play, they should also take advantage of point-ending opportunities when they arise.

- Give angry or hurried opponents more opportunities to lose control. An opponent who is agitated will have difficulty thinking clearly and hitting accurately.

- Keep communicating as a team. Communication helps partners determine what is working best that day and helps them play the same style and play to the weakest position or the weaker player.

At a Glance

The following parts of the text offer additional information on keeping the ball in play:

Serve-and-Volley (Singles and Doubles)

The serve-and-volley style is the most offensive style of play in the sport of tennis. The serve is followed by a rush to the net with the intent to end the point quickly at the net with a volley or overhead. This tactic is especially effective when the player has a powerful serve that consistently results in weak returns. It is also effective for players who are more aggressive than patient because the points will not last as long. This section looks at the decisions the serve-and-volley player must make for serve placement, spin, and power along with the first volley options either as a setup for the final shot or going for a winner.

 WATCH OUT!

The following tendencies in your athletes may cause poor play:

- Rushing by not getting physically, mentally, and emotionally prepared to serve. The serve is the only shot in tennis that players have complete control of, so they should slow down and be focused and completely prepared to serve and play their next shot. Even though the points don't last long, players must take the time to prepare for and hit good first serves.

- Becoming predictable. Players should mix their serve placement, spin, and speed to keep their opponents off-balance.

- Not noticing the opponent's position. The opponent may change position slightly, either right, left, forward, or back, to make a better return. Players should observe these changes and be able to exploit the new weakness.

- Counting on a fast serve. Using the fast serve might overpower an opponent early in the match, but the opponent could adjust to the speed. Also, the balls will get slower as the match progresses. Players should rely on more than just power later in the match.

READING THE SITUATION

Serve-and volley players should do the following:

- Serve the ball to the opponent's weakness.
- Plan their first serve placement, depth, speed, and spin, along with the first volley, before hitting the serve.
- Go to the net after a successful first serve.
- Develop a serve and follow-through that causes them to move forward after the hit.
- Hit the first volley based on the height of the ball at contact. They can go for a winner on a high ball, but they must play a deep volley on a low ball.
- "Follow the ball" by moving in and to the side where the return is hit.

ACQUIRING THE APPROPRIATE KNOWLEDGE

To use the serve-and-volley, players must understand the following:

Rules

Players need to know several rules when serving and volleying:

- Rules about playing to the pace of the server

REMINDER!

When trying to decide when to use serve-and-volley, players must understand the match strategy and game plan. They should also consider the questions on page 140.

- o Rules about foot faults
- o Rules about walking or running before the serve

Physical Playing Conditions

The physical playing conditions can significantly affect the game. Thus, players should pay attention to the following conditions when serving and volleying:

- o Court speed. For example, if the court is smooth and fast, the server might hit a big, fast serve on both first and second serves because this would result in a serve return error or weak return.
- o Ball speed. Depending on the court surface and the amount of spin the players are using, the felt nap could fluff up and slow the ball down considerably.
- o Wind direction. Serving and volleying is even better with the wind blowing from the server to the receiver. Both serves and volleys will have more pace, and returns will have less speed. However, when the wind is into the server's face, serving and volleying is more difficult because the big serve is slowed by the wind. A crosswind gives the server the opportunity to hit wide serves that drift even wider by the wind.

Strengths and Weaknesses of Opponents

Players must account for their opponents' strengths and weaknesses to know how to gain the best advantage when serving and volleying. They should consider the following about their opponents:

- o Can the opponent hit a return that drops below the top of the net so the onrushing server is forced to volley the ball up on both the forehand and backhand side? To do this, the opponent must be able to hit a topspin return of serve or a low chip return that just clears the net and drops at the server's feet.
- o Can the opponent move out of the way on the serve hit at the body, or does this serve jam them so they pop up a weak return? The serve at the body is very effective because the swing is cramped and the ball is generally blocked back with an open racket face. If this happens, it gives the server a high and soft ball to volley. A quick opponent can move out of the way and hit the return with a complete swing, which could result in a more forceful and controlled return.
- o Does the opponent begin in a starting position well behind the baseline to allow more time for the return? The deeper the opponent stands, the closer to the net the server can get to play the first volley. The returner is also vulnerable to the wide serve when she begins in a very deep serve return ready position.
- o Does the opponent have a strong and weak side? Most serves and first volleys should be directed at the weaker side so the server can play easy shots at the net.

Self-Knowledge

In addition to being aware of their opponents' strengths and weaknesses, players need to know their own abilities. When serving and volleying, players should answer the following questions:

- o Can you take into account the wind, court speed, and your opponent's weaknesses; play the right serve; and follow up with an effective first volley? As conditions change, so must the serve. On a windy day, the server might decide to serve and volley only when the wind is at her back. The serve will have more speed and the opponent's return will have less, so it should make the volley an easier shot. Also, a player using the serve-and-volley might not be as effective on a slow court. She may decide to use this tactic only on a first serve. Balls change during the course of a match. Sometimes they get slower as the felt fluffs up, making it more difficult for the serve-and-volley style of play. Sometimes the balls wear down and become lighter, smoother, and faster, which would favor the serve-and-volley style.

(continued)

○ Can you accurately hit serves, in both deuce and ad sides, to the alley corners of the service court, at the body, and to the center T of the service court? Being able to do this will enable the server to vary the serve and keep the opponent from developing a rhythm on the return. Sometimes the returner alters his position to cover up a weakness, which exposes an opening either to the alley or center side. A serve directly at the body will almost always produce a weak return that is easy for the server to volley.

Decision-Making Guidelines

When deciding whether to use the serve-and-volley, players should be sure to consider the previous information. They should also consider the following guidelines:

○ Always plan ahead, including planning the placement of the serve and the direction of the first and second volleys. Serves with no plans are very predictable and often fail to hit the appropriate areas of the court.

○ Make the correct decisions on the first volley by either going for an outright winner on the first volley or playing the first volley deep in the court and closing in to the net for a put-away shot from the next return. If the return is low, the player must play the volley easy and deep. If the return is high, she can hit the volley hard and down into the open court.

○ Make sure the second serve has enough speed, spin, and depth to be effective. Following a second serve to the net is more difficult because the returner usually has additional time to hit a more aggressive return.

○ Move in after the serve to play floating returns. Even if the player is not comfortable going to the net after the serve, it is a very good option when the returner is simply blocking back returns high and deep in the court. Such returns make for easy volleys that force the opponent to hit lower and with more speed on future returns.

○ Watch for the position of the receiver. If the receiver moves forward to receive the serve, the ball will come back much quicker and the server will not have as much time to move forward and be in a good position to make the first volley. A good response to this position is to hit the serve at the body of the returner because she will have less time to get out of the way to make an effective return.

At a Glance

The following parts of the text offer additional information on the serve-and-volley:

Open Volley Stance	31
Crossover Volley Stance	33
Continental Grip	41
Applying Backspin	51
Controlling Shot Angle	57
First Serve	86
Second Serve	92
Volley	105
Swinging Midcourt Volley	110

The swinging midcourt volley is the answer to how to beat the pusher, the player who hits very cautious soft, high, and deep shots that have very little risk and are intended to keep the ball back in the court and the opponent behind the baseline. The opponent who is content to float every return back with great margin of error over the net and deep in the court is frustrating to play and gives most players a great deal of difficulty. If the player waits in the backcourt, he will often have to retreat to play the return shot well behind the baseline and must supply his own power. It is easy to fall into this style and trade moonball (soft, high, and deep) groundstrokes with an opponent, causing each point to be a marathon. Rather, the player should strive to move in and hit that floating ball out of the air to break the opponent's rhythm and force the opponent into playing a different, less comfortable style.

WATCH OUT!

The following tendencies in your athletes may cause poor play:

○ Being discouraged by an occasional error. The player using the swinging midcourt volley is forcing the play and changing the pace of the game. Even with an error now and then, the player can begin to dictate the style of play more toward her liking.

○ Not anticipating and moving quickly and decisively. If the player hesitates, he won't be able to move in as close to the net as necessary for an offensive return, or the ball might drop below the top of the net forcing the return to be hit up and defensively rather than down and offensively.

○ Hitting the midcourt volley cautiously so it lands short in the court. The midcourt volley must be hit with a full stroke, unlike a placement volley played close to the net. If the stroke is only a punch or block rather than a full stroke, the ball will land short in the court and it will be easy for the opponent to play the next shot.

ACQUIRING THE APPROPRIATE KNOWLEDGE

To use a swinging midcourt volley, players must understand the following:

Physical Playing Conditions

The physical playing conditions can significantly affect the game. Thus, players should pay attention to the following conditions when using a swinging midcourt volley:

○ Wind at the back. Aggressive midcourt volleys are very effective with the wind at the back. However, players must hit these shots with some topspin to pull the ball down in the court.

READING THE SITUATION

Players should do the following when playing a swinging midcourt volley:

- Anticipate the shot and get a rolling start so they can play the ball high and well inside the baseline once they know the opponent will hit a floating return.

- Hit with a full swing and either flat or with topspin. This shot must be hit firmly.

- Hit the swinging midcourt volley to the open court, away from the opponent.

- If the midcourt volley is poorly hit, either move quickly to the net or retreat to the baseline.

- Keep steps quick and short to adjust to a ball moving in the wind.

REMINDER!

When trying to decide when to use a swinging midcourt volley, players must understand the match strategy and game plan. They should also consider the questions on page 140.

(continued)

○ Wind in the face. Players should use a flatter hit when they are facing the wind. Too much spin will drop the ball short in the court for an easy return by the opponent.

○ Court speed. If the courts are smooth and fast, an aggressive midcourt volley with extra pace is very effective. The faster court will allow the player to hit the midcourt volley firmly and aggressively, sending the ball through the court. A rougher, slower court will cause the ball to slow down after contacting the court. For this reason, the faster and smoother court is preferred for this shot.

Strengths and Weaknesses of Opponents

Players must account for their opponents' strengths and weaknesses to know how to gain the best advantage when using a swinging midcourt volley. They should consider the following about their opponents:

○ Can the opponent change from a very conservative game with high-bounding groundstrokes to a more aggressive hard-driving game, if pressured? This will determine whether the player will hit midcourt volleys and move in for a put-away shot or hit and return to the baseline if an opening is not apparent.

○ Does the opponent play conservatively? If a conservative style of play is the only option the opponent has, the player should keep the pressure on because the opponent can't hurt her with more powerful shots. Letting the opponent determine the style and pace of the game will frustrate players and force them to play their opponent's style of play.

○ Does the pusher play defensively? Usually, pushers play more defensively when under pressure, so players should be prepared to hit overheads if they move to the net behind an aggressive midcourt volley.

○ What type of shots does the opponent hit? Many players hit high and deep shots when forced either out of the court or very deep behind the baseline. Players should take advantage of these shots by moving forward and hitting midcourt volleys to end these points quickly.

Self-Knowledge

In addition to being aware of their opponents' strengths and weaknesses, players need to know their own abilities. When using a swinging midcourt volley, players should answer the following questions:

○ How quickly do you react, move, and prepare for the midcourt volley? The contact point for this shot must be above the top of the net so the player can hit the volley hard and deep.

○ Can you move in to finish the point with a volley or overhead if necessary, or are you more comfortable moving back and waiting for another opportunity? If the player stays back, the points will be long—probably just what the opponent wants.

○ Can you make the correct decision to hit to the open court, play an angled volley, or play an approach volley, depending on the situation and court position of the opponent? If the opponent is off the court, there is an opportunity to play an angled midcourt volley into the open court to end the point. If the opponent is in a good position, the approach volley is the best option with the player hitting the midcourt volley and moving immediately to the net position.

○ Can you hit the ball with enough topspin? To hit the ball hard enough for a winner, a player needs some topspin to keep the ball in the court. Players need to learn to hit with some spin, but not so much that the ball will land short with little pace.

Decision-Making Guidelines

When deciding whether to use a swinging midcourt volley, players should be sure to consider the previous information. They should also consider the following guidelines:

- React quickly as soon as the ball is hit to get into the proper position before hitting the shot. Players cannot play an aggressive midcourt volley from well behind the baseline, even if the return is a real floater. They must move up to or inside the baseline.

- If the midcourt volley is hit in the middle of the court, play the shot back to the opponent's weak side.

- Angle the midcourt volley if the ball is high and off center. Balls that are high and off center offer a good angle opportunity.

- Determine a two-shot sequence to end the point, such as a down-the-line midcourt volley followed by an angled volley hit from a closer position to the net, away from the opponent.

- Hit behind the opponent if she anticipates the direction of the midcourt volley and begins to move early to cover the open court.

- Keep pressure on the opponent by playing every floating return back before it bounces. Players should avoid letting the opponent get into a rhythm and force them into long, floating groundstroke rallies.

At a Glance

The following parts of the text offer additional information on the swinging midcourt volley:

Semi-Western Grip	37
Applying Topspin	47
Controlling Shot Angle	57
Controlling Shot Height	59
Controlling Shot Speed	61
Volley	105

Approach Shot (Singles and Doubles)

An approach shot allows the player to move from a rallying position at the baseline to a volley position at the net. Playing an effective approach shot positions the player in an offensive position at the net and forces the opponent to hit a passing shot or lob. The better the approach shot is, the weaker the passing shot or lob from the opponent will be. For the best execution, the player must know when to play the approach shot and where to direct it. In addition, the player should also consider spins and speeds for maximum effectiveness.

WATCH OUT!

The following tendencies in your athletes may cause poor play:

- Stopping and hitting, rather than running through approach shots. A player will not make it to an ideal volley position if she stops to hit the shot before running to the net.

- Watching just the ball and not being aware of the opponent and the openings on the court.

- Hitting the ball so hard that there's less time to get to the net before hitting the volley. Hard-hit shots also give the opponent pace to use on the return shot.

ACQUIRING THE APPROPRIATE KNOWLEDGE

When hitting the approach shot, players must know about the following:

Physical Playing Conditions

The physical playing conditions can significantly affect the game. Thus, players should pay attention to the following conditions when playing approach shots:

- Wind direction. With the wind at the player's back, approach shots are extremely effective because passing shots and lobs are difficult to hit effectively against the wind.

- Court speed. Slower courts give the opponent more time to set up and hit better passing shots

READING THE SITUATION

Players should do the following to gain the best advantage when hitting approach shots and keeping the opponent on defense:

- Make sure the ball is short enough so they can play the approach shot and be in an ideal volley position before the opponent plays the next shot. The short ball permits the player to move forward in the court to play the approach shot. After the shot she needs to take only a few quick steps to get to the net position.

- Keep moving through the approach shot so they can get to the net before the opponent can return the ball.

- Know the opponent's strengths and weaknesses. Is the forehand or backhand his best side? Does he press when the ball is high and hard or low and soft? Unless there is a glaring weakness, players should hit the approach shot deep and either down the line or down the center of the court.

- If the player hits a short approach shot, she should take a split step before the opponent plays the next shot, even if she is not yet at the net.

or lobs. The player will have to select shorter balls before hitting the approach shot when the courts are slow. Balls tend to skid more on smooth courts and stay low. Rough or textured courts cause the ball to bounce higher. Keeping the ball lower on smooth courts forces the opponent to hit up on passing shots.

o Ball speed. As the match progresses and the felt nap of the ball fluffs up, the ball slows down. The player needs to be more selective and choose short balls before hitting the approach shot and moving forward to the net since the opponent has more time to prepare when the balls are slow.

> **REMINDER!**
>
> When trying to decide when to use approach shots, players must understand the match strategy and game plan. They should also consider the questions on page 140.

Strengths and Weaknesses of Opponents

Players must account for their opponents' strengths and weaknesses to know how to gain the best advantage when playing approach shots. They should consider the following about their opponents:

o Does the opponent like to use the speed of the oncoming shot to generate power on his return? If so, soft and deep approach shots are the best choice. Some players are very good at using an opponent's speed to generate power on their returns. Players should deny such opponents the luxury of their speed by hitting their approach shots deep and soft so opponents have to generate all of their own power.

o What does the opponent tend to do when under pressure to lob or hit a passing shot? If the opponent lobs, the player doesn't have to get as close to the net after hitting the approach shot. If the opponent prefers to drive passing shots, the player should close in to the net for easier volleys.

o Does the opponent have a strong and weak side, either forehand or backhand? Hitting to the opponent's weakness will result in an error or a soft return. These soft balls are easy to hit, either with a volley or an overhead.

o Is the opponent slow or tired? The player up against a slow or tired opponent can pull him wide with an approach shot and force him to hit a weak return.

o Does the opponent move forward well? Short, low approach shots are not usually recommended, but they can be very effective against a player who does not move forward well. An opponent who does not move forward well is forced to lift or scoop the short approach shot. This ball will lack speed and come in high over the net, making it easy for the player at the net to hit a volley or overhead.

Self-Knowledge

In addition to being aware of their opponents' strengths and weaknesses, players need to know their own abilities. When hitting approach shots and moving to the net, players should answer the following questions:

o Are you comfortable at the net? If the player likes to volley, she should hit an approach shot on the first relatively short ball. She should wait for a very short ball if she is not as comfortable at the net.

o Do you know the possible angles of return? The player should position himself in the middle of the possible angle of return. If he approaches down the center of the court, the ideal volley position is in the center of the court. He should move to the same side of the center service line as the direction of the approach shot.

o Do you know how to hit an approach shot on a very low ball? A low ball requires the player to hit with an open racket face producing backspin. She should work on these shots so the ball stays low and doesn't sail long.

(continued)

○ Do you know to split step just before the opponent hits? The purpose of the approach shot is to move forward from the baseline to the net for a point-ending volley or overhead. The player must split step just before the opponent hits so he can react forward and side to side for a volley or back for an overhead.

Decision-Making Guidelines

When deciding whether to play approach shots and move to the net, players should be sure to consider the previous information. They should also consider the following guidelines:

○ If the opponent likes the oncoming ball with speed so she can hit back hard in return, slow the ball down when hitting the approach shot. The opponent will have to generate her own power, and the player will have more time to get into an ideal volley position.

○ Keep the approach shot low to force the opponent to hit up and provide an easier volley opportunity. The low approach shot makes the opponent hit up with an open racket face. This high return is much easier to volley than a ball hit with topspin that drops over the net at the volleyer's feet.

○ If you can overpower the opponent and force weak returns, wait for the best shot so you can set up and go for it. The player should make sure she continues to play until she puts away the weak passing shot or lob.

○ If you hit a poor approach shot, get to the net quickly and be ready for an aggressive passing shot or offensive lob. The player can't realistically retreat to the baseline, so she should get ready for some quick action at the net!

At a Glance

The following parts of the text offer additional information on approach shots:

Volley and Overhead (Singles and Doubles)

Once a player is at the net, he is in an excellent position to end the point. When he can hit an overhead or a volley from inside the service court and over the top of the net, he is able to drive the ball into the court and should be able to win with one shot.

Even though volleys and overheads should be point-ending shots, this is not always the case. Players should also understand when they need to play a more neutral or even defensive shot and also what to do to improve their position so they can end the point with the next shot. The hard work is done, and the player has arrived at the net so she can end the point with one shot. She must understand how to maintain this offensive position and end the point with a winning overhead or volley as quickly as possible.

WATCH OUT!

The following tendencies in your athletes may cause poor play:

○ Playing a cautious shot and failing to end the point with one shot when at the net.

○ Getting excited and overplaying a volley or overhead by hitting much too hard for the desired results, making an error on an easy ball.

○ Not playing until the point is over. The player may think he hit a point-ending put-away, only to watch the ball go by because he is out of position for the opponent's return.

ACQUIRING THE APPROPRIATE KNOWLEDGE

To hit successful volleys and overheads, players must understand the following:

Rules

Players need to know several main rules when hitting volleys and overheads:

○ Rules pertaining to touching the net with the racket or clothing

○ Rules about making contact with the ball before it crosses the net

Physical Playing Conditions

The physical playing conditions can significantly affect the game. Thus, players should pay attention to the following conditions when playing volleys and overheads:

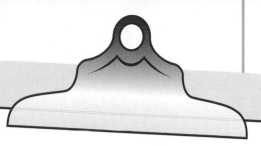

READING THE SITUATION

Players should do the following to control points at the net with volleys and overheads:

- In windy conditions or with very high lobs, let the ball bounce before hitting an overhead.

- Hit high volleys down and angled away from the opponent. Low volleys should be played deep and either down the center or down the line.

- Hit overheads from behind the service line deep in the court. Follow up by closing on the net to the side where the ball will be returned.

- Hit overheads from close to the net sharply down and bounce them over the opponent's head.

- Any time the opponent is out of position, hit the volley or overhead to the open court.

REMINDER!

When trying to decide when to use volleys and overheads, players must understand the match strategy and game plan. They should also consider the questions on page 140.

(continued)

- Wind strength. Because the wind can cause the ball to move while in flight, players should focus on the ball and make contact in front of the body. The ball moves quickly from a passing shot, so tracking is important for solid contact when it is being blown around by the wind.
- Wind at the back. The wind can play havoc with a lob and make it very difficult to time and hit with solid contact. When the wind is at his back and the lob is high, the player should let the ball bounce and adjust to the lower-bouncing ball rather than trying to hit it out of the air.
- Crosswind. Players can use the angle of the shot plus the wind to hit the ball away from the opponent. They should be careful about playing angles into a crosswind because the wind will blow the ball back toward the opponent.
- Clear sky. A clear sky hinders depth perception when hitting an overhead. Letting the ball bounce, especially from high lobs, makes the ball easier to see, time, and hit.
- Sun direction. A lob hit directly into the sun is very difficult to see, not to mention hit. Players should either let the ball bounce, shade the sun with their nonracket hand, or position themselves slightly off center so they can see the ball better.

Strengths and Weaknesses of Opponents

Players must account for their opponents' strengths and weaknesses to know how to gain the best advantage when hitting volleys and overheads. They should consider the following about their opponents:

- What shot does the opponent prefer to hit when your player is at the net? Would he rather hit a passing shot or a lob? If the opponent would rather hit a passing shot, your player should be ready to move forward and across to reach these shots so he can play a firm volley back into the open areas of the court. If the opponent prefers to hit a lob, your player can position himself closer to the service line so that he is ready to move back and play an aggressive overhead.
- Is the opponent slow or tired? Both overheads and volleys can be hit with a greater margin of error inside the lines if the opponent is either slow or tired. Because the opponent can't cover as much court, the player can hit safer shots to the open court.
- Does the opponent have a strong side and weak side? If the passing shot is hit off the weaker side, the player will have a better opportunity to either lob or drive away because the weaker side generally hits with less speed and spin. The return from the weak side is usually a higher and softer ball making for an easy volley or overhead by the player at the net.
- Does the opponent have enough power to hit the ball past the person at the net? Some players lack the power to win points if they are forced to hit powerful shots, especially from behind the baseline.
- Does the opponent panic and rush? Just being at the net causes some opponents to panic and rush either a passing shot or a lob. An opponent who rushes his shots is more likely to fail to even get the ball back over the net and in the court.

Self-Knowledge

In addition to being aware of their opponents' strengths and weaknesses, players need to know their own abilities. When playing at the net and hitting volleys and overheads, players should answer the following questions:

- Can you move quickly right and left to reach wide balls, and forward to close in on the net and end the point? Can you move back quickly for an overhead if your opponent lobs? Quick reaction times are necessary when at the net. The player at the net can end any point with one shot into the open court. However, she has less than half the time to react to the return. She must be ready to intercept shots to the right or left. She must move forward to volley a ball before it drops below the top of the net and move back to put away lobs with an overhead.

- Can you hit volleys that are played below the top of the net? Most people can hit firm, crisp volleys, but players also need to develop soft hands for those volleys that need to be hit up and still land in the court.
- Related to the above point, can you hit a drop volley that just goes over the net and dies when it hits the court? This is an excellent shot when the opponent is deep in the court and the player is playing a volley below the top of the net. The volley hit below the top of the net must be hit up. The drop volley is hit up with just enough speed to clear the net. If this same volley is hit deeper in the court, the opponent should have time to get to the ball and hit a strong return.
- Can you hit with control and direction? Many players like to hit overheads hard, but many times good placement with moderate speed is more than adequate.
- Can you determine the spin of the ball off the opponent's racket? Topspin will drop, so the player must move forward to play the volley before it drops below the top of the net. Backspin will stay in the air longer, so the player must realize that a hard-hit ball with backspin will probably travel beyond the baseline.

Decision-Making Guidelines

When hitting volleys and overheads, players should be sure to consider the previous information. They should also consider the following guidelines:

- Determine when to play an overhead in the air, and when to let it bounce. Letting the lob drop and playing it after the bounce is prudent when the lob is very high, the ball will land close to the net, the ball is in the sun, the ball is blowing in the wind, or the player is just not prepared to play the ball in the air.
- Identify which ball to hit sharply for a winner and which to hit gently as a drop volley or soft but deep in the court. Although the intent is to win the point when at the net, sometimes the opponent can neutralize an offensive position by hitting low shots that force the player to hit the volley up and much softer.
- Keep playing until the point is over. This means that even after good overheads and volleys, the player must work to get into the best possible position, just in case the opponent can get to the ball and return it back in the court. There is nothing worse than hitting a solid overhead or volley only to have the opponent block the ball weakly back into the open court.
- Stay back behind the baseline to prepare for the next shot if the lob is effective and hit deep into the backcourt. If the player has to retreat to play an overhead, most of the time he will return to the net and be ready for the next shot. Sometimes, however, he might be in a better position if he stays behind the baseline when the overhead is hit from very deep in the court.

At a Glance

The following parts of the text offer additional information on volleys and overheads:

Offensive Lob (Singles and Doubles)

The lob is not always a defensive shot. At the right time and in the right situation a player can use the lob to win the point. The lob is an easy shot to execute and can exploit an opponent's poor position or condition. It can also be an excellent alternative to a passing shot and can be hit as a variation if the opponent is anticipating a passing shot and is moving forward.

 WATCH OUT!

The following tendencies in your athletes may cause poor play:

○ Predictably lobbing all the time. When a player lobs predictably, the opponent can adjust and be ready to move back and hit an overhead.

○ Not hitting a safe lob without a lot of topspin if there is a large opening in the backcourt. The extra topspin requires better timing on contact, and too much spin will make the ball drop short in the court.

○ Not being cautious about using the lob when well inside the baseline. Players well inside the baseline don't have as much court to hit into safely.

○ Overhitting when using the lob. The lob is a controlled shot that does not demand a lot of racket head speed.

READING THE SITUATION

Players should do the following to gain the best advantage when hitting offensive lobs:

- Know when the opponent is too close to the net.
- Be in a good enough position to set up and swing with a full follow-through.
- Get enough height to clear the opponent's racket. A high lob will give the opponent time to move back and play an overhead.
- Know that topspin will bring the ball into the court and bounce it away from the opponent toward the back fence.
- Be aware that all lobs are more difficult in windy conditions. Players should play with topspin when the wind is at their backs and hit hard and deep when the wind is in their faces.

ACQUIRING THE APPROPRIATE KNOWLEDGE

To use the offensive lob, players must know about the following:

Physical Playing Conditions

The physical playing conditions can significantly affect the game. Thus, players should pay attention to the following conditions when contemplating an offensive lob:

○ Wind in the face. A player with the wind in his face will have difficulty hitting an effective offensive lob. Even if it gets over the opponent's head, the ball will not bounce and travel beyond the baseline with a stiff oncoming wind. However, this lob is effective because it neutralizes the opponent's offensive net position and drives him back to the baseline.

○ Wind at the back. The wind at one's back is ideal for an offensive lob. A carefully placed lob that gets over the opponent at the net will be very difficult to run down because the wind will carry the ball toward the back fence after the bounce.

○ Crosswind. Players must learn to use a crosswind to their advantage. They may even have to aim the lob outside the sideline and let the wind blow the ball back in the court. Even if this lob is short, it will make hitting a solid overhead very difficult.

REMINDER!

When trying to decide when to use offensive lobs, players must understand the match strategy and game plan. They should also consider the questions on page 140.

Strengths and Weaknesses of Opponents

Players must account for their opponents' strengths and weaknesses to know how to gain the best advantage when using an offensive lob. They should consider the following about their opponents:

- Is the opponent quick? A player has to hit a perfect offensive lob if her opponent can prepare quickly and move back for an overhead.
- Is the opponent winded or tired? A winded or tired opponent will have little desire to run for a ball that is lobbed over his head.
- Does the opponent have a weak overhead or dislike playing an overhead at all? This is not uncommon, especially in players who prefer to hit groundstrokes from the baseline.
- Do you know the opponent's weak side? Offensive lobs are most effective when hit over the weak, backhand side. Directing the lob over the backhand side is very effective because the backhand overhead is generally much weaker than the forehand overhead. Even if the opponent can play a backhand overhead, the player should have an easy ball to hit from the return, either another lob or a passing shot into the open court.
- Is the opponent slow? Almost any lob that gets over a slow opponent's head will be difficult to run down and return.

Self-Knowledge

In addition to being aware of their opponents' strengths and weaknesses, players should know their own abilities. When hitting an offensive lob, players should answer the following questions:

- Can you disguise the shot so your opponent cannot read whether it will be a drive or lob? Disguise is a great benefit and will freeze the opponent at the net and give the player more room for the lob in the backcourt.
- Do you plan the offensive lob situation by drawing the opponent to the net and following up with a lob over his head? Hitting a drop shot or very short ball forces the opponent to move forward to play the shot near the net, opening up the backcourt for an easy offensive lob.
- Can you hit a lob with topspin that will bring the ball down in the court and have it run toward the back fence after the bounce? The topspin lob is the perfect offensive lob and only needs to get over the net player's head to be effective.
- Do you have a favorite side? A player should set up and hit most offensive lobs on her best side. Occasionally she might have to resort to hitting a more defensive and higher lob from her weaker side.

Decision-Making Guidelines

When deciding whether to use an offensive lob, players should be sure to consider the previous information. They should also consider the following guidelines:

- Hit it over the opponent's head and into the backcourt when the opponent is in a poor court position very close to the net.
- Determine whether to hit a drive or a lob partially based on the opponent's position on the court.

(continued)

At a Glance

The following parts of the text offer additional information on offensive lobs:

Applying Topspin	47
Controlling Shot Height	59
Controlling Shot Speed	61
Lob	126

Players must not only watch the ball but also be aware of the opponent and court openings.

○ Do not attempt to hit an offensive lob when very deep in the court or pulled wide and out of the court. The offensive lob may not be the best shot when the player is not in a good court position. In this situation, a higher defensive lob would be the better option.

Although not every passing shot is an offensive opportunity, at times players can use it more offensively than defensively. If the opponent comes to the net after a poor approach shot, or if the opponent hits a poor volley, an accurate passing shot can result in a one-shot winner. Other offensive opportunities are available when the opponent fails to be in the correct position at the net, thus creating a large opening for a passing shot.

 WATCH OUT!

The following tendencies in your athletes may cause poor play:

- Getting greedy with passing shots and trying to go for winners. Players should remember that opponents have the offensive advantage when they are at the net. Players should not be too aggressive if they are out of position or well behind the baseline.
- Having difficulty hitting passing shots on low balls. Players must hit passing shots up to get them over the net and give them enough topspin to drop into the court.
- Hitting passing shots hard, but not accurately.

ACQUIRING THE APPROPRIATE KNOWLEDGE

To hit effective passing shots, players must understand the following:

Physical Playing Conditions

The physical playing conditions can significantly affect the game. Thus, players should pay attention to the following conditions when playing passing shots:

- Wind at the back. In this situation, players should hit solid passing shots without overhitting. Even if the shot is not an outright winner, the opponent will have difficulty volleying with much pace against the wind.
- Wind in the face. In this case, offensive passing shots are more difficult because the wind will slow the ball down before it can get by the opponent at the net. Hitting with topspin against the wind will make the ball drop even faster. A neutral passing shot with a little topspin is probably the best option.
- Crosswind. A player can use a crosswind to her advantage. She can hit the passing shot wide of her opponent's reach, and the wind will blow the ball back into the court.

READING THE SITUATION

Players should do the following to hit effective passing shots:

- Know the opponent's position at the net.
- Know the opponent's stronger side for volleys.
- Move to the ball quickly to play it in the ideal contact zone.
- Keep the ball low so the opponent will have to hit the volley up.
- Hit directly at the opponent to reduce his angle at the net.

REMINDER!

When trying to decide when to use passing shots, players must understand the match strategy and game plan. They should also consider the questions on page 140.

(continued)

Strengths and Weaknesses of Opponents

Players must account for their opponents' strengths and weaknesses to know how to gain the best advantage when playing a passing shot. They should consider the following about their opponents:

- Is the opponent agile or mobile? If not, the player can hit passing shots with a greater margin of error because the opponent will not be able to cover much court.

- Does the opponent have a strong and weak side? If so, the player should direct as many passing shots as possible to the weak side. Even if the passing shot does not get by the opponent, he will probably hit a weak volley if he is using his less favorite side.

- Does the opponent move early to cover the open court? Early movement creates an opportunity to hit behind the opponent.

- Does the opponent hit a very easy ball that is short and high? In this case, the player could choose to go right back at the opponent. If she moves right or left in anticipation of the shot, she will be out of position. If she remains stationary, she will be forced to play a very weak volley just to protect her body.

Self-Knowledge

In addition to being aware of their opponents' strengths and weaknesses, players need to know their own abilities. When playing passing shots, players should answer the following questions:

- Can you hit with enough topspin to pull the ball down into the court on a ball hit with a little extra speed? Because the player is trying to hit the ball past the person at the net, extra power is beneficial, but only if the player can add extra topspin to pull the harder-hit shot down in the court.

- Can you disguise the shot so the opponent can't tell whether to prepare for a passing shot or lob? Disguising the shot will freeze the opponent long enough that he doesn't get a quick start to the oncoming shot.

- Can you play aggressive passing shots when hitting from your best side and more neutral passing shots or lobs from your less potent side? Players should hit their most aggressive passing shots from their favorite side. The less powerful side should be used to hit shots with less speed and more net clearance, and that are more safely inside the lines, or simply lobbed over the opponent at the net.

- Can you move forward quickly to play the ball early and at the top of the bounce? Players cannot hit effective passing shots if they wait for the ball to come to them at or behind the baseline. If they wait at the baseline, two things happen: They are forced to hit the ball up, and the ball must travel a longer distance to get to the net player. Both of these make it easy for the opponent to volley from a position at the net.

Decision-Making Guidelines

When deciding whether to use a passing shot, players should be sure to consider the previous information. They should also consider the following guidelines:

- Be aware of court position. Even if the player has a ball he can play in a very comfortable hitting zone, if he is well behind the baseline, he will have to hit an almost perfect passing shot to get it by the net player.

- Don't get caught just watching the ball. When an opponent is at the net, the exchange of shots is much quicker. The player has to watch not only the ball but also her opponent, her movement, and the open court.

- Make quick decisions on low balls to either drive offensively with topspin or play a defensive or neutral shot with backspin. It is possible to play a low ball firmly and hit it up and over the net and into the open court with topspin. However, if the player must contact the ball a few inches lower, he will be forced to open the racket face and hit under the ball to get it up and over the net. He should not hit this shot hard because it has backspin and will tend to sail long if hit with enough speed to get by the opponent.

- The player should keep playing until the point is over, even if she thinks she has hit a great passing shot. The opponent might be able to get enough racket on the ball to hit a weak return that just gets over the net and dies quickly on the court. The player who hits good passing shots should immediately prepare for any possible return.

At a Glance

The following parts of the text offer additional information on passing shots:

Unless a player can break the opponent's serve, he will not be able to win matches. Because the server has the advantage of hitting the first shot of the point with complete control of speed, spin, and direction, players have to take advantage of opportunities in which they can return the serve aggressively and offensively.

In most, but not all, matches, opportunities to return aggressively and offensively occur on second serves. Servers usually hit second serves farther inside the lines and with more spin and less speed than first serves. These factors allow receiving players to move into a good position and hit an aggressive return from their better side. Hitting offensively might also occur when the server is very predictable so the returner can anticipate and play an offensive return.

 WATCH OUT!

The following tendencies in your athletes may cause poor play:

○ Not being patient and waiting to attack the right ball, given that the server has the advantage.

○ Not being aware that a slow serve may be difficult to attack. Returners should watch out for a high bounce or a ball spinning away from them or into them.

○ Not being aware that some servers have weak serves and are content to put the ball in play and are ready to play when the return is hit. These servers probably prefer to hit groundstrokes and are not intimidated when a return is hit aggressively back at them.

○ Being wild, not just aggressive. Players should not be losing points when returning weak serves because they make unnecessary errors.

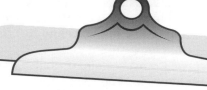

READING THE SITUATION

Players should do the following to gain the best advantage by attacking a weak second serve:

- Quickly move forward to play a weak serve.
- Learn the situations in which the opponent hits a weak serve.
- Hit either an aggressive approach shot or a sharp-angled shot from a short and weak serve.
- Play the shot on their favorite side when the serve is not hit hard.
- Be aggressive and hit with topspin to keep the ball in the court.

ACQUIRING THE APPROPRIATE KNOWLEDGE

To attack weak serves, players must know about the following:

REMINDER!

When trying to attack a weak serve, players must understand the match strategy and game plan. They should also consider the questions on page 140.

Physical Playing Conditions

The physical playing conditions can significantly affect the game. Thus, players should pay attention to the following conditions when contemplating attacking a weak serve:

○ Wind at the back of the server. When the wind is at the back of the server, returners will have a much more difficult time attacking even a weak serve. The serve will tend to land deeper in the service court, and the return will lack the speed because it is being hit into the wind.

- Wind in the server's face. The returner can go for more offensive returns when the wind is blowing into the server's face. Not only does the serve tend to land short, but all of the returns will be wind assisted and have better depth and speed because the wind is at the back of the returner.

- Court speed. A smooth, fast surface will make the ball skid low and get past the returner very quickly. If the court is rough, or slow, a topspin serve will kick up high and be more difficult to attack.

- Sun angle. The angle of the sun can make it difficult for the server to see the ball when he tosses it for the serve. When this happens, the server is just trying to get the ball in play, and the returner should be ready for the opportunity to attack.

Strengths and Weaknesses of Opponents

Players must account for their opponents' strengths and weaknesses to know how to gain the best advantage when attacking a weak serve. They should consider the following about their opponents:

- Does the opponent have a strong and weak side? The player should determine this and attempt to attack the weaker side whenever possible. The weaker side will either produce more errors or a much softer return that will be easy to attack.

- Does the server prefer to serve and stay back and hit groundstroke rallies? Sometimes the best shot is not an aggressive shot deep in the court, but a short, soft shot forcing the opponent to move toward the net. If the server doesn't like to come to the net, the returner can bring her in with her return.

- Does the opponent like to hit a huge first serve and follow it up by just popping a second serve into the court? In this case, the returner should make the server pay the price for hitting a very weak second serve and force him to take some speed off the first serve so he can get that serve in play and avoid being attacked on the second serve. If a player has a very weak second serve, he is forced to take speed off the first serve to get the ball in play. He loses some offensive advantage from a powerful first serve, but he avoids losing points because the weak second serve is an easy put-away shot by the player returning the serve.

- Can the opponent hit a serve with a lot of spin that kicks high after the bounce? This might look like an easy shot to attack, but the high-bounding kick serve is difficult to drive because of the high and long bounce.

- Does the opponent almost always use the same type of serve or serve it to the same place? In this case, the returner can set up and hit the best return by getting that slight head start toward the ball.

Self-Knowledge

In addition to being aware of their opponent's strengths and weaknesses, players need to know their own abilities. When attacking weak second serves, players should answer the following questions:

- Do you know how to put topspin on the ball to bring it down in the court? Players should learn to hit with enough spin to pull the ball into the court but not so much that the shot will lack speed and depth. Any time a player is hitting hard, she must impart additional topspin to pull the ball down into the court. However, too much topspin will take speed off the ball and it will bounce up high so the opponent can return the shot rather than having it run through the court and past the opponent.

- Are you aware of the angles? A wide and weak serve can be returned by an even wider serve return. Players should work on sharp-angled serve returns.

- Do you hit weak serves on your best side? Because players returning the serve have to cover only half of the court (the service court), they should be able to move quickly and attack a weak serve using their best side, either forehand or backhand.

(continued)

○ Can you start well inside the baseline to return the serve? This puts more pressure on the server to hit a deep serve and could force her into more errors.

○ Do you watch to see if the server is angry or discouraged? If the server is angry or discouraged, all the returner may have to do is get the ball back in the court and let the opponent self-destruct with the next shot. The returner may not have to hit an aggressive return if the server is not in a position or frame of mind to play a solid return.

At a Glance

The following parts of the text offer additional information on attacking a weak serve:

Square Groundstroke Stance	22
Open Groundstroke Stance	25
Semi-Western Grip	37
Applying Topspin	47
Controlling Shot Angle	57
Controlling Shot Speed	61
Serve Return	95
Approach Shot	100
Forehand as a Weapon	122

Decision-Making Guidelines

When deciding whether to attack a weak serve, players should be sure to consider the previous information. They should also consider the following guidelines:

○ Decide in advance where to return the weak serve. The returner should have a plan and look for the right opportunity and go for his shot.

○ Decide where to go after attacking a weak serve. The player must decide to follow up the return by moving to the net to play a winning volley or overhead, or to move back to play an aggressive groundstroke.

○ Mix up returns when playing easy balls. Not every shot needs to be hit with power. Players should try mixing in a sharp-angled return or even a drop shot.

Playing With Two Players at the Net (Doubles)

When playing doubles, the formation of two players at the net is the most aggressive and offensive position available to a team. Both players have the opportunity to hit a point-ending shot with an overhead or a volley. This formation leaves little room for opponents to hit between or on either side of the team at the net, and a short or medium-depth lob is usually an easy overhead to hit hard and accurately for an aggressive team.

The two players at the net can put pressure on the opposing team. The team controlling the net can quickly and firmly hit either forcing volleys and overheads or sharp-angled shots for winners. If the opposing team has one person at the net, the two-up team can isolate and hit to the person at the net and end points quickly.

 WATCH OUT!

The following tendencies in your athletes may cause poor play:

○ Being wild rather than aggressive with shots. A team is in a good position to win the point when both players are at the net. They should not lose points as a result of hitting sloppy shots.

○ Not keeping the pressure on the opponents. If ball comes back after a volley or an overhead, the team should be ready and in position to finish the point with the next shot.

○ Not playing the right shot. Players at the net should hit openings with an angle or down the middle between the opponents. Even strong shots hit back to the player behind the baseline will probably be returned.

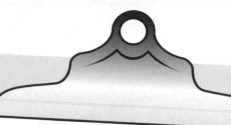

READING THE SITUATION

Players should do the following to play aggressively when both are at the net in doubles:

• Be ready for both a drive and a lob. Because play is fast when two players are at the net, these players will have to react much more quickly than if they were at the baseline.

• Know the tendencies of both opponents. Players should know whether their opponents prefer to drive or lob, what they will do when hitting on the backhand side, and whether they play shots to the middle of the court or to the doubles alleys.

• Play shots to the side of the closer opponent, especially one at the net.

• Move in quickly if opponents hit with heavy topspin. Balls hit with heavy topspin will go over the net and drop, forcing players to hit up. Players should move forward and get to the ball while it is still above the top of the net.

○ Not being extra quick. Opponents might try to hit one-shot winners even from a poor court position, so the team at the net should be ready for anything.

○ Crowding the net. If the players at the net get too close to the net, opponents can easily hit lobs over them.

ACQUIRING THE APPROPRIATE KNOWLEDGE

To be successful with both players at the net, doubles teams must understand the following:

Rules

Players need to know several rules when both players are at the net in doubles.

REMINDER!

When two players are at the net, they must understand the match strategy and game plan. They should also consider the questions on page 140.

(continued)

- Rules about touching the net after hitting a volley or an overhead
- Rules about volleying a ball before it crosses the net
- Rules about both players simultaneously hitting the ball

Physical Playing Conditions

The physical playing conditions can significantly affect the game. Thus, doubles teams should pay attention to the following conditions when playing with both players at the net:

- Wind in the face. If the wind is at the opponent's back, the balls will come at the players quickly. When opponents lob with the wind, any balls your players can't hit in the air will be very difficult to catch up to after the bounce.
- Wind at the back. The team can move closer to the net when the wind is blowing at the opponents. Lobs are difficult to hit deep, and soft and medium-speed drives should be volleyed when the ball is close to and above the net before the wind blows the ball down below the top of the net.
- Sun in the face. A lob hit up into the sun can be very difficult to see and hit. Players might need to let the ball bounce so they can see it better before hitting an overhead.

Strengths and Weaknesses of Opponents

Players must account for their opponents' strengths and weaknesses to know how to gain the best advantage when they are both at the net in doubles. They should consider the following about their opponents:

- Can the opponents lob effectively? If the opponents are not proficient with the lob, both net players can position themselves closer to the net for better angles on the volley. They will be able to hit before the ball drops below the top of the net.
- Do the opponents lob often? A ready position closer to the service line might be the ideal starting point when opponents lob frequently because the players won't have to move as far to play the overhead. When players start at the service line, it is almost impossible for a lob to get over their heads and land in the court.
- Do the opponents hit flat or with backspin? A ball hit flat will stay up when it crosses the net rather than dropping when hit with topspin. A hard-hit ball with backspin will probably go long.
- Do the opponents recover well? If opponents don't recover well, players at the net should volley wide and hit their next shot to the opening in the center of the court. The wide volley will draw the opponent out of the court and leave a large opening in the center for a point-ending volley.
- Are the opponents caught with one player in the backcourt and one at the net? In this situation, the players at the net should isolate the opponent at the net. An isolated opponent at the net will have very little chance of returning any balls that are volleyed or smashed to his side.

Self-Knowledge

In addition to being aware of their opponents' strengths and weaknesses, players need to know their own abilities. They should answer the following questions when two players are at the net in doubles:

- Are you aggressive? Do you play firm overheads and volleys? Any weak shot will give opponents an opportunity to hit the ball back quickly and hard because weak shots are slow and land short in the court.

- Can you hit volleys on the forehand and backhand sides? Can you hit balls hit directly at you using the backhand side of the racket? Players need the complete volley arsenal: They must be able to play volleys on the wide right and left and also on the backhand side when the ball is hit directly at the body.

- Can you take speed off the ball if you have to volley the ball up to get it over the net? This shot should be played back deep in the court to keep opponents back behind the baseline. To hit the ball up, the player must hit softly so it lands in the court but deep near the baseline so the opponent cannot attack a short ball.

- Can you identify the positions of your opponents? Players should be able to hit the openings with the first volley or overhead. An opponent might be in a position close to the net or out of the court. Players need to recognize when they have openings in the court so they can hit volleys and overheads in these gaps or at the person who could not handle the return and win points with one shot.

Decision-Making Guidelines

When deciding how to play aggressively with both players at the net, players should be sure to consider the previous information. They should also consider the following guidelines:

- Keep thinking offensively. Players should end the points as soon as possible. They don't want to be in an offensive position and extend points; rather, they want to end points as quickly as possible so their opponents don't force any unnecessary errors or have an opportunity to hit a winning shot.

- Attack the weaker player or isolate the player closer to the net.

- Get back into position if forced to play a wide volley or a deep overhead. Players should return to the net position so their opponents won't be able to hit to any openings.

- Don't assume your partner is going to get the ball that is hit down the middle. It is better to have both players go for the ball than to have both players standing still and watching the ball go between them.

At a Glance

The following parts of the text offer additional information on playing with two players at the net:

Controlling Shot Angle	57
Controlling Shot Speed	61
Volley	105
Overhead	113

chapter 7

Defensive Tactical Skills

This chapter covers the defensive tactical skills players must know to be successful. In this chapter, you will find the following skills:

Returning a well-placed, hard-hit first serve should be considered a defensive tactic. Players should be thinking about getting the ball back in play to neutralize the server's advantage. They can also neutralize the server with a deep return if the server is staying back, or with a ball hit at the server's feet if the server is following the serve to the net.

WATCH OUT!

The following tendencies in your athletes may cause poor play:

- Hitting offensively if the server has an effective serve. This will only result in too many unforced errors.
- Not watching their own court position. If a player is being overpowered, he should take a step or two back and give himself extra time for the return.
- Getting caught covering a weakness. A player who moves to cover her weaker side exposes some extra court for the server to hit.
- Not being ready to hit an offensive return. If the server hits a safe serve, the returner should return the ball from a comfortable hitting position.

READING THE SITUATION

Players should do the following to gain the best advantage by returning a powerful or well-placed serve:

- Know the best place to stand when preparing to return the serve.
- Focus on and identify the flight, speed, and spin of the ball at contact.
- Determine whether the server is coming to the net or staying at the baseline.
- Move across and forward to cut off the angle on a wide slice serve.
- Keep the backswing short to return hard-hit serves.
- After the return, quickly recover to the center of the court behind the baseline and be prepared for the next shot.

ACQUIRING THE APPROPRIATE KNOWLEDGE

To return the serve effectively, players must know about the following:

Rules

Players need to know several main rules when returning the serve:

- Rules pertaining to being ready when the server is ready
- Rules about calling faults and double faults
- Rules about let serves

REMINDER!

When deciding how to gain the best advantage with the serve return, players must understand the match strategy and game plan. They should also consider the questions on page 140.

Physical Playing Conditions

The physical playing conditions can significantly affect the game. Thus, players should pay attention to the following conditions when returning the serve in various game situations:

- Court speed. The speed of the court determines the amount of time the receiver has to make the return. Because smooth, fast courts make aggressive returns difficult, players should use defensive returns instead.
- Wind direction. Wind conditions affect the ball speed. If the server has the wind at his back, the serve will have more speed and the return will have less pace going back.
- Crosswinds. Crosswinds can pull the returner well out of the court and create a huge opening for the server. Returners must get the ball back in play crosscourt and deep when pulled off the court with a crosswind.
- Ball speed. The ball speeds up as the nap wears down. The advantage goes to the server, so returners must play these faster serves more defensively.

Strengths and Weaknesses of Opponents

Players must account for their opponents' strengths and weaknesses to know how to gain the best advantage when returning the serve. They should consider the following about their opponents:

- Does the opponent come to the net after hitting a hard serve? If so, the player should force her to play the volley up by dropping her return at the feet of the oncoming server.
- Does the opponent stay back? The returner will be able to hit an easy return with plenty of net clearance as long as the ball lands deep in the court.
- Does the opponent serve predictably? Even if the serve is hit hard, if it is predictable, the returner should be able to time his swing to hit more aggressively.
- Does the opponent have a weak side? The returner should figure out the server's weak side and return to that side when possible, both when the server stays back and when he comes to the net. Playing shots to the weak side is always preferable to hitting shots to a player's strong side. The weaker side will produce more errors. Shots played on the weaker side are hit with less confidence and usually lack consistency in power, spin, and direction. The weaker side will also break down under pressure more frequently than the stronger side will.

Self-Knowledge

In addition to being aware of their opponents' strengths and weaknesses, players need to know their own abilities. When returning the serve, players should answer the following questions:

- Can you take speed off the ball by either chipping with backspin or hitting with a compact stroke with some topspin? Players should develop some variety against various styles of play. Using variety by changing spins and speeds makes it more difficult for opponents to time their swings and develop a rhythm and confidence on their strokes. They will be forced to think about correct positioning, preparation, contact, and follow-through rather than performing automatically and thinking about placement and tactics.
- Can you modify your stroke and play with a much shorter backswing so you can make contact out in front, even on a hard-hit serve? The shorter backswing allows the player to make good contact in front of the body because it takes less time to prepare and make the forward swing.
- Can you pick up the flight of the ball right off the server's racket so you can move quickly and make good contact? If the movement is slow, the return will be weak. If the player recognizes the direction of the serve as the ball leaves the racket and moves quickly to the ball, she will be in the best possible position and on balance to hit her best return with power, direction, and spin.

(continued)

Decision-Making Guidelines

When deciding how to gain the best advantage with the serve return, players should be sure to consider the previous information. They should also consider the following guidelines:

○ Be aware of possible angles of return. For example, a serve out wide should be returned crosscourt because a defensive down-the-line return creates a big opening for the server's next shot.

○ Be aware of the fact that a big server can't always follow up with a volley or aggressive groundstroke. The returner can decide to just block the ball back deep in the court, taking the advantage away from the big server and making him play another shot.

○ Get into rhythm before attempting any return with much spin or angle. A player may need a game or two to adjust to the speed of a powerful serve; as she does, she can gain the confidence and rhythm to return these powerful serves. If the player is not accustomed to returning a fast serve, she will need to make some adjustments in her starting position, movement, and backswing. She must make sure she can get to and make good contact with the fast-moving ball so she can get it back in the court before attempting any additional spin or angle.

○ Always be ready for a weak serve. If the server delivers an easy ball, the returner should always be ready to take advantage of the mistake.

○ Don't forget to use the chip return. With a chip return, the ball stays low and forces the server to move in and hit up.

When the opponent is at the net and the player is at the baseline, the player must be thinking about playing good defense. She must be able to get the ball back in play. If she is in the right position and can hit the ball in a comfortable hitting area, she may be able to neutralize her opponent. She has the option of hitting a passing shot for an outright winner (which is unlikely if she is behind the baseline), making the opponent volley the ball up if she can drop her passing shot below the top of the net, or lobbing the ball over the opponent's head (which will be covered in Playing Defensively Using the Lob).

When forced to volley up, the opponent can't hit the ball hard to the open court or easily angle the ball off the court. If she volleys the ball up, soft, and short, the player should be in a much better position to hit a passing-shot winner to the open court from a position inside the baseline.

WATCH OUT!

The following tendencies in your athletes may cause poor play:

○ Getting greedy and trying for too much speed or angle when behind the baseline.

○ When deciding on a shot, not being aware of the opponent's position, the open court, and whether they can play the ball in a comfortable hitting zone. Players should be aware of all three variables.

○ Counting on a one-shot passing shot as a winner. Players should be thinking at least two or three shots ahead for best results.

○ Stopping playing and not being prepared for the return because the player thought he hit a great passing shot. A player should not lose the point because the opponent could get just enough racket on the ball to return it weakly back in the court, where he is standing and not ready to return.

READING THE SITUATION

Players should do the following to gain the best advantage when playing defensively using the passing shot:

- Know how close to the net the opponent is positioned.
- Determine whether the opponent is comfortable at the net and can hit volleys effectively on both sides.
- Determine whether the opponent is quick or tired and slow.
- Play their best shots with good contact once they can picture the situation. They should stay away from changing their stroke just before hitting the ball.
- Be ready to play the next shot. A volley by an opponent will come back twice as fast as a groundstroke.

ACQUIRING THE APPROPRIATE KNOWLEDGE

To play defensively using the passing shot, players must know about the following:

Physical Playing Conditions

The physical playing conditions can significantly affect the game. Thus, players should pay attention to the following conditions when playing defensively using the passing shot:

○ Court speed. The speed of the court has a huge impact on the type of passing shot the player can hit. When the courts are smooth and fast, a deep approach shot hit with good pace will be very difficult to handle. The combination of smooth courts and a low approach shot hit with backspin

REMINDER!

When playing defensively using the passing shot, players must understand the match strategy and game plan. They should also consider the questions on page 140.

(continued)

will make the ball skid and stay very low, which makes a passing shot difficult because it must be hit up just to get over the net.

○ Wind in the face. A wind blowing in the player's face slows down the passing shot and gives the opponent more time to move in for the volley. Also, with an oncoming wind, any ball played by an opponent at the net will have extra wind-aided speed to get by quickly.

Strengths and Weaknesses of Opponents

Players must account for their opponents' strengths and weaknesses to know how to gain the best advantage when defending against the net person by hitting passing shots. They should consider the following about their opponents:

○ Does the opponent have a strong and a weak side? Because the opponent will be volleying at the net, the player should play the passing shots to the weaker side if possible. Playing to the weak side is always preferable because the strong side generally hits with more confidence and with greater speed, accuracy, and spin.

○ Is the opponent tired and slow? When the opponent is tired and slow, the player should hit passing shots with plenty of margin of error inside the sidelines. Even if the opponent reaches the ball, he should give the player a big opening for his next shot. If the opponent is slow, the player doesn't have to hit risky shots close to the lines to create an opening. If the opponent can't recover quickly after playing a shot from the side of the court, there will be ample room for the player to hit his next shot to the opposite side.

○ How well does the opponent handle high or low balls? Many players have a weakness in playing high backhand volleys. Players should force opponents to hit this shot even when they are in a good position. Another common weakness is the low volley especially for tall players or players who use the Western grip. With opponents who struggle with low volleys, players should give them a steady diet of low passing shots.

○ Is the opponent timid and not comfortable at the net, or does he hit a two-handed backhand volley? (A shot hit directly at an opponent is difficult to execute with a two-handed grip.) A player can hit at the body in either of these situations. If the opponent is not comfortable at the net, the last thing she wants to see are balls hit directly at her. The reaction is to do whatever it takes to avoid getting hit rather than thinking about volleying the ball to the open court. The two-handed backhand volley is almost impossible to hit without releasing one hand when the ball is directed at the body. Even a strong two-handed player is ineffective when forced to play with one hand.

Self-Knowledge

In addition to being aware of their opponents' strengths and weaknesses, players need to know their own abilities. When playing defensively using the passing shot, players should answer the following questions:

○ Can you hit with topspin on both sides? Players' options are very limited if they can't hit with topspin with both forehand and backhand groundstrokes. Topspin allows a passing shot to be hit hard and still drop into the court. Without topspin, the player cannot hit the ball fast and so his options are to lob or hit passing shots with very little margin of error close to the top of the net and just inside the lines.

○ Can you drive high and low balls on both sides? If a player has a weakness, her opponent is sure to exploit it so she can play easy shots at the net. If the player has a weakness hitting high backhand passing shots, and if the opponent recognizes this and hits high-bouncing approach shots to the backhand side, the player should lob in this situation to push her opponent away from the net. Uncomfortable balls that are either high, low, or wide in the hitting zone are best played as lobs because hitting a weak passing shot will result in an easy volley from the opponent.

- Are you calm under pressure? Can you execute a solid passing shot, or do you get excited when being attacked and either rush or overhit? Rushing and overhitting result in a large number of errors and give the opponent points without even having to play a volley. If the player can stay calm when being attacked, he will not rush and make unforced errors. He will use better judgment and hit the right shot if he doesn't panic and overhit.

Decision-Making Guidelines

When deciding how to gain the best advantage when playing defensively using the passing shot, players should be sure to consider the previous information. They need to be prepared to make these decisions on their own when the opportunities arise. They should also consider the following guidelines:

- Be aware of the opponent's position, the openings in the court, and the ball in the contact zone. Players must understand all three of these things before deciding what shot to use and where to hit it.

- Determine quickly what type of passing shot to hit. The player must decide whether to hit right back at the net person, to hit a topspin shot that drops below the top of the net, to hit to the weak volley side, or to hit a high ball to the weak side. He must make this decision quickly based on his opponent's strengths and weaknesses, his opponent's court position, and his own ability to hit the passing shot. If he can set up and play his best shot, he can go directly back at the opponent if he is timid at the net, drop the ball below the top of the net if the opponent is too far away from the net, or hit to the opponent's weak side if the opponent is in good position for the volley. The player may even decide to go for an outright winner if the opponent at the net is not covering the court properly and there is an open court.

- Think two or three shots ahead. If the opponent is very predictable, the player should hit her passing shot and recover to where she likes to volley the return so she is ready for the second passing shot.

- Don't just watch the ball. The opponent might be getting in a perfect position for the return, or he might be out of position and give the player an opening. On the other hand, the player should be careful not to just watch his opponent to see where he is and the direction in which he is moving. If he does, he might be late getting to and playing the ball.

At a Glance

The following parts of the text offer additional information on playing defensively using the passing shot:

Controlling Shot Angle	57
Controlling Shot Height	59
Controlling Shot Speed	61
Forehand Groundstroke	66
One-Handed Backhand Groundstroke	73
Two-Handed Backhand Groundstroke	80
Passing Shot	131

Playing Defensively Using the Lob (Singles)

The lob is hit to drive the opponent away from the net, where he has the best opportunity to hit hard or with a sharp angle to win the point. The lob also gives the player time to recover from a poor court position, either very deep or very wide in the court. The lob is the most defensive shot, but if played properly, it will give the player time to recover back into a good court position and move the opponent away from the net.

 WATCH OUT!

The following tendencies in your athletes may cause poor play:

- Being afraid to hit the ball high. Even if it is short, a high ball will give the player time to recover to a good court position. The opponent might even miss with the next shot.

- Giving up. Even if the opponent is in the best position and the player is in the worst, she should play a few more shots and be ready to run the ball down to keep it in play. She should make the opponent play additional shots by running for every overhead or volley (even if helplessly out of position), hitting a high lob, recovering to a better position, and getting ready for the next shot.

- Not taking something away from the opponent, even in the worst situation. Even if the lob is low and short, the player can at least move to the biggest or most logical part of the court for a possible next shot.

- Panicking and rushing the lob once the opponent is in a good position at the net.

READING THE SITUATION

Players should do the following to gain the best advantage when playing defensively using the lob:

- Know where the opponent is in relation to the net.

- If at all possible, lob the ball over the opponent's backhand side.

- Be aware of the wind. The wind will blow a lob around, but it is also very difficult to hit good overheads in windy conditions.

- Transition quickly if the opponent plays an overhead and does not recover to a good position. One option is to dip the next shot at the opponent's feet.

- When behind the baseline or pulled out wide, make solid contact and get the ball high in the air so there is time to recover before playing the next shot.

ACQUIRING THE APPROPRIATE KNOWLEDGE

REMINDER!

When trying to play defensively using the lob, players must understand the match strategy and game plan. They should also consider the questions on page 140.

To play defensively using the lob, players must know about the following:

Physical Playing Conditions

The physical playing conditions can significantly affect the game. Thus, players should pay attention to the following conditions when playing defensively using the lob:

- Wind direction. The wind is a huge factor when lobbing. With the wind at her back, the player may only need to get the ball up and let the wind carry it over her opponent's head. It is very difficult to hit a successful lob with a stiff oncoming wind. An oncoming wind will keep the ball both short and low.
- Angle of the sun. The lob does not have to be great when there is a bright midday sun. The player can simply hit the lob up and let his opponent battle the sun to even see the lob.
- Clear sky or lights at night. A clear sky or playing at night under the lights makes it very difficult to establish good depth perception for returning the lob. Cloudy skies are much better for judging where lobs will land because the player has better depth perception.

Strengths and Weaknesses of Opponents

Players must account for their opponents' strengths and weaknesses to know how to gain the best advantage when playing defensively using the lob. They should consider the following about their opponents:

- Can you lob the ball over the opponent's backhand side when she is at the net? In almost all situations, lobbing the ball over the backhand side will send it to the opponent's weaker side. Very few players have effective backhand overheads.
- Is the opponent great at hitting volleys but weak with the overhead? Players should lob to these opponents. Forcing the opponent at the net to hit a weak overhead will cause more errors than letting him hit strong volleys.
- Can the opponent move back quickly for an overhead? If the opponent is slow, tired, or uncomfortable moving back, the player has more court to hit the lob into. A slow or tired opponent at the net will not be able to retreat fast enough to hit an overhead, so the lob is very effective. It will get over the opponent's head and land well out of the opponent's reach in the backcourt.

Self-Knowledge

In addition to being aware of their opponents' strengths and weaknesses, players need to know their own abilities. When playing defensively using the lob, players should answer the following questions:

- Can you slow the ball down by taking a very short backswing and using a compact stroke? The lob requires the player to take speed off the ball. A complete player hits lobs equally well on both the forehand and backhand side. If she has a weakness, a smart opponent will play shots to her weak side to force more errors. This is especially true when lobbing back a hard-hit overhead. All the backcourt player needs to do is block the ball back with an open racket face to hit an effective lob.
- Can you hit defensively on both sides? Players should be able to lob equally well on both the forehand and backhand side.
- Do you understand open-court percentages? For example, hitting a lob crosscourt gives the player more court to hit compared to a down-the-line lob. Hitting from the same spot but going crosscourt gives him 82 feet, 9 inches (25 m) of court. The higher-percentage shot is the one that is hit to the larger area of the court.
- Can you hit a defensive lob and run down the opponent's overhead? Doing so lengthens the point and puts pressure on the opponent to hit harder and closer to the lines to win the point.

(continued)

At a Glance

The following parts of the text offer additional information on playing defensively using the lob:

Decision-Making Guidelines

When deciding how to gain the best advantage when playing defensively using the lob, players should be sure to consider the previous information. They should also consider the following guidelines:

- Determine the best lob to hit. High and crosscourt is the best choice when the player is out of position. However, when the player can set up and play the ball in a comfortable position, the lob over the backhand side of the opponent is the best option.

- Drive, rather than lob, when the opponent is anticipating a lob and is in a ready position close to the service line. By making the opponent volley up from a deep volley position, the player should have an easy ball for the next shot.

- Keep the ball in play and give the opponent a chance to make mistakes. Many high school players can win points if they play good defense. If they are patient, select good shots, and play every ball back in the court, they can force their opponents to make errors.

 s discussed in chapter 6, aggressive baseline play is the most popular style of play in the game today. Although both players might prefer this style, at times players will need to play defensively. Good shot selection and court positioning are essential when defending against the aggressive baseline player to stay in the point and in a position to take advantage when the opponent hits an ineffective return.

⚠ WATCH OUT!

The following tendencies in your athletes may cause poor play:

o Trying to attack an attacker. When the opponent has the advantage, trying offensive shots from a defensive position is a formula for defeat.

o Not playing defense. Players can't always be in an offensive position.

o Not being prepared to hit an easy shot. Players must be ready to go from defense to offense if they get an easy ball to return.

o Not thinking about going from defense to neutral before hitting offensively. Rarely does a player have the opportunity to go from defense to offense in one shot.

READING THE SITUATION

Players should do the following to gain the best advantage when defending against an aggressive baseline player:

- Know their position on the court.
- Be aware of the opponent's favorite and strongest shots.
- Even when the opponent has the advantage, make him work to win every point by getting to and returning every ball.
- Always be aware of an opening if the opponent hits a poor shot or fails to recover quickly.
- Play more defensively the farther behind the baseline the player is.

ACQUIRING THE APPROPRIATE KNOWLEDGE

To defend against an aggressive baseline player, players must know about the following:

Physical Playing Conditions

The physical playing conditions can significantly affect the game. Thus, players should pay attention to the following conditions when defending against the aggressive baseline player.

o Court speed. It is easier for an opponent to attack when the courts are smooth and fast.

o Wind in the face. The opponent can take advantage when he has the wind at his back. It is also more difficult to defend when the wind is in the player's face.

o Ball speed. Tennis balls have different characteristics as the match progresses. If the balls fluff up, they become slower and give players more time to get to and set up for returns. If the balls get worn down and smooth, they become faster, thus giving the advantage to the aggressive baseline opponent.

REMINDER!

When defending against an aggressive baseline player, players must understand the match strategy and game plan. They should also consider the questions on page 140.

(continued)

Strengths and Weaknesses of Opponents

Players must account for their opponents' strengths and weaknesses to know how to gain the best advantage when defending against the aggressive baseline player. They should consider the following about their opponents:

- Do you know how to move around a weak return to play an aggressive shot? The player should be ready to neutralize her opponent if she has poor shot selection, poor court positioning, or both, after playing the shot.

- Is the opponent predictable? If the opponent likes to hit the same area of the court when he gets an easy ball to return, the player can position himself to give his opponent less room in which to hit his favorite shot.

- Does the opponent move in for a volley or overhead as a follow-up to an effective approach shot? Is the opponent comfortable hitting both overheads and volleys? If there is a weakness at the net, it would be a good tactic to draw the opponent into the net rather than let her play aggressive groundstrokes.

- If the opponent stays back, does he overhit a deep return? Many players become impatient and try for too much when they are forced to play the ball from deep in the court.

Self-Knowledge

In addition to being aware of their opponents' strengths and weaknesses, players need to know their own abilities. When defending against an aggressive baseline player, players should answer the following questions:

- Can you change the speed of your shots to give the opponent his least favorite ball? Aggressive baseline players prefer to attack slower balls or like to use the pace of the opponent. Some players like to use the speed of the opponent's shots to generate the power on their shots. Others prefer a slower ball so they can set up and drive the ball from a controlled and balanced position.

- Do you rush when under pressure? Players need to stay focused and play solid, high-percentage shots when the pressure is on. It is easy to rush and try to hit a powerful shot back with even more speed when under pressure. Obviously, rushing and overhitting will result in many unforced errors, so players should work on playing controlled and steady shots when under pressure.

- Can you play the ball on the rise and not retreat well behind the baseline? Playing the ball on the rise gives the opponent less time between shots and allows the player to maintain a better court position.

Decision-Making Guidelines

When deciding how to gain the best advantage when defending against an aggressive baseline player, players should be sure to consider the previous information. They should also consider the following guidelines:

- Keep the ball in play until the opponent makes an error. This is a good strategy with an opponent who likes to hit aggressive groundstrokes but is inconsistent. With this strategy, the player doesn't have to take any risks or play shots close to the lines.

- Always be ready to play aggressively if the opponent is on the offensive but hits a weak return. Even though a player is in a good position to attack, he may mis-hit or misjudge a shot so it will be weak. The player can go from defense to offense if he is prepared to capitalize on this opportunity to attack this weak shot.

- Change speeds, height, and spin to keep the opponent from getting in a comfortable groove or rhythm.
- As much as possible, play error-free tennis, even when the opponent is attacking. Make the opponent work to win every point.

At a Glance

The following parts of the text offer additional information on defending against an aggressive baseline player:

Defending Against the Serve-and-Volley (Singles)

The server who follows her serve to the net is constantly putting pressure on the returner to make an effective serve return so the returner can follow up with a passing shot or lob. When the server comes to the net, it forces the returner to do more than block the ball back in play with ample net clearance. The returner should hit solidly and either wide to make the onrushing server reach, or low to make her volley the ball up to get it over the net.

 WATCH OUT!

The following tendencies in your athletes may cause poor play:

- Hitting the return too defensively or cautiously. This gives the server an easy ball to volley.

- Hitting the return too aggressively. The server will probably win points due to the errors that will result from trying to hit hard returns from a fast serve.

- Getting discouraged early in the match because the server is winning points with either the serve or volley. The player should keep the pressure on by making returns. He might need only a couple of good returns in one game to break serve.

REMINDER!

When defending against the serve-and-volley, players must understand the match strategy and game plan. They should also consider the questions on page 140.

READING THE SITUATION

Players should do the following to gain the best advantage when defending against the serve-and-volley:

- Be aware of how quickly the server gets to the net. The returner should notice whether the server is inside or behind the service line when playing the first volley. The closer to the net the server gets, the lower the returner needs to hit to force the server to volley the ball up rather than hitting it with power down in the court.

- Determine whether the server likes to come in on wide serves, makes down-the-center serves, or serves into the body. The opponent might like to move to the net after hitting a wide serve because she has a large open court for the volley. The serve down the center is difficult to return with any angle. The serve hit at the body is difficult to return with much power.

- Determine whether the opponent is vulnerable to the lob because he gets too close to the net.

- Determine whether the opponent moves closer and to the side where the ball is hit for the second volley.

ACQUIRING THE APPROPRIATE KNOWLEDGE

To defend against the serve-and-volley, players must know about the following:

Physical Playing Conditions

The physical playing conditions can significantly affect the game. Thus, players should pay attention to the following conditions when defending against the serve-and-volley:

- Court speed. Fast, smooth courts make it more difficult to control the serve because the ball will not slow down as much when it hits the court. This creates an advantage for the server playing the serve-and-volley style. Rough, slow courts make the ball bounce slower, but extra spin on the serve could also make the ball bounce high, making for a difficult serve return.
- Wind in the face. The wind at the server's back makes the serve faster and slows down the return.
- Crosswind. A crosswind can force players out of the court and create a huge opening for the first volley.

Strengths and Weaknesses of Opponents

Players must account for their opponents' strengths and weaknesses to know how to gain the best advantage when defending against the serve-and-volley. They should consider the following about their opponents:

- When the server follows the serve to the net, how well can he play the low volley? Can he hit it firmly and deep in the court, does he have trouble getting under the ball to hit it up and back over the net, or does he pop up the ball weakly? The first option against the serve-and-volley is to return the ball low at the feet of the server moving to the net. If the server plays this shot weakly by scooping and popping the ball up, there is no need to change the return. If he plays the low volley well and can hit it back deep in the court, the returner will be forced to make the return lower or wider to get the opponent to move and reach either right or left.
- Does the server split step and cover balls both to the right and left? If the opponent is moving forward too fast or split steps too late, she will have difficulty moving either right or left. The player should exploit this weakness by hitting returns to either side of the server to make her reach for the first volley.
- Even if the server moves well to both his right and left, does he have a strong and weak side when executing the volley? The player should try to hit as many returns as possible to the server's weak side. The weak side will produce more errors than the strong side.
- Is the opponent tired or slow? Slow or tired opponents often hit the first volley from a deep volley position. They can't do much harm from that area of the court because it is difficult to hit a hard, well-placed volley from behind the service line.

Self-Knowledge

In addition to being aware of their opponents' strengths and weaknesses, players need to know their own abilities. When defending against the serve-and-volley, players should answer the following questions:

- Can you hit with topspin? Topspin from both the forehand and backhand side is necessary to drop the ball low to the feet of the onrushing server, forcing her to volley the ball up and easy rather than with power.
- Can you hit a chip return (a very short swing with the racket face open)? Sometimes a chip return is very effective. Players should hit chip returns against the serve-and-volley opponent, especially when hitting from the side where they have the most trouble imparting topspin. Chip returns are not hit hard, and there is very little racket motion before and after the hit. They are effective against the hard-hit serve. If a player has confidence in this return, it is very effective. If the chip return is high, it is a very easy ball for the server to volley, so the effective chip return is low.
- Do you play the returns early by standing on or inside the baseline? Playing returns early gets the ball back quicker and gives the server less time to move forward to a more advantageous position closer to the net.

(continued)

At a Glance

The following parts of the text offer additional information on defending against the serve-and-volley:

Applying Topspin	47
Applying Backspin	51
Controlling Shot Angle	57
Controlling Shot Height	59
Controlling Shot Speed	61
Serve Return	95
Lob	126

o Do you play high-percentage serve returns? The highest-percentage return is the crosscourt return. Crosscourt returns go over the lowest part of the net and require the shortest distance for recovery. Down-the-line returns must be hit higher and open up more court for the first volley.

Decision-Making Guidelines

When deciding how to gain the best advantage when defending against the serve and volley, players should be sure to consider the previous information. They should also consider the following guidelines:

o Be aware of the server's style to be in a position to set up for the next shot. Quick thinking is essential when playing against the serve-and-volley. The returner should notice, for example, that the server hits firmly to the open court when she gets a high ball, or that she hits low balls deep and down the line.

o Consider the lob if the server is serving well and able to move in quickly for a high return. Because the server is closing in on the net quickly, he may have difficulty stopping and retreating for the lob.

o Consider hitting directly back at the server if she is moving in quickly. The server may not be able to move either right or left fast enough to play a good return when she is moving quickly.

o Don't forget to try a chip serve return. The chip return takes speed off the serve and forces the server to hit the first volley up.

When playing doubles, the most aggressive and offensive position is for both players to be at the net. This formation puts both players in a position to win the point with one shot, either an overhead smash or a volley. When playing against this formation, players must understand that this is the time to play defensive tennis. Shot selection and court positioning are essential for success against this well-positioned doubles team.

 WATCH OUT!

The following tendencies in your athletes may cause poor play:

- Not hitting the first shot to neutralize the opponents before trying to hit offensive shots.
- Trying to win the point with one shot.
- When the opponents are in a good position at the net, not making sure their own team is in a solid defensive position at the baseline.
- Panicking and trying to overpower the opponents with wild shots. Players should choose to hit well-placed lobs and passing shots instead.

ACQUIRING THE APPROPRIATE KNOWLEDGE

To defend against two players at the net, players must know about the following:

Physical Playing Conditions

The physical playing conditions can significantly affect the game. Thus, players should pay attention to the following conditions when defending against two players at the net:

- Wind direction and speed. Lobs blow around in the wind, but players can hit them effectively if they make allowances for the speed and direction of the wind.
- Location of the sun. If the sun is high in the sky, players will have difficulty playing overheads because the ball will be in the sun.
- Ball speed. As balls fluff up, play becomes slower and passing shots will not have as much pace. When balls wear down and become smooth, they move through the air with more speed, but spins are not as effective.

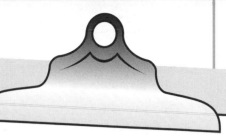

READING THE SITUATION

Players should do the following to gain the best advantage when defending against two players at the net:

- Know their opponents' strengths and weaknesses.
- Hit lobs if the opposing team has weaker overheads than volleys.
- Hit passing shots if the opposing team has better volleys than overheads.
- Isolate and hit to the weaker player.
- Direct passing shots to the middle of the court over the lowest part of the net.
- Always be ready and in position to play another shot. Players should be prepared to hit a series of shots to create an opening rather than try to win points with one shot against a team in an offensive position.

REMINDER!

When defending against two players at the net, players must understand the match strategy and game plan. They should also consider the questions on page 140.

(continued)

Strengths and Weaknesses of Opponents

Players must account for their opponents' strengths and weaknesses to know how to gain the best advantage when defending against two players at the net. They should consider the following about their opponents:

- Is one opponent stronger and one weaker? Players should determine the stronger and weaker players at the net and direct shots at the weaker player. It is a good tactic to hit at the weaker player, who is more likely to make errors than the stronger player.

- Does the opposing team prefer to hit overheads? When playing against teams that prefer overheads, players should force them to hit volleys. Or, if the opponents like to hit volleys, players can force them to hit overheads. When a team is at the baseline in a defensive position and the opponents are at the net in an offensive position, the team at the baseline will have a better chance of winning points if its opponents are playing their least favorite shots because these will produce more errors.

- After the opponents play their first shot, either an overhead or volley, does the person who played the shot quickly recover to a good position at the net? If the person who played the shot does not recover to a good position, the defending team can catch her out of position and exploit the player in the weak court position.

- Do the opponents at the net prefer to hit angles, or do they try to hit hard and overpower their opponents? The defending team should study their opponents' preferences so they can anticipate their returns. If the opponents like to overpower, players can adjust by moving back a step or two in the backcourt. If the opponents use angled volleys, players need to anticipate shorter and wider volleys.

Self-Knowledge

In addition to being aware of their opponents' strengths and weaknesses, players need to know their own abilities. When defending against two players at the net, doubles teams should answer the following questions:

- Can you hit well-placed passing shots under pressure? Hitting passing shots low and down the middle of the court will neutralize the return from the opponents and give the team an easier shot on the next return.

- Can you hit soft, high, and deep defensive lobs? Such lobs will make the offensive team at the net retreat to a defensive position.

- Do you know and hit high-percentage shots when on defense? There is more open court when lobs are hit crosscourt because the distance is greater crosscourt compared to down the line or straight ahead. When players force a team at the net to volley, hitting down the middle is a higher-percentage shot because it goes over the lowest part of the net and the players avoid the very risky shot to the doubles alley.

- Can you recognize when an opponent is out of position? If one player is out of position or recovers slowly, the team should make that person play the next shot from a poor court position. A couple of situations are common. In one, a player is positioned closer to the service line than the net. Hitting an effective volley this far away from the net is difficult. Also, the team at the baseline can hit the ball at her feet. In another situation, one player gets too close to the net. This creates a large opening in the backcourt; hitting a lob over that player's head is easy because there is so much open court to hit into.

- Can you hit and recover quickly? Because defending teams rarely win points with the first shot, they must develop the skills of hitting, recovering quickly, and moving quickly to the next shot.

Decision-Making Guidelines

When defending against two players at the net, players should be sure to consider the previous information. They should also consider the following guidelines:

o   Be patient and know that more than one shot is usually required to win the point.

o   Choose the right shot. When the players are behind the baseline, they should hit lobs. If they are hitting from inside the baseline, passing shots are the better option.

o   Take away the angles available to the players at the net by hitting down the middle of the court.

o   Isolate the weaker player and hit shots at that player when possible. More specifically, defending players should hit to the weakest shot from the weaker player.

At a Glance

The following parts of the text offer additional information on defending against two players at the net:

Applying Topspin	47
Controlling Shot Angle	57
Controlling Shot Height	59
Controlling Shot Speed	61
Lob	126
Passing Shot	131

Doubles formations vary from two players at the net to two players at the baseline to one player at the net and one at the baseline. The majority of high school doubles teams use the one-up, one-back formation, so this skill will address the best way to defend against teams in this formation by teams who are also in this formation. The player at the net on either team is in an offensive position and should be thinking aggressively because she can end points with one shot, either a volley or an overhead. The player in the backcourt needs to think more defensively and play safe shots that the net player cannot hit. The backcourt player should direct shots back to the opposite deep player (deep to deep) or hit a lob over the opposing player at the net.

 WATCH OUT!

The following tendencies in your athletes may cause poor play:

o Backcourt players not playing defensive shots. Trying to hit winners from behind the baseline will produce many unforced errors.

o Backcourt players not keeping an eye on net players. The net player might anticipate your return to the deep player and move across to intercept your shot from the backcourt.

o Changing their minds about what shot to hit or where to hit it at the last moment because of movement from their opponents. Changing just before contact will almost always result in an error.

o Net players not playing aggressively. Players at the net need to play aggressively. Backcourt players, on the other hand, should play more conservatively to avoid unforced errors.

READING THE SITUATION

Players should do the following to gain the best advantage when defending against one player at the net and one player in the backcourt:

- When at the baseline, know their target before hitting the shot. The target is usually either away from or over the head of the player at the net. However, a player can hit at the person at the net if that person doesn't volley well or is out of position.

- Don't hesitate to wear the opponents down. Lobbing over the player at the net will force the backcourt partner to run from side to side to return the lob.

- Don't forget the short target in front of the person at the baseline. A soft, short-angled shot or drop shot might be very effective if the baseline player is tired or slow.

ACQUIRING THE APPROPRIATE KNOWLEDGE

To defend against one player at the net and one player in the backcourt, players must know about the following:

Physical Playing Conditions

The physical playing conditions can significantly affect the game. Thus, players should pay attention to the following conditions when playing against one player at the net and one player in the backcourt:

> **REMINDER!**
>
> When defending against one player at the net and one player in the backcourt, players must understand the match strategy and game plan. They should also consider the questions on page 140.

- Wind direction and speed. Players should watch the wind and make allowances for speed and direction, especially when hitting lobs. Lobs are most affected by the wind because they are hit higher and with less speed than most other shots. Players should allow for this when hitting lobs.

- Location of the sun. Even if a lob is not hit perfectly, hitting an overhead when the ball is lobbed up in the sun is always difficult because it is difficult to see the ball clearly when it is in the sun.

- Ball speed. As the cover of the ball fluffs up, players have to hit harder to keep the ball deep in the court because the ball becomes larger and has more friction through the air.

Strengths and Weaknesses of Opponents

Players must account for their opponents' strengths and weaknesses to know how to gain the best advantage when defending against one player at the net and one player in the backcourt. They should consider the following about their opponents:

- Is the player at the baseline comfortable hitting groundstrokes? If so, the lob from side to side is a good option. It forces the baseline player to move and hit shots from a high-bouncing ball.

- Is the baseline player slow or tired? If so, the short target just over the net is a good option because it forces the baseline player to run a long way to get to and return the ball.

- Is the player at the baseline uncomfortable at the net? If so, players should bring her in with a short ball and force her to hit a volley or an overhead with her next shot. Many players are very steady when hitting groundstrokes but very error prone when they are drawn to the net and forced to hit volleys and overheads.

- Does the opposing player at the net volley or hit overheads confidently? Does he move well and hit point-ending shots with both volleys and overheads? If so, players should direct shots to the person in the backcourt so the net player won't have the opportunity to hit point-ending shots. If the net player is not confident, it may not be necessary to avoid him.

- How consistent is the opponent at the baseline? If the baseline player is inconsistent, the focus should be on keeping the ball away from the partner at the net and directed at the player at the baseline. If the backcourt player is comfortable at the baseline, lobs over the person at the net will force the backcourt player to move side to side and hit balls from a more difficult high bounce.

Self-Knowledge

In addition to being aware of their opponents' strengths and weaknesses, players need to know their own abilities. When defending against one player at the net and one player in the backcourt, players should answer the following questions:

- Can you hit deep shots away from the net player from the baseline position? This will keep the net player from hitting point-ending volleys and overheads and force the baseline player to win points from the backcourt.

- Can you hit the lob over the player at the net and prevent her from hitting strong overheads? This will also force the backcourt player to move side to side and play the more difficult high-bouncing groundstrokes or lobs.

- Can you hit a short ball in front of the opposing baseline player? This will force the backcourt player forward to make the shot. If he is more comfortable in the backcourt, this takes him out of his comfort zone and forces him to play his next shot at the net with a volley or an overhead.

- Is the baseline player steady and consistent? A team with a player that is consistent from the baseline can win most of the team's points by simply engaging in a rally from the backcourt and letting the backcourt opponent lose points as a result of making more errors than the team's own baseline player.

(continued)

At a Glance

The following parts of the text offer additional information on defending against one player at the net and one player in the backcourt:

Decision-Making Guidelines

When deciding how to play against one player at the net and one player in the backcourt, players should be sure to consider the previous information. They should also consider the following guidelines:

- If the net player can't hurt your team with a volley or an overhead, don't take unnecessary risks to keep the ball away from her. Teams need not avoid a player if she can't hurt them from the position she is in. Not having to direct shots away from the player at the net provides the team with more court to hit to.

- If opponents are of equal skill level, play shots to the player at the baseline to keep the ball away from the offensive player at the net.

- Don't be too predictable. Teams should mix up groundstrokes away from the net player and lobs over the net player.

- If one player is weak, slow, discouraged, or out of rhythm, force that player to play more shots. This player will make more errors.

- Have the backcourt player keep the ball in play long enough for the net player to play an offensive shot. The priority for the player in the backcourt is to force a return so his partner at the net can hit an easy winning shot.

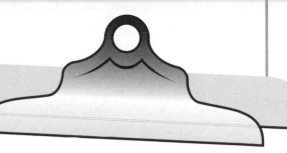

When playing doubles, the formation of two players in the backcourt is a definite defensive position. Both players will be hitting neutral or defensive shots to try to force the opponents to make an error to win the point. This formation rarely gives players opportunities to win points by hitting openings in the court. Both players must be willing to play longer points that will ultimately end when the opponents make errors.

The two players in the backcourt formation can be an effective position if the opponents are winning points quickly at the net by isolating the net person or by hitting the opening between the two players. By moving both players to the baseline, the team deprives its opponents of a close player target and greatly reduces the opening in the middle of the court. Opponents are forced to hit angled volleys and overheads or use more speed to overpower the players.

 WATCH OUT!

The following tendencies in your athletes may cause poor play:

- ○ Not realizing that they are in a defensive position and should play defensive shots.
- ○ Not being patient and willing to play longer points.
- ○ Trying to hit winning shots to end points.
- ○ Not making opponents work hard. Opponents will hit winning shots at times, but teams at the baseline should make them work hard for every point and pressure them into unforced errors.

ACQUIRING THE APPROPRIATE KNOWLEDGE

To defend with two players in the backcourt, players must know about the following:

Physical Playing Conditions

The physical playing conditions can significantly affect the game. Thus, players should pay attention to the following conditions when defending with two players in the backcourt:

- ○ Wind direction. If the wind is blowing into the opponents' faces, they will have difficulty generating speed to hit

READING THE SITUATION

Players should do the following to gain the best advantage when defending with two players in the backcourt:

- Have both solid groundstrokes and solid lobs to force the opposing team to hit many shots every point. If the opponents become impatient, they will try to hit too hard or close to the lines and increase the likelihood of an error.
- Lob when opponents crowd the net to move the ball over their heads.
- When opponents are closer to the service line, hit groundstrokes with lower net clearance so these shots land at the opponents' feet.
- Play to the center of the court to go over the lowest part of the net and to reduce the angles for the opponents' volley.
- Direct shots at the weaker player.
- Hit balls to get the weaker returns, either weak volleys or overheads.

REMINDER!

When defending with two players at the net, players must understand the match strategy and game plan. They should also consider the questions on page 140.

(continued)

forcing volleys and overheads. Windy conditions make lobs difficult, but when played effectively, they make overheads very difficult for the opposing team.

○ Clear sky. A clear and sunny day makes overheads very difficult because the ball can be lost against the sun. Tracking the ball is also difficult with a clear sky because of the lack of depth perception. Players should lob the ball up in the sun. Even if a player can track and return a ball hit into the sun, the next shot can be difficult because the opponent's eyes are still adjusting to the intense light.

○ Ball speed. As balls fluff up, they become slower and make points last longer.

Strengths and Weaknesses of Opponents

Players must account for their opponents' strengths and weaknesses to know how to gain the best advantage when defending with two players in the backcourt. They should consider the following about their opponents:

○ Can both opponents hit effective overheads? If not, the players should hit a large number of lobs to force the opponents to play a lot of overheads.

○ Are both opponents effective at volleying? Do they try to hit hard volleys to overpower the team at the baseline or soft and sharp-angled volleys? Teams at the baseline must be ready for their opponents' preferred shots. If opponents prefer powerful shots, players in the backcourt can move back an extra step or two to have more time to react. If the opponents prefer sharp-angled volleys, baseline players must be prepared to move forward and wide to return their shots.

○ Does the opposing team have a weaker player? A team in the backcourt should try to make the weaker opponent hit most of the shots at the net. The weaker player could be either the less skilled or the more frustrated or tired player. This person will produce more errors than the stronger or more consistent player.

Self-Knowledge

In addition to being aware of their opponents' strengths and weaknesses, players need to know their own abilities. When defending with two players in the backcourt, teams should answer the following questions:

○ Are you patient and willing to play lots of shots before your opponents make errors? Players in the backcourt cannot expect to win points in one or two shots; they will win many points by producing errors from their opponents. Such teams must be patient and consistent to give their opponents plenty of opportunities to make errors.

○ Can you lob well? If the opponents move very close to the net, backcourt players should lob. When the opponents are close to the net, they expose a large open area in the backcourt to hit lobs into. If the opponents are closer to the service line, backcourt players should hit groundstrokes with low net clearance at their feet.

○ Do you hit the right shots, either lobs or groundstroke drives, depending on which is more effective? The choice of shot is determined by the strengths of the opponents, either volleys or overheads, and their position. If the opponents are very close to the net, backcourt players should hit lobs over their heads; if the opponents are closer to the service line, backcourt players should hit low groundstrokes that land at their feet.

○ Do you play every point hard and never give up? Players never know when opponents will miss an easy shot. Backcourt players must be willing to never give up on any shot and be prepared to get every ball back in play. This puts pressure on the opponents to not make errors on any shots. They will also have a tendency to hit harder and closer to the lines to end points quickly.

Do you play smart and not take unnecessary risks that will produce unforced errors by getting to every ball and then playing shots that produce the fewest number of unforced errors? This is the formula for players in the backcourt. Opponents become frustrated when they have to hit good shot after good shot, only to have the ball keep coming back over the net by the players in the backcourt.

Decision-Making Guidelines

When deciding how to play defensively with two players in the backcourt, players should be sure to consider the previous information. They should also consider the following guidelines:

- Force the weaker opposing player to hit point-ending shots. Because the weaker opponent will make more errors, backcourt players should force that person to play the majority of the shots.

- Mix up shots with drives and lobs to keep the opponents out of rhythm. Backcourt players should not allow their opponents to get comfortable with all volleys or all overheads. They should add variety to keep the opponents from getting on a roll and winning several points in a row with the same shots.

- Let opponents make errors. Teams in the backcourt don't have to hit winners to win points. They should stay in every point by getting the ball back in play. If the opponents get frustrated, they will make even more errors as they attempt to hit harder or closer to the lines.

At a Glance

The following parts of the text offer additional information on defending with two players in the backcourt:

Controlling Shot Angle	57
Controlling Shot Speed	61
Forehand Groundstroke	66
One-Handed Backhand Groundstroke	73
Two-Handed Backhand Groundstroke	80
Lob	126

Planning for Teaching

Part IV helps you apply what you learned in the previous chapters to developing a plan for the upcoming season. By having a season plan that outlines your practices for the year and then creating specific practice plans that make up your season plan, you will be ready to coach and get the most out of your season.

Chapter 8 explains how to create your season plan, which is a framework for the practices that make up your season. Besides teaching you about the six essential steps to developing the season plan, this chapter provides a sample season plan using the games approach. A sample season plan using the traditional approach can be found in the *Coaching Tennis Technical and Tactical Skills* online course.

After you have created your season plan, you must create what is called a practice plan, which outlines how you will approach each practice. Chapter 9 helps you do this by explaining the components of a good practice plan and then providing samples of the first eight practices of your season based on the season plans using the games approach. A sample practice plan using the traditional approach can be found in the *Coaching Tennis Technical and Tactical Skills* online course.

chapter 8

Season Plans

The preceding chapters of this book describe the game of tennis and the multitude of skills you must teach to develop your players. Teaching these numerous and varied skills to a variety of players requires a comprehensive, systematic approach. Putting a team together is like assembling a jigsaw puzzle. When you open the puzzle box and dump the pieces on the table, you may feel overwhelmed at the prospect of making order out of the chaos. Facing the job of teaching dozens of skills to players of varying abilities, you may feel similarly overwhelmed.

Before touching any of the pieces in a jigsaw puzzle, you must have a vision of the completed project—what the puzzle will look like—which is provided by the picture on the cover of the box. For you as a tennis coach, this picture is your coaching philosophy, or what you want your team to look like, which you garner from your own experience and exposure to other coaches' ideas through clinics, workshops, and conversations. You must decide if you will emphasize consistency and keeping the ball in play, an all-court game with both backcourt and net play, or an aggressive attacking style by getting your players to the net to end points quickly. You must decide how you want your team to dress, on and off the court; how much to try to control their emotions and reactions, on and off the court; how regimented to be with policies and practice sessions; and how involved you want to be in their lives away from tennis. You must consciously and systematically review your philosophy every year so that you have an up-to-date blueprint for your program. Just as the picture on the puzzle box constantly guides you as the puzzle takes shape, you should frequently refer to your coaching philosophy to be sure your teaching strategies are producing the team you desire.

Once you have the picture of the jigsaw puzzle, you must organize and prioritize the pieces of the puzzle so that the project has some starting points. You first find all the pieces with at least one straight edge to create the borders. Next, you sort the pieces into groups by colors and design. Finally, you analyze the particular lines and curves of each piece and work diligently to match that piece with its adjacent pieces. This chapter provides the straight edges and color groupings of your coaching project, giving you a place to start planning and a method for prioritizing your teaching. Then, with the plan in place, you can take each piece of the puzzle—each isolated skill required to play the game—and fit it into the larger picture. Just as the completed puzzle transforms a chaotic pile of cardboard pieces into a beautiful picture, the well-coached tennis team, built by players all following an organized plan, miraculously blends diverse skills into a fascinating, systematic team effort.

Six Steps to Instructional Planning

As with building a puzzle, using a systematic approach can help you put together your season plan. After you have articulated your philosophy, you can begin planning for the season ahead by following the Six Steps to Instructional Planning:*

Step 1: Identify the skills that your athletes need

Step 2: Know your athletes

Step 3: Analyze your situation

Step 4: Establish priorities

Step 5: Select methods for teaching

Step 6: Plan practices

Step 1: Identify the Skills That Your Athletes Need

The first step in organizing the season plan is to identify the specific skills that the athletes must be able to execute for the team to be successful, as shown in column one of figure 8.1. This list of skills is based on the technical and tactical skills in this book as well as the information on communication and physical, character, and mental skills from *Successful Coaching, Third Edition*. In the following steps, you will examine the list of skills and add others if necessary. Step 4 of the planning process explains further how you can put this list to work.

Step 2: Know Your Athletes

The next step in the planning process is to refine the list of skills that you are planning to teach, based on an evaluation of the strengths, weaknesses, and abilities of the athletes in your program. For example, assume that you want your singles players to play an aggressive baseline style of play because you think they will be successful if they can work toward ending points from the backcourt when the

---

*Reprinted, by permission, from R. Martens, 2004, *Successful Coaching*, 3rd ed. (Champaign, IL: Human Kinetics), 237.

Figure 8.1   Identifying and evaluating skills

STEP 1	STEP 4							
	Teaching priority			Readiness to learn		Priority rating		
Skill	Must	Should	Could	Yes	No	A	B	C
Foundational skills								
Square groundstroke stance	M	S	C	Yes	No	A	B	C
Open groundstroke stance	M	S	C	Yes	No	A	B	C
Closed groundstroke stance	M	S	C	Yes	No	A	B	C
Open volley stance	M	S	C	Yes	No	A	B	C
Crossover volley stance	M	S	C	Yes	No	A	B	C
Eastern forehand grip	M	S	C	Yes	No	A	B	C
Semi-Western grip	M	S	C	Yes	No	A	B	C
Western grip	M	S	C	Yes	No	A	B	C
Continental grip	M	S	C	Yes	No	A	B	C
Eastern backhand grip	M	S	C	Yes	No	A	B	C
Two-handed backhand grip	M	S	C	Yes	No	A	B	C
Applying topspin	M	S	C	Yes	No	A	B	C
Applying backspin	M	S	C	Yes	No	A	B	C
Applying sidespin	M	S	C	Yes	No	A	B	C
Controlling shot angle	M	S	C	Yes	No	A	B	C
Controlling shot height	M	S	C	Yes	No	A	B	C
Controlling shot speed	M	S	C	Yes	No	A	B	C
Controlling shot depth	M	S	C	Yes	No	A	B	C
Strokes and shots								
Forehand groundstroke	M	S	C	Yes	No	A	B	C
One-handed backhand groundstroke	M	S	C	Yes	No	A	B	C
Two-handed backhand groundstroke	M	S	C	Yes	No	A	B	C
First serve	M	S	C	Yes	No	A	B	C
Second serve	M	S	C	Yes	No	A	B	C
Serve return	M	S	C	Yes	No	A	B	C
Approach shot	M	S	C	Yes	No	A	B	C
Volley	M	S	C	Yes	No	A	B	C
Swinging midcourt volley	M	S	C	Yes	No	A	B	C
Overhead	M	S	C	Yes	No	A	B	C
Drop shot	M	S	C	Yes	No	A	B	C
Forehand as a weapon	M	S	C	Yes	No	A	B	C
Lob	M	S	C	Yes	No	A	B	C
Passing shot	M	S	C	Yes	No	A	B	C
Groundstroke from deep in the court	M	S	C	Yes	No	A	B	C
Offensive tactical skills								
Aggressive baseline play (singles)	M	S	C	Yes	No	A	B	C
Drop shot (singles)	M	S	C	Yes	No	A	B	C
Keeping the ball in play (singles)	M	S	C	Yes	No	A	B	C

(continued)

Figure 8.1 *(continued)*

STEP 1	STEP 4							
	Teaching priority			Readiness to learn		Priority rating		
Skill	**Must**	**Should**	**Could**	**Yes**	**No**	**A**	**B**	**C**
Offensive tactical skills *(continued)*								
Keeping the ball in play (doubles)	M	S	C	Yes	No	A	B	C
Serve-and-volley (singles and doubles)	M	S	C	Yes	No	A	B	C
Swinging midcourt volley (singles and doubles)	M	S	C	Yes	No	A	B	C
Approach shot (singles and doubles)	M	S	C	Yes	No	A	B	C
Volley and overhead (singles and doubles)	M	S	C	Yes	No	A	B	C
Offensive lob (singles and doubles)	M	S	C	Yes	No	A	B	C
Passing shot (singles and doubles)	M	S	C	Yes	No	A	B	C
Attacking weak serves (singles and doubles)	M	S	C	Yes	No	A	B	C
Two players at the net (doubles)	M	S	C	Yes	No	A	B	C
Defensive tactical skills								
Serve return (singles)	M	S	C	Yes	No	A	B	C
Playing defensively using the passing shot (singles)	M	S	C	Yes	No	A	B	C
Playing defensively using the lob (singles)	M	S	C	Yes	No	A	B	C
Defending against aggressive baseline players (singles)	M	S	C	Yes	No	A	B	C
Defending against the serve-and-volley (singles)	M	S	C	Yes	No	A	B	C
Defending against two players at the net (doubles)	M	S	C	Yes	No	A	B	C
Defending against one player at the net and one player in the backcourt (doubles)	M	S	C	Yes	No	A	B	C
Defending with two players in the backcourt (doubles)	M	S	C	Yes	No	A	B	C
Physical training skills								
Strength	M	S	C	Yes	No	A	B	C
Speed	M	S	C	Yes	No	A	B	C
Agility	M	S	C	Yes	No	A	B	C
Power	M	S	C	Yes	No	A	B	C
Flexibility	M	S	C	Yes	No	A	B	C
Other	M	S	C	Yes	No	A	B	C
Mental skills								
Emotional control—anxiety	M	S	C	Yes	No	A	B	C
Emotional control—anger	M	S	C	Yes	No	A	B	C
Maturity	M	S	C	Yes	No	A	B	C
Self-confidence	M	S	C	Yes	No	A	B	C

STEP 1	STEP 4							
	Teaching priority			Readiness to learn		Priority rating		
Skill	**Must**	**Should**	**Could**	**Yes**	**No**	**A**	**B**	**C**
Motivation to achieve	M	S	C	Yes	No	A	B	C
Ability to concentrate	M	S	C	Yes	No	A	B	C
Experience	M	S	C	Yes	No	A	B	C
Other	M	S	C	Yes	No	A	B	C
Communication skills								
Sends positive messages	M	S	C	Yes	No	A	B	C
Sends accurate messages	M	S	C	Yes	No	A	B	C
Listens to messages	M	S	C	Yes	No	A	B	C
Understands messages	M	S	C	Yes	No	A	B	C
Receives constructive criticism	M	S	C	Yes	No	A	B	C
Receives praise and recognition	M	S	C	Yes	No	A	B	C
Credibility with teammates	M	S	C	Yes	No	A	B	C
Credibility with coaches	M	S	C	Yes	No	A	B	C
Character skills								
Trustworthiness	M	S	C	Yes	No	A	B	C
Respect	M	S	C	Yes	No	A	B	C
Responsibility	M	S	C	Yes	No	A	B	C
Fairness	M	S	C	Yes	No	A	B	C
Caring	M	S	C	Yes	No	A	B	C
Citizenship	M	S	C	Yes	No	A	B	C

From *Coaching Tennis Technical and Tactical Skills* by ASEP, 2009, Champaign, IL: Human Kinetics. Adapted, by permission, from R. Martens, 2004, *Successful Coaching*, 3rd ed. (Champaign, IL: Human Kinetics), 250-251.

opportunity presents itself. Before teaching this style of play, you must evaluate the ability of the singles players in your program to determine if they have the consistency necessary to keep the ball in play long enough to force a short ball from the opponent. You also need to know whether they have the power and accuracy to put a short ball away once they get the opportunity to move forward and return aggressively.

As you learned previously, player evaluation takes many forms. You should study your players in drills and matches to determine their strengths and weaknesses. Simple charting and postmatch reports can also provide useful information.

Using all this information, you need to add or delete skills on the list that you began developing in Step 1, based on the ability of the players in your program.

Step 3: Analyze Your Situation

As you prepare for the season, you must also weigh the external factors that will both guide and limit you. Budgetary issues and related fund-raising options will affect scheduling, off-court training facilities, practice equipment, and court time.

Administrative and community support will influence goal setting and expectations. Teaching loads will set parameters for both off-season and in-season programming. Clearly, then, many factors influence your planning. In evaluating these factors, you will find it helpful to spend some time working through the questions in figure 8.2 on page 224.

Figure 8.2   Evaluating your team situation

How many practices will you have over the entire season? How long can practices be?

How many matches will you have over the entire season?

What special events (team meetings, parent orientation sessions, banquets, tournaments) will you have and when?

How many athletes will you be coaching? How many assistants will you have? What is the ratio of athletes to coaches?

What facilities will be available for practice?

What equipment will be available for practice?

How much money do you have for travel and other expenses?

What instructional resources (videos, books, charts, CDs) will you need?

What other support personnel will be available?

What other factors may affect your instructional plan?

From *Coaching Tennis Technical and Tactical Skills* by ASEP, 2009, Champaign, IL: Human Kinetics. Reprinted, by permission, from R. Martens, 2004, *Successful Coaching,* 3rd ed. (Champaign, IL: Human Kinetics), 247-248.

Step 4: Establish Priorities

Steps 1, 2, and 3 of the Six Steps to Planning describe general factors that provide an important base of information regarding your players and your program. Now, in Step 4, you must make a decision about where to start and how to progress in the teaching of skills. Refer back to figure 8.1 beginning on page 221 and notice the three columns under "Step 4." You are asked to evaluate each essential skill based on two factors—teaching priority and the athletes' readiness to learn. To assess the teaching priority, think of your overall scheme and plan for the season and, for each skill, ask yourself, Is this a skill that I must, should, or could teach? Then, think about each skill and your athletes and ask yourself, Are my athletes ready to learn this skill?

Take some time now to rate the skills on your form. These ratings will divide the skills into three groups. Skills that are A-rated are obviously priority skills that you must teach immediately and emphasize. Include B-rated skills in the planning process and teach them periodically. Finally, depending on the progress of the season and of the athletes, you can incorporate instruction for the C-rated skills.

Step 5: Select Methods for Teaching

Now you should go through the schedule and determine the methods you will use in daily practices to teach the skills you have decided are necessary to your team's success. As you learned previously, the traditional approach to practice emphasizes technical skill development and usually involves using daily drills to teach skills, interspersed with group and team drills. In the games approach, players learn to blend decision making with skill execution as you add the elements of pressure, competition, and match-day nuance to the performance of essential skills.

The traditional method might cover all the techniques of tennis adequately and may even cover most of the skills players would typically use during matches, but it has at least two glaring shortcomings: First, traditional practice sessions by their very nature emphasize techniques at the expense of tactics, and second, they involve too much direct instruction. Typically, a coach explains a skill, shows the players how they are to perform the skill, and then sets up situations in which the players can learn the skill, without placing that skill in the context of match day, tactical decision making.

Recent educational research has shown that students who learn a skill in one setting (e.g., the library) have difficulty performing it in another setting (e.g., the classroom). Compare this finding to the common belief among coaches that today's young players don't have tennis sense, the basic knowledge of the sport that players used to have. For years, coaches have been bemoaning the fact that players don't react as well to match situations as they used to, blaming video games, television, the Internet, and the popularity of other sedentary activities. But external forces may not be entirely to blame for the decline in tennis logic. Bookstores offer dozens of drill books to help coaches teach the technical skills of tennis, and players around the country practice those drills ad infinitum. If drills are so specific, numerous, and clever, why aren't players developing that elusive tennis sense? Perhaps just learning techniques and performing drill after drill creates not expertise but simply the ability to do drills.

An alternative way to teach tennis skills is the games approach. As outlined in chapter 1, the games approach allows players to take responsibility for learning skills. The games approach in sports can be compared to the holistic method of teaching writing. Traditional approaches to teaching students to write involved doing sentence-writing exercises, identifying parts of speech, and working with various types of paragraphs. After drilling students in these techniques, teachers assigned topics to write about. Teachers used this method of teaching for years. When graduating students could not write a competent essay or work application, educators began questioning the method and began to use a new approach, the holistic method. In the holistic method of teaching writing, students wrote compositions without learning parts of speech or sentence types or even ways to organize paragraphs. Teachers looked at the whole piece of writing and made suggestions for improvement from there, not worrying about spelling, grammar, or punctuation unless it was germane. This method emphasized seeing the forest instead of the trees.

This holistic approach is applicable to teaching tennis skills as well. Instead of breaking down skills into their component parts and then waiting until match day for the players to put the pieces together, you can impart the whole skill to the players and then let them discover how the parts relate. This method resembles what actually occurs in a match more than the traditional drill method does, and learning occurs at match speed.

The games approach does not take you out of the equation; in fact, you must take a more active role. You must shape the play of the athletes to get the desired results, focus their attention on the important techniques and components of the match, and enhance the skill involved by attaching various challenges to the games they play.

You can use the games approach to teach almost any area of the game. For example, instead of having players work endlessly on crosscourt groundstroke drills, you can create games around backcourt play and encourage competition.

Step 6: Plan Practices

In Step 6 you sketch out an overview of what you want to accomplish during each practice for your season using all the information you have gathered from the previous steps.

Figure 8.3 shows a season plan for the games approach (for a sample season plan for the traditional approach, please refer to the *Coaching Tennis Technical and Tactical Skills* online course). Although this season plan was created in isolation, you can use it in your season planning. You may find that you are more comfortable teaching the drop shot using the traditional approach but that the games approach works best for teaching players to serve and volley. Use these season plans as templates to help you create the plan that works best for you and your team.

In the sample season plan, notice that the first two weeks are completed. After the matches begin in the season, the practice plans are more open ended so you can focus on problems that occur in matches and develop practices accordingly. We have also identified some technical and tactical skills that are important to teach during later practices. Keep those skills in mind as you are further fine-tuning your practices during the season. The main objective of your practices at this point is to focus on your players' game plans, but as time permits, you should fit in these key skills to help your players continue to learn throughout the season.

After you have developed your season plan, you can further refine individual practices. We will help you do that in chapter 9 by showing you the components of a practice and providing sample practice plans for the games approach.

Figure 8.3 Games approach season plan

	Purpose	New skills to introduce
Practice 1	Rally skills using the forehand groundstroke	Forehand groundstroke (p. 66), movement, tracking, recovery
Practice 2	Rally skills using the forehand and backhand groundstrokes	Forehand groundstroke (p. 66), backhand groundstroke (pp. 73 and 80), movement, tracking, recovery
Practice 3	Serve and return	First serve (p. 86), second serve (p. 92), serve return (p. 95), positioning, movement, recovery
Practice 4	Volley	Volley (p. 105), positioning, movement, hitting to targets
Practice 5	Overhead and lob	Overhead (p. 113), lob (p. 126), positioning, movement, recovery
Practice 6	Approaching the net	Approach shot (p. 100), approach volley, movement, split step, positioning at the net
Practice 7	Singles positioning and tactics	Shot selection, court positioning, recovery
Practice 8	Doubles positioning and tactics	Formations, shot selection, court positioning, recovery, playing as a team
Practice 9	Serve tactics	First serve (p. 86), second serve (p. 92), preparation, direction, spin
Practice 10	Serve return tactics	Serve return (p. 95), positioning, recovery
Practice 11	Serve and volley	First serve (p. 86), second serve (p. 92), movement, split step, swinging midcourt volley (p. 110), volley (p. 105)
Practice 12	Doubles tactics with one player at the net and one player in the backcourt	Positioning, shot selection, volley (p. 105), overhead (p. 113), forehand groundstroke (p. 66), backhand groundstroke (pp. 73 and 80) defending against one player at the net and one player in the backcourt (p. 210)
Practice 13	Aggressive baseline tactics	Forehand groundstroke (p. 66), backhand groundstroke (pp. 73 and 80), movement, recovery, shot selection, power
Practice 14	Doubles tactics with two players at the net	Volley (p. 105), overhead (p. 113), court positioning, working as a team, two players at the net (p. 187), defending against two players at the net (p. 207)
Practice 15	Defensive singles tactics	Forehand groundstroke (p. 66), backhand groundstroke (pp. 73 and 80), positioning, lob (p. 126), recovery
Practice 16	Doubles tactics with two players in the backcourt	Forehand groundstroke (p. 66), backhand groundstroke (pp. 73 and 80), lob (p. 126), shot selection, positioning, recovery

(continued)

Figure 8.3 *(continued)*

	Purpose	New skills to introduce
Practice 17	Patterns of play	Shot selection, forehand groundstroke (p. 66), backhand groundstroke (pp. 73 and 80), approach shot (p. 100), volley (p. 105), positioning, recovery
Practice 18	Second serve tactics	Second serve (p. 92), spin, direction, preparation
Practice 19	Emergency situations	Lob (p. 126), reflex volley, movement, recovery
Practice 20	Alternative doubles formations	Australian formation, I-formation, communicating with partner
Practice 21	High-percentage tactics from the backcourt	Forehand groundstroke (p. 66), backhand groundstroke (pp. 73 and 80), lob (p. 126), targets, shot selection, positioning
Practice 22	Transitioning from defense to offense	Anticipation, movement, shot selection
Practice 23	Easy point-ending shots	Volley (p.105), overhead (p. 113), short groundstrokes
Practice 24	Isolating a vulnerable doubles player	Shot selection, volley (p. 105), overhead (p. 113), forehand groundstroke (p. 66), backhand groundstroke (pp. 73 and 80)
Practice 25	Aggressive net play	Volley (p. 105), overhead (p. 113), movement, recovery
Practice 26	Taking speed off the ball	Drop shot (p. 118), drop volley, chip serve return
Practice 27	Neutral, defensive, and aggressive groundstrokes	Forehand groundstroke (p. 66), backhand groundstroke (pp. 73 and 80), positioning, shot selection
Practice 28	Playing in windy conditions	Spin, shot selection, height, depth
Practice 29	Slow court tactics	Forehand groundstroke (p. 66), backhand groundstroke (pp. 73 and 80), drop shot (p. 118), shot selection, shot patterns, lob (p. 126)
Practice 30	Fast court tactics	First serve (p. 86), volley (p. 105), swinging midcourt volley (p. 169), shot selection

chapter 9

Practice Plans

To get the most out of your practice sessions, you must plan every practice. Completing the season plan, as described in chapter 8, helps you do this. But you have to take that season plan a step further and specify in detail what you will be doing at every practice.

As described in *Successful Coaching, Third Edition*, every practice plan should include the following:

- Date, time of practice, and length of practice session
- Practice objective
- Equipment needed
- Warm-up
- Practicing previously taught skills
- Teaching and practicing new skills
- Cool-down
- Coaches' comments and evaluation of practice

Using these elements, we developed eight practice plans based on the games approach season plan in chapter 8, beginning on page 227.

Note that we have developed these practice plans to work with teams that include both singles and doubles players. In many situations you will be responsible for coaching several players on multiple courts so it is important to design drills, activities, and games that your players can start and direct themselves.

At times, especially during the warm-up and the practice-ending game or activity, all of your players will be on one or two courts. Take this opportunity to mix all of the players on your team regardless of skill level. This gives them the opportunity to interact with one another in a setting that is more relaxed than a match or challenge situation. These are great times for team building and are very important for the development of your team.

The following games-approach practice plans are based on the season plan from chapter 8. The early practices focus on tennis as a whole, including the essential tactical skills. Then, as players need to refine technical skills, you can bring those skills into the practices. When athletes play focused games early in the season, they quickly discover their weaknesses and become more motivated to improve their skills so that they can perform better in match situations.

PRACTICE 1

Date:

Monday, August 15

Practice Start Time:

8:00 a.m.

Length of Practice:

2 hours, 15 minutes

Practice Objective:

To practice rally skills using forehand groundstrokes

Equipment:

Tennis balls, low-compression balls, foam balls, flat targets (spots or donuts)

Time	Name of activity	Description	Key teaching points
8:00-8:15 a.m.	Prepractice meeting	Review coach's expectations of players	
8:15-8:30 a.m.	Warm-up	Partners perform various racket and ball drills such as roll and catch; toss and catch; toss and trap; and toss, turn, and trap.	• Balance • Movement • Contact point
8:30-9:15 a.m.	*New skill:* Forehand groundstroke	Introduce the forehand groundstroke. Players practice the skill by performing the following: self rally, partner rally to a target spot, partner rally over the net, partner rally to targets (side to side), partner rally to targets (short and deep), and step-back rally.	• Movement • Recovery • Contact point • Direction • Depth • Consistency
9:15-9:30 a.m.	Serve and return	Partners serve and return the ball over the net.	
9:30-10:00 a.m.	*Game:* Tag Team (singles)	Separate the team into two groups and play the game in challenge matches.	• Consistency • Cooperation • Control
10:00-10:10 a.m.	Cool-down	*Dynamic stretching:* The entire team stretches on one court; the coach leads the team in the stretching exercises.	
10:10-10:15 a.m.	Coach's comments	Review practice, collect challenge match results and scores, distribute match schedule, outline travel procedures and policies, announce topic of next practice, take suggestions for after-practice sessions.	• Working as a team • Hustling • Intensity

Date:

Tuesday, August 16

Practice Start Time:

8:00 a.m.

Length of Practice:

2 hours, 15 minutes

Practice Objective:

To practice rally skills using forehand and backhand groundstrokes

Equipment:

Tennis balls, low-compression balls, foam balls, flat targets (spots or donuts)

Time	Name of activity	Description	Key teaching points
8:00-8:10 a.m.	Prepractice meeting	Review coach's expectations of players.	
8:10-8:25 a.m.	Warm-up	Partners warm up by performing various racket and ball drills such as roll and catch; toss and catch; toss and trap; and toss, turn, and trap.	• Balance • Movement • Contact point
8:25-8:35 a.m.	*Skill review:* Forehand groundstroke	Players perform step-back forehand groundstrokes with a partner.	
8:35-9:15 a.m.	*New skill:* Backhand groundstroke	Introduce the backhand groundstroke. Players practice the skill by performing the following: self rally, partner rally to a target spot, partner rally over the net, partner rally to targets (side to side), partner rally to targets (short and deep), and partner rally alternating with forehands and backhands.	• Movement • Recovery • Contact point • Direction • Depth • Consistency
9:15-9:30 a.m.	Serve and return	Partners serve and return the ball over the net.	
9:30-10:00 a.m.	*Game:* Champion of the Court (singles)	Separate the team into two groups and play the game in challenge matches.	• Constructing points • Using strengths • Identifying and exploiting an opponent's weakness
10:00-10:10 a.m.	Cool-down	*Dynamic stretching:* The entire team stretches on one court; the coach leads the team in the stretching exercises.	
10:10-10:15 a.m.	Coach's comments	Review practice, explain importance of groundstroke base, announce topic for next practice, take suggestions for after-practice sessions.	

PRACTICE 3

Date:
Wednesday, August 17

Practice Start Time:
8:00 a.m.

Length of Practice:
2 hours, 15 minutes

Practice Objectives:
To practice the serve and serve return

Equipment:
Tennis balls, low-compression balls, foam balls, flat targets (spots or donuts)

Time	Name of activity	Description	Key teaching points
8:00-8:10 a.m.	Prepractice meeting	Review coach's expectations of players.	
8:10-8:25 a.m.	Warm-up	Partners rally with a foam ball from service line to service line using groundstrokes.	• Movement • Balance • Consistency
8:25-8:35 a.m.	*Skill review:* Forehand and backhand groundstroke	Partners rally using alternating forehand and backhand groundstrokes.	
8:35-9:15 a.m.	*New skill:* Serve and serve return	Introduce the serve and serve return. Players practice the skill by performing the following: throw to partner; toss, touch, and freeze; serve and trap; serve, return, and trap; serving to targets A-B-C; step-back serve, return, return and trap.	
9:15-9:30 a.m.	Serve and return	Partners serve and return the ball over the net.	
9:30-10:00 a.m.	*Game:* Serve Relay	Separate the team into two groups and play the game in challenge matches.	• Preparation • Serving under pressure
10:00-10:10 a.m.	Cool-down	*Dynamic stretching:* The entire team stretches on one court; the coach leads the team in the stretching exercises.	
10:10-10:15 a.m.	Coach's comments	Review practice, collect results and scores of challenge matches, review importance of preparation for the serve and consistency for serve and return, take suggestions for after-practice sessions, announce topic for next practice.	

Date:

Thursday, August 18

Practice Start Time:

8:00 a.m.

Length of Practice:

2 hours, 15 minutes

Practice Objective:

To practice the volley

Equipment:

Tennis balls, low-compression balls, foam balls, flat targets (spots or donuts)

Time	Name of activity	Description	Key teaching points
8:00-8:10 a.m.	Prepractice meeting	Review coaches' expectations of players.	
8:10-8:25 a.m.	Warm-up	Partners alternate forehand and backhand groundstrokes with foam balls from service line to service line.	• Balance • Movement • Direction • Control
8:25-8:35 a.m.	*Skill review:* Serve and return	Review the serve and return (step-back serve, return, return, trap).	
8:35-9:15 a.m.	*New skill:* Volley	Introduce the volley. Players practice the skill by performing the following: volley progression with partner holding halfway down the handle; volley progression with partner holding handle; volley with partner on backhand side; groundstroke and volley combination; step-back volley–groundstroke after four-ball rally.	• Contact point • Racket direction • Hand facing target—before, during, and after the hit • Hand and racket togother • Crossover step
9:15-9:30 a.m.	Serve and return	Partners serve and return the ball over the net.	
9:30-10:00 a.m.	*Game:* One Ball Live	Separate the team into two groups and play the game in challenge matches.	• Consistency • Attacking the short ball • Ending the point with a volley
10:00-:10:10 a.m.	Cool-down	*Dynamic stretching:* The entire team stretches on one court; the coach leads the team in the stretching exercises.	
10:10-10:15 a.m.	Coach's comments	Review practice, collect results and scores from challenge matches, discuss styles of play, take suggestions for after-practice sessions, announce topic for next practice.	

PRACTICE 5

Date:

Friday, August 19

Practice Start Time:

8:00 a.m.

Length of Practice:

2 hours, 15 minutes

Practice Objectives:

To practice the overhead and lob

Equipment:

Tennis balls, low-compression balls, foam balls

Time	Name of activity	Description	Key teaching points
8:00-8:10 a.m.	Prepractice meeting	Review coach's expectations of players.	
8:10-8:25 a.m.	Warm-up	Partners rally using groundstrokes with foam balls from service line to service line and using groundstrokes to volley rallies with foam balls in the service court.	
8:25-8:35 a.m.	*Skill review:* Volley	Review volleys. Players practice the skill by performing the following: step-back volley to groundstroke starting at the service line and moving back after each successful four-ball rally.	
8:35-9:15 a.m.	*New skill:* Overhead and lob	Introduce the overhead and lob. Players practice the skill by performing lobs, overheads, and overhead–lob combinations.	• Preparation • Good contact point • Maintaining balance • Recovery
9:15-9:30 a.m.	Serve and return	Partners serve and return the ball over the net.	
9:30-10:00 a.m.	*Game:* Team Doubles	Separate the team into two groups and play the game in challenge matches.	• Moving together as a team • Hitting groundstrokes deep to deep • Hitting volleys close to close • Setting up the person at the net to win the point
10:00-10:10 a.m.	Cool-down	*Dynamic stretching:* The entire team stretches on one court; the coach leads the team in the stretching exercises.	
10:10-10:15 a.m.	Coach's comments	Review practice, collect challenge match results and scores, take suggestions for after-practice sessions over the weekend, announce topic for next practice.	

PRACTICE 6

Date:

Monday, August 22

Practice Start Time:

8:00 a.m.

Length of Practice:

2 hours, 15 minutes

Practice Objective:

To practice approaching the net

Equipment:

Tennis balls, low-compression balls, foam balls, flat targets (spots or donuts)

Time	Name of activity	Description	Key teaching points
8:00-8:10 a.m.	Prepractice meeting	Review coach's expectations of players.	
8:10-8:25 a.m.	Warm-up	Partners hit groundstrokes with foam balls from service line to service line. They work a series of shots—all topspin, all backspin, down the line, crosscourt.	• Contact point • Recovery after each shot
8:25-8:35 a.m.	*Skill review:* Overhead and lob	Review the overhead and lob. Partners practice the skill by performing a series of shots under control. The player at the net hits a forehand volley, backhand volley, and overhead. See how many three-shot sequences can be played consecutively.	
8:35-9:15 a.m.	*New skill:* Approach shot and approach volley	Introduce the approach shot and approach volley. Players practice the skill by performing the following: approach shot from a coach or player bounce; approach shot from a coach or player toss; approach volley from a coach or player toss; approach shot or volley, move forward and split step, volley to open court.	• Moving through the shot • Accelerating to the net
9:15-9:30 a.m.	Serve and return	Partners serve and return the ball over the net.	
9:30-10:00 a.m.	*Game:* Champions of the Court (doubles)	Separate the team into two groups and play the game in challenge matches.	• Moving quickly to the net as a team
10:00-10:10 a.m.	Cool-down	*Dynamic stretching:* The entire team stretches on one court; the coach leads the team in the stretching exercises.	
10:10-10:15 a.m.	Coach's comments	Review practice, collect results and scores of challenge matches, review status of challenge matches and doubles teams, announce topic for next practice.	

PRACTICE 7

Date:

Tuesday, August 23

Practice Start Time:

8:00 a.m.

Length of Practice:

2 hours, 15 minutes

Practice Objectives:

To practice singles positioning and tactics

Equipment:

Tennis balls, low-compression balls, foam balls, flat targets (spots or donuts)

Time	Name of activity	Description	Key teaching points
8:00-8:10 a.m.	Prepractice meeting	Review coach's expectations of players.	
8:10-8:25 a.m.	Warm-up	Partners rally with foam balls from service line to service line. Player A must match all spins applied by player B; partners volley a foam ball back and forth from the ideal volley position (players halfway between the service line and the net); partners volley from service line to service line using low-compression balls.	
8:25-8:35 a.m.	*Skill review:* Approach shot and approach volley	Review the approach shot and approach volley. The coach or a player tosses a ball and players run through an approach shot, volley, and overhead sequence on both forehand and backhand sides.	
8:35-9:15 a.m.	*New skill:* Singles positioning and tactics (situation tennis)	Using players on both sides of the court, give player A the situation to play. Player B must determine the best style to play to beat player A.	• Keeping the ball in play
9:15-9:30 a.m.	Serve and return	Partners serve and return the ball over the net.	
9:30-10:00 a.m.	*Game:* Champion of the Court (singles)	Separate the team into two groups and play the game in challenge matches.	• Varying tactics depending on the champion's style of play
10:00-10:10 a.m.	Cool-down	*Dynamic stretching:* The entire team stretches on one court; the coach leads the team in the stretching exercises.	
10:10-10:15 a.m.	Coach's comments	Review practice, collect challenge match results and scores, discuss importance and differences in styles of play for singles players, take suggestions for after-practice sessions, announce topic for next practice.	

Date:

Wednesday, August 24

Practice Start Time:

8:00 a.m.

Length of Practice:

2 hours, 15 minutes

Practice Objectives:

To practice doubles positioning and tactics

Equipment:

Tennis balls, low-compression balls, foam balls, flat targets (spots or donuts)

Time	Name of activity	Description	Key teaching points
8:00-8:10 a.m.	Prepractice meeting	Review coach's expectations of players.	
8:10-8:25 a.m.	Warm-up	Partners rally service line to service line using foam balls; partners volley using low-compression balls; partners serve and return using low-compression balls.	• No errors • Good preparation for shots • Hitting and recovering • Good contact point on every shot
8:25-8:35 a.m.	*Skill review:* Singles positioning and tactics	Using players on both sides of the court, give player A the situation to play. Player B must determine the best style to play to beat player A.	• Keeping the ball in play
8:35-9:15 a.m.	*New skill:* Doubles positioning and tactics (all position doubles)	Doubles teams are stationed on both sides of the court. Team A plays points in a designated formation and style, and team B defends against that style.	• Keeping the ball in play
9:15-9:30 a.m.	Serve and return	Partners serve and return the ball over the net.	
9:30-10:00 a.m.	*Game:* Deep Desperation	Separate the team into two groups and play the game in challenge matches.	• Moving and playing as a team • Keeping the ball in play • Communication
10:00-10:10 a.m.	Cool-down	*Dynamic stretching:* The entire team stretches on one court; the coach leads the team in the stretching exercises.	
10:10-10:15 a.m.	Coach's comments	Review practice, collect challenge match results and scores, solicit comments on doubles formations, take suggestions for after-practice sessions, announce topic for next practice.	

PART V

Match Coaching

You can plan and have your players practice all day long, but if they do not perform to the best of their abilities during matches, what has all that planning done for you? Part V helps you prepare players for match situations.

Chapter 10 teaches you how to prepare long before the first match, addressing issues such as communication, scouting opponents, and creating a match plan. Chapter 11 teaches you how to prepare your players to make decisions before and during the match about issues such as choosing to serve or receive first, deciding the end of the court to begin the match, playing at the right pace, handling errors, dealing with line calls, and keeping focused between points.

After all the preparation you have done, match day is when it really becomes exciting, especially if you and your players are ready for the challenge.

chapter 10

Preparing for Matches

A tennis team's performance on match day reflects its preparation. A well-prepared team has players ready to play using their strengths as singles players, doubles players, or both. They are confident because they have prepared for handling their opponents' various styles of play and formations. Following are the areas that you should consider when preparing yourself and your team for a match.

Communication

As a coach, you must communicate well at many levels—with players, team captains, your coaching staff, school and community officials, parents, officials, students, and the media. You must be aware of your nonverbal communication, which can be just as loud as what you say.

Players

When you communicate well with your players, you engage them in the learning process. When you make players partners and give them a stake in their own development, you become a facilitator, not merely a trainer. The players' participation in the learning process is the key to the games approach and what makes it such a valuable approach to coaching. Although shaping, focusing, and enhancing play can be more challenging than using the traditional approach to coaching, doing these things is ultimately more rewarding because it allows players to take ownership of their development.

As part of the communication process, you should assemble a team manual that covers basic styles of play for singles and doubles formations, including the strengths and weaknesses of each style and formation. The manual should also include the season plan, match dates, and practice schedules while also outlining a basic practice and the procedures to follow for practice on inclement weather days. The longer the manual is, the less apt the athletes are to read it, so make it short. Meet with players often and encourage them to study the manual thoroughly.

Before the beginning of a season, prepare a list of expectations that outlines the policies you expect players to follow. The term *expectations* is preferable to the term *rules,* which conveys a sense of rigidity. The term *expectations* also communicates to players that they are responsible for living up to them. You and the other members of your coaching staff must reinforce expectations daily so that they become second nature to the team. Handle any breaches of discipline that arise immediately and evenhandedly. You must treat all players alike, starters no differently than subs. Finally, make sure that your list of expectations covers any situations that may occur in your school or community.

You may decide to have the team elect captains, who can then assist you in communicating to the team. Emphasize to captains that their main role is to help make their teammates better players, not to order them around. Show captains the many ways to accomplish that—by encouraging teammates, helping them work on their skills, supporting them, and modeling good practice habits.

Parents

Before the season begins, schedule a preseason meeting with the parents of all players, separate from the meeting that most schools already sponsor during each sport season. A few weeks before the season begins, mail a letter to the homes of players with an RSVP enclosed. This personal touch will pique the interest of parents and make them feel valuable to the program. A special invitation letter should go to the superintendent, the principal, and the athletic director, who should be present to explain school policies, athletic codes, and general school issues.

Prepare a simple agenda for this meeting and follow it to keep the meeting on track and to convey to parents a sense of your organizational ability. Besides setting an agenda, you should prepare and distribute a simple list outlining the roles of parents, players, and coaches. Parents want to be involved in their children's progress, so stating the method of communication between parent and coach is important.

Coaching Staff

Many tennis teams do not have assistants or other coaches. If you are a head coach with a coaching staff, you need to communicate well with your assistants or fellow coaches. Each season, hold a formal preseason meeting with your coaching staff to outline expectations. Discuss your coaching philosophy and specific techniques you will emphasize during the season, especially if changes have occurred from the previous year or if new members have joined the staff. You should spell out, or even write out, the roles of assistants or volunteer coaches, including how to deal with parents (they should be referred to you). Assistants should be firm and immediate in noting breaches of discipline and bringing them to your attention.

Officials

In many dual matches, coaches also serve as officials. Officials are often used in larger events such as league championships or district, regional, or state tournaments, so you should know how to communicate well with them. Treat officials with respect at all times. Players will model your behavior with officials. Because most states and leagues provide outlets for official evaluations, you can address shortcomings and commendations of officials through that process.

Community and Media

Involvement with the community and the media demands that you be a good communicator. You speak each day with your demeanor. If you are irritated by the lack of media coverage, players will assume that demeanor. If you are enthusiastic, positive, and accommodating, the players will be that way too. In most communities, tennis is not the focus of the local media, so be appreciative when your players or matches are covered.

You should be accommodating to the press and instruct players in tactics for talking to the media. Players need to understand that the role of the media may be in conflict with the goals and expectations of the team. Players should respectfully answer questions that deal with matches but defer questions about philosophy or opponents to the coaching staff.

Scouting an Opponent

Football and basketball teams develop scouting reports by watching video recordings of opponents or even by watching games in person. Because tennis teams do not usually do this, coaches must rely on observations of the opponents in previous matches or even in previous years.

The important elements to note are the opponent's style of play and physical strengths and weaknesses. It is also helpful to note the emotional stability of an opponent. Does he self-destruct after a few errors, or is he calm, even when he is struggling or losing momentum? You may be able to decipher not only the speed and quickness of an opponent but also her physical condition. Does she play well in a third set, or do long matches spell disaster for her? Also, although you may not be able to observe opponents in person, it can be helpful to collect match scores for all of your opponents. These scores might indicate whether a player starts quickly and fades in a long match, or whether a player or a team starts slowly but finishes strong because they are in exceptional physical condition.

Often your players will have to do their own scouting during the warm-up to a match. Teach them to look for strengths and weaknesses. Does the opponent prefer to hit a forehand or backhand when the ball is coming directly at him? Does he prefer to play the ball low or high in the strike zone? Is she more comfortable at the net or at the baseline? When she warms up at the net, which shot is stronger, the volley or overhead? Your players can determine how well their opponents move from side to side and up and back by hitting balls to different areas of the court during the warm-up period. When taking practice serves, players should notice the speed, spin, and direction of the serve. Can the opponent change the speed and spin of the serve?

All of this information is extremely helpful when your players have to develop game plans based on 10-minute warm-ups. Teach them to do more than physically warm up during this time. They should also develop a critical eye for the strengths and weaknesses of their opponents so they can select the best tactics to use beginning with the first game of the match.

Because matches occur frequently during the course of the season, scouting opponents in advance is very difficult. However, the more information you have about opponents, the better you can prepare your team during practices and the better your plans for each match will be.

Coaches are generally rotating from court to court on match day, monitoring matches, collecting scores, offering advice, and providing encouragement. This leaves little time to observe and analyze the players on the opposing team. One way to get this information is to have each player complete a postmatch analysis of the player or doubles team they just competed against. They can write this information on a card immediately after every match (see figure 10.1). Create a file for every opponent; this will serve as a scouting report for the next time your players play that opponent.

Developing the Game Plan

After gathering as much information about each player or doubles team as you can, you must provide guidance on how to play this particular player or doubles team. Take into consideration your players' strengths and preferences. Give them tactics to use when playing each opponent. Consider the opponents' physical condition and emotional stability. If your players can force a few errors, or play some long points, the opponent might self-destruct mentally or give up physically from fatigue.

If you are forced to plan for a match without knowing much or anything about the opponent, focus on maximizing your player's strengths. Help her recognize her strengths and have her focus on using them for the first set of the match. If she wins, have her maintain the same game plan for the second set. If she loses the first set, she will have to change something, either a tactic or style of play, to change the momentum.

Structuring Practices

Because matches occur frequently during the tennis season, each practice is important for skill development and understanding and using various tactics in matches. Devote time to controlled repetitions to build solid strokes and develop confidence in your players.

It is not possible to practice all shots in any practice, but all practices should include some time for the serve and the serve return. These two shots are the most important shots in the game, and your players will be successful if they develop consistent returns and serves hit with direction, various spins, and speed. You may have a tendency to work on weaknesses, but don't forget to strengthen and sharpen your players' best shots and develop them into weapons. The weapon might not be a hard-hit ball, but rather, movement around the court or pinpoint accuracy.

Figure 10.1   Sample postmatch analysis card

Opponent's name: _____ Date: _____

School: _____ Grade: _____

Right handed _____ Left handed _____

Physical condition: *Poor* _____ *Fair* _____ *Good* _____ *Excellent* _____

Foot speed: *Poor* _____ *Fair* _____ *Good* _____ *Excellent* _____

Reaction and speed at the net: *Poor* _____ *Fair* _____ *Good* _____ *Excellent* _____

WEATHER CONDITIONS

_____

_____

Temperature: _____ Wind speed: _____

OPPONENT INFORMATION

Opponent's strongest or best shot: _____

Opponent's weakest shot: _____

Opponent's favorite area of the court: Net _____ Backcourt _____

Style of Play

Hard hitter (ends points quickly) _____

Retriever (lets opponent make the errors) _____

Serve-and-volley _____

Shot Threshold

Points end, win or lose, in how many shots?   *2 shots* _____ *4 shots* _____ *6 shots* _____ *more* _____

EMOTIONAL STABILITY

Showed no emotion _____

Occasional frustration _____

Quick temper _____

QUALITY OF SERVE

Excellent first and second serves _____

Good first serve, poor second serve _____

Consistent and accurate first and second serve _____

Your name: _____ Score: _____   *Win or Lose*

Comments (e.g., What did I do to win today? What will I do differently if I play this opponent again?):

_____

_____

_____

_____

From *Coaching Tennis Technical and Tactical Skills* by ASEP, 2009, Champaign, IL: Human Kinetics.

Your players must be aware of their most effective style of play in singles and practice this style against a variety of opponents. Playing games that emphasize a certain style of play or one or two tactics are fun for your players and teach them to play against various players and styles of play. Point play is an effective way to prepare for matches. Structure games that replicate match situations so you can work on both skills and tactics. You can teach consistency by not allowing anyone to win a point until the ball crosses the net four times. You can encourage players to move to the net by rewarding them with two points for a put-away volley.

Some teams have players who play both singles and doubles. Other teams have players who specialize in either singles or doubles because they can't play both in high school matches. Make sure your practices include doubles drills and give your teams opportunities to play points in various formations against a variety of players and positions.

Controlling Your Team's Performance

By establishing a consistent routine on match day, you help your athletes prepare themselves physically, mentally, and emotionally for their best possible performance. You have great flexibility in designing your prematch ritual. Whatever routine you choose, staying with it for the entire season is more important than its actual elements. When the team is on the road, the outline should remain as similar as possible to the routine at home. This regularity produces consistency in performance that might not exist if the timetable were erratic. See Sample Prematch Routine for a routine that you may want to use with your team.

SAMPLE PREMATCH ROUTINE

Your team's routine should become part of the events leading up to the match itself to breed a comfortable atmosphere and help players feel relaxed and ready to give their best. Following is a suggested routine for the hours leading up to a match.

Four Hours Before the Match

Players should eat a training meal that provides them with the proper nutrition for optimal performance. This meal should include moderate portions of carbohydrate, be low in fat, and contain no sugar. Players should get into a habit of eating the same meal at the same time before every match so they can regulate how much they eat and feel their best throughout the match. For more information on your athletes' diet, refer to chapter 16, Fueling Your Athletes, beginning on page 357 of Rainer Marten's *Successful Coaching, Third Edition*.

One Hour Before the Match

Players should arrive at the courts an hour before the match. They should check all their equipment to make sure rackets, strings, and grips are in good condition. All players should do some dynamic warm-up with movement in dynamic stretching. After this group warm-up, singles players should hit with each other to get a feel for the court, the balls, and weather conditions. This should be easy hitting as part of a dynamic warm-up. Doubles teams should hit with other doubles teams to get comfortable with the court and weather conditions. After this easy hitting with partners, players should leave the court at least 10 minutes prior to the match to prepare for the team introductions and court assignments.

Team Building and Motivation

Team building in tennis can be a challenge because competition is made up of individual singles and doubles matches. Individual results count for the success or failure of the team. Individuals will play better, be more motivated, and handle individual challenges better if they feel they are an important part of the team.

Each practice can include team participation and team-building activities. Several great warm-up activities are available for the team to use as a group on one court. Also, you can use cooperative partner drills and activities for all ability levels; these work well when players change partners frequently. These partner drills keep everyone active and give players lots of repetitions to develop strokes and consistency. The final activity of every practice can be an exciting group game that mixes all ability levels and has everyone on the team leaving energized and excited about coming to practice or playing a match the next day.

The underlying point is that you must motivate your players to practice so that they will be motivated to play well in the match. They have to know why it is important for them to grasp the concepts and learn how to execute them. They must make the connection between preparation and performance and realize that they can reach their goals only if they practice diligently. Then, when the match comes, they are confident in their abilities, committed to the goal, and ready to play hard for the entire match.

Despite your best efforts to plan and prepare your team, one factor trumps everything else. One of the main reasons high school students play on a tennis team is that they enjoy the friendship, camaraderie, competition, and life lessons that they share with their teammates. Because they go through both tough and exciting experiences together, they develop deep and committed bonds of friendship. The commitment of team members to each other is the most powerful form of motivation in sport. You must strive to find ways to encourage and enhance opportunities for players to spend time together, work to break down barriers between isolated groups on the team, and help players develop the kind of friendships that move mountains.

chapter 11

During and After the Match

One of the great challenges of coaching tennis is the fact that the season comprises many matches and few practice days in comparison to other sports such as football or basketball. In many instances a team will play dual matches and get the opportunity to play that same opponent in a larger conference or district tournament at the end of the season. As the coach, you must manage the practices wisely so each player can work on the skills and tactics needed to be prepared and equipped for each match.

The three-step tactical triangle approach to analyzing a match situation detailed in chapter 1 creates a blueprint for you and your players to follow in making important decisions during a match. While the match is in progress, players must be able to accurately read the cues presented, apply technical and tactical knowledge on the spot, adjust the plan accordingly, and make immediate decisions. The logical format of the triangle helps them slow the speed of the match and apply organized, logical thinking to the situation.

Leadership does not just happen; it is a gradual process of education and experience. You should prepare your team to be led by telling them how you expect them to behave. Describe to the team your expectations for them on match day—how they should act on the court; how they should talk to officials, coaches, and opponents; how they should react to adverse situations; and how they should respond to success. Then, follow up by insisting on those behaviors through reinforcement during and after the match. Everything your team does on match day is the result of something you have taught or something you have allowed to happen. Teach match day the right way, and your team will perform admirably.

During the Match

Communicating with your players during the match is very important. This takes place in brief on-court meetings and before the racket spin or coin toss.

Meetings

Although the rules for on-court meetings vary from state to state, most high school coaches can talk with their players during the 90-second time on the odd-game changeover period, between sets, or both. Make sure your players know the location and purposes of your meetings with them on the court. Establish meeting locations, either on the court or through the fence, depending on the court situation. Because these meetings are very short, instruct them to give you a brief update on the progress of the match, including the score, who is serving, match momentum, injuries, and the physical and emotional condition of themselves and their opponents.

It is also important for each player or doubles team to know the game plan, style of play, and formation that works best for them. They should start with a well-defined plan. If this plan is successful, there is no need to change during the course of the match. If the player is not successful, you need to determine whether the plan is valid for that particular player against the opponent that day. If a player loses a close first set, you may tell her to stay with her plan but try to execute it better by reducing the number of unforced errors. If the style of play is simply not working against the opponent, you may instruct the player to go to another plan to see if she can develop a rhythm or disrupt the opponent's momentum.

Racket Spin or Coin Toss

A racket spin or coin toss is done on each court prior to the match to determine who will serve and what side of the court each player will begin on. Meet with your players before the racket spin or coin toss to help them decide whether to serve or receive and which side of the court to take if they win the spin or toss. Some players like to serve, and others are more comfortable receiving the first game. Your player may have a preference of side depending on the position of the sun or direction of the wind. Also remember that your players' and doubles teams' strengths and weaknesses can influence their decision if they win the spin or toss. Review these strengths and options before the match so each player or team has a plan and can make a well-thought-out decision to get off to the best possible start.

After the Match

At the conclusion of every match, players should go to the net and shake hands. When your players meet their opponents at the net, their actions will reflect the training, or lack thereof, that you have given them about this custom. Long before this moment, preferably at the beginning of the season before the first match, you should address this situation with your players. A simple formula for the handshake is to be brief and, in defeat, to extend congratulations and quickly move on. Any further comments could be perceived as either provocative or patronizing.

After your players shake hands with their opponents, you have the opportunity to meet with them as they come off the court. Remember to think before you speak, and be aware of your emotional condition and theirs. In defeat, console your players and praise their effort. This is the perfect time to recognize improvements they made since the previous match. Find positives to build on and move forward to the next opponent. In victory, let them know that you are happy and point out any areas in which they performed especially well—following the plan, good mental focus, few unforced errors, or great determination in getting to all balls. Reinforce how their hard work in conditioning and practice prepared them for their performance.

At this time, win or lose, your players should not disappear to the bus or locker room. Instead, they should go to another court where a match is in progress to encourage and support teammates who are still playing. Even though their individual match is over, the team outcome is more important than an individual result. You should stress this attitude at team meetings and require all players to stay and support their teammates until the last match has concluded.

When all matches are over, each player on your team should take time to congratulate the opposing coach for a win, or thank him or her for a good match in defeat. A handshake by all members of your team is a first-class acknowledgment that they respect the opposing coach's dedication. If officials were used, especially in larger tournaments, make sure your team thanks these officials before leaving the site.

After all of the individual matches are concluded, your team will gather on the bus or in the locker room. This is your time to praise their effort and congratulate them. Acknowledge some individuals for outstanding individual performances, even if they lost. Point out that their hard work in practices is moving them in the right direction. Be happy for your team in victory. If the match went in your favor, tell them how proud you are and how happy you are for them. If the match ended in a loss, tell them how proud you are and how much you appreciated their effort. Your players will vividly remember these postmatch moments. They will never forget that you coached them in life as much as you did in tennis.

Players who speak to the team at the postmatch meeting often provide the most poignant messages. At the beginning of the year, set up a team policy that players' comments must be positive and sincere. Players should keep their comments brief, compliment teammates who played hard and well, and try to motivate the team for the next match.

All players who played in the match should fill out the scouting cards while the match and opponents are still fresh in their minds. You may want to add a few comments on each card before you file them for reference in future matches. These cards will help you determine what your players need to work on during upcoming practice days. Even the best season plan will change direction based on the results and needs of your players at that point in the season. You may be able to accelerate into more advanced tactics, or you might have to return to the basics.

Note: The italicized *f* following page numbers refers to figures.

about the authors

Kirk Anderson, who is the United States Tennis Association's director of recreational coaches and programs, started playing competitively when he was a sophomore at Parchment High School in Parchment, Michigan, a suburb of Kalamazoo. He attended Western Michigan University in Kalamazoo and graduated with a major in physical education.

Kirk spent 12 years as a club professional in Michigan in Holland, Battle Creek, and Kalamazoo and one year as a resort professional in Hawaii. Along the way he returned to Western Michigan University and earned a master's degree in exercise science. In the mid-1980s, Anderson joined the Midwest Tennis Association and became the schools director in Springfield, Ohio, where he remained for 6 years before moving to Atlanta to work for Penn Racquet Sports as its promotions manager.

He then joined the United States Professional Tennis Association as its director of education, a post he held for 2 years before coming to the USTA in 1996 as the manager of the Play Tennis America program. But throughout his journey within the tennis industry, this premier tennis teacher has never stopped learning. Kirk is one of only a handful of tennis teaching pros worldwide who are designated as master professionals in both the Professional Tennis Registry and USPTA. And Anderson's goal to become the best tennis teacher possible was recognized in 2003 when the International Tennis Hall of Fame honored him with its Tennis Educational Merit Award.

Anderson, who lives in New Fairfield, Connecticut, frequently is a featured presenter, both on court and off, at industry conventions. And he is one of the codirectors of the USTA Tennis Teachers Conference, the annual gathering held at the beginning of the US Open that attracts hundreds of teaching pros from the United States and around the world. In 2006 the TTC drew nearly 750 attendees, the largest number since 2001. Kirk also is in charge of the on-court activities for the yearly Arthur Ashe Kids' Day, which takes place at the USTA Billie Jean King National Tennis Center on the Saturday before the US Open begins. In 2005 more than 33,000 kids attended the event.

In his role as USTA director of recreational coaches and programs, one of Anderson's key initiatives is the Recreational Coach Workshops (www.usta.com/

coaches), which involve parents and other volunteers in teaching and coaching players at the recreational level. This national program, presented in cooperation with the USPTA and PTR, offers training to help develop recreation coaches.

Both the PTR and the USPTA praise Anderson for his leadership in the Quick-Start Tennis format that uses slower balls, lower nets, smaller courts, shorter rackets, and modified scoring for children ages 10 and under.

The United States Tennis Association (USTA) is the national governing body for the sport of tennis and the recognized leader in promoting and developing the sport's growth on every level in the United States, from local communities to the crown jewel of the professional game, the US Open.

Established in 1881, the USTA is a progressive and diverse not-for-profit organization whose volunteers, professional staff, and financial resources support a single mission: to promote and develop the growth of tennis. The USTA is the largest tennis organization in the world, with 17 geographical sections, more than 750,000 individual members and 7,000 organizational members, thousands of volunteers, and a professional staff dedicated to growing the game.

The American Sport Education Program (ASEP) is the leading provider of youth, high school, and elite-level sport education programs in the United States. Rooted in the philosophy of "Athletes first, winning second," ASEP has educated more than 1.5 million coaches, officials, sport administrators, parents, and athletes. For more than 25 years, local, state, and national sport organizations have partnered with ASEP to lead the way in making sport a safe, successful, and enjoyable experience for all involved. For more information on ASEP sport education courses and resources, call 800-747-5698, visit www.ASEP.com, or look inside this book.

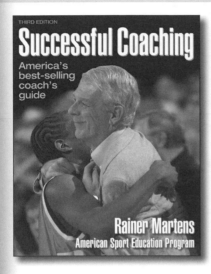
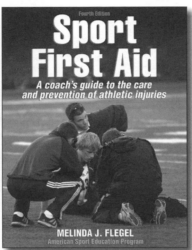

You'll find other outstanding tennis resources at

http://tennis.humankinetics.com

In the U.S. call 1-800-747-4457

Australia 08 8372 0999 • Canada 1-800-465-7301
Europe +44 (0) 113 255 5665 • New Zealand 0064 9 448 1207

 HUMAN KINETICS
The Premier Publisher for Sports & Fitness
P.O. Box 5076 • Champaign, IL 61825-5076 USA